T0276295

ALSO WRITTEN OR CO-WRITTEN BY DAN ROBSON

Ignite
Unlock the Hidden Potential Within
(with Andre De Grasse)

Crossroads
My Story of Tragedy and Resilience as a Humboldt Bronco
(with Kaleb Dahlgren)

Measuring Up
A Memoir of Fathers and Sons

Change Up
How to Make the Great Game of Baseball Even Better
(with Buck Martinez)

The Crazy Game
How I Survived in the Crease and Beyond
(with Clint Malarchuk)

Killer
My Life in Hockey
(with Doug Gilmour)

Quinn
The Life of a Hockey Legend

Bower
A Legendary Life

The Beautiful Dream

A Memoir

Atiba Hutchinson

WITH DAN ROBSON

VIKING

VIKING

an imprint of Penguin Canada, a division of Penguin Random House Canada Limited

Canada • USA • UK • Ireland • Australia • New Zealand • India • South Africa • China

First published 2024

Copyright © 2024 by 1000062426 Ontario Inc.

All rights reserved. Without limiting the rights under copyright reserved above,
no part of this publication may be reproduced, stored in or introduced into
a retrieval system, or transmitted in any form or by any means (electronic,
mechanical, photocopying, recording or otherwise), without the prior written
permission of both the copyright owner and the above publisher of this book.

www.penguinrandomhouse.ca

LIBRARY AND ARCHIVES CANADA CATALOGUING IN PUBLICATION

Title: The beautiful dream : a memoir / Atiba Hutchinson ; with Dan Robson.
Names: Hutchinson, Atiba, author. | Robson, Dan, 1983- author.
Identifiers: Canadiana (print) 2023046873X | Canadiana (ebook) 20230468756 |
ISBN 9780735247352 (hardcover) | ISBN 9780735247376 (EPUB)
Subjects: LCSH: Hutchinson, Atiba. | LCSH: Soccer players—Canada—Biography. |
LCGFT: Autobiographies.
Classification: LCC GV942.7.H88 A3 2024 | DDC 796.334092—dc23

Book design by Matthew Flute
Typeset by Terra Page
Cover design by Matthew Flute
Cover photo © Canada Soccer / Beau Chevalier
Interior illustrations: (jersey) © Sansom / Adobe Stock Images;
(net and soccer ball) © cako74 / Getty Images
Images are courtesy of the author unless stated otherwise.

Printed in Canada

10 9 8 7 6 5 4 3 2 1

Penguin
Random House
VIKING CANADA

This book is dedicated to my children—
Noah, Nava, Ayo, and Lily-Rose.
Nothing brings me more joy than being your father.

Contents

Prologue

A few steps away from the end of the tunnel, I closed my eyes and wondered whether I'd wake up. It was a scene I'd imagined so many times before but it felt entirely unfamiliar. The nerves hit two days earlier and were reaching a level I'd never experienced in two decades as a professional footballer.

A couple months shy of my fortieth birthday, I was a grandfather in a young man's game. I'd played the sport a decade longer than most. It was now the last season of my football life. Soon I would walk into the wide-open space that exists on the other side of any pro athlete's career. Since I was a boy, soccer had been my identity. It was always who I was—the singular pursuit that gave me passion and purpose. But now I was nearing middle age, still playing the game I first fell in love with as a boy. I had a family—my wife, three young sons, and a baby girl on the way. I had everything I'd wanted, everything I could need in life. On the pitch, I'd achieved everything I was capable of and knew that I'd done everything possible in my career to make that happen.

Everything but this.

And now I stood a few steps away.

Just beyond the tunnel beneath the stands at Ahmad bin Ali Stadium in Qatar was a green pitch, bright lights, more than forty thousand fans, and television cameras that would send us around the globe. Behind me stood a team who represented the most talented collection of Canadian male soccer players the country had ever produced—a team with youth, raw ability, and passion. They represented a new generation of men's football in Canada, one that had earned a level of respect the national team had never before received.

For years, this very scene had seemed impossible. A faraway hope that had diminished with time, disappointment after disappointment.

We'd been mocked and humiliated.

We'd been harassed.

We'd been ignored.

We'd been robbed.

We'd failed.

We'd overcome—and then failed again and again.

We'd been, it seemed, the only people on the planet who believed that we belonged. And even that belief had grown frail.

After so much frustration, I'd almost walked away. Almost. But I'd remained, because I knew that we were more than the world believed, and I had one last chance to help prove it.

The ninety-ninth time I'd run across a pitch for Canada.

We'd made it this far—farther than any Canadian men's team in nearly four decades, and only the second to ever get here.

The World Cup.

The biggest stage in sport. On the other side of this tunnel, we'd meet the number two ranked team on the planet.

The whole world watching. All eyes on us.

I felt like a kid, naive enough to have enormous ambitions and believe that those dreams were possible. I remembered those long-ago days, playing out those visions on a patchy field, feeling a joy that would grow into passion. Back then, I'd imagined this moment so many times, scoring goals and hoisting trophies in a fantasy land.

"Could this be real?" I wondered. My heart pounded. The roar beyond the tunnel called.

I opened my eyes near the end of a beautiful dream.

Part I

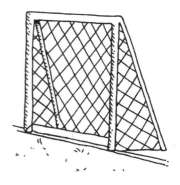

1

The World Cup of Brampton's Own

We came from around the corner and across the world. From Winterfold Drive and Pluto Drive, Ashurst Crescent and Hockley Path—from streets that sound like they could be in any suburban town, but laid the course towards our childhood dreams.

We'd known each other all our young lives, running and biking down these sleepy roads, always finding our way to the same field. We'd met two months after birth, in the first grade, in the seventh grade—a collection of childhood friendships that would become life-long bonds. No matter where we'd wind up, decades on, entire lives lived, we'd always be able to return to where it began and everything would be just as it was—as so it always would be.

The centre of our universe was a lumpy, patchy sandlot; a cracked dirt archipelago scattered with grassy islands. Every time we kicked the ball over the fence, it tumbled down the slope of a massive gravel pit on the edge of the subdivision in the heart of Brampton, where we lived alongside dozens of other kids whose families also came to Canada from somewhere else. It was the kind of field you'd find behind any elementary school in the city in the 1990s, and it was the best quality we could hope for in a soccer pitch at the time. The field behind Arnott Charlton Public School was our home.

Our group of about half a dozen friends mostly lived within throwing distance of the field. Alex Della Sciucca, a best friend since we were six, was probably the furthest away: he lived a couple of blocks over.

Any day in the summer, or any day after school, you could ride your bike by Arnott Charlton and be guaranteed to find at least three friends—but up to as many as a dozen—playing some kind of sport. Every day. That was the spot. It was the shared backyard for all the kids in the neighbourhood. And it was like an Olympic Park: you would see kids playing soccer on the field, or you could go over to the concrete pad next to the school and kids would be playing hand-ball. There would be kids climbing up on the roof to hang out and watch all the action from the best seats around.

It didn't matter what sport we were playing, Arnott Charlton hosted our battles for our adolescent bragging rights. There were arguments and fights, insults and showboating. There were boastful winners and sore losers. Everybody wanted to win. But nobody wanted to win more than me.

I was short and skinny then, probably the slightest among my group of friends. My brother, Haldon, who is five years older than me, often joked that I seemed malnourished. I also suffered from asthma, which just gave him more material to work with.

I had a lot of confidence for a twig with breathing issues. I might have always been the slenderest kid in whatever sport we were play-ing, but I was able to hold my own. I was determined to, even if I was playing against kids who were much bigger and older.

Sometimes we'd play basketball on a Fisher-Price net that we brought to the Arnott Charlton parking lot from our house. It was meant for little kids, but we were well into our middle-school years by then. I don't know what we were thinking—we were as tall as the net itself. Those games were basically just people trying to dunk on each other. It was a set-up for us to get into fights.

One afternoon, things got a little too heated and my next-door neighbour hit me with a hard foul and then refused to accept the call. In the accepted standards of adolescent Fisher-Price-net schoolyard basketball, this was an egregious violation. We got in each other's faces and were about to fight, when our friends pulled us back.

"Who wants to play some basketball?" my friend shouted, over and over. It pissed me off. I was done.

"Alright," I said. "That's it. It's game over."

I picked up the Fisher-Price net and walked home with it. If I wasn't going to play, no one else was going to play either.

I had a very short fuse. I *hated* to lose. It didn't matter what sport I was playing or whether or not I was good at it.

My disdain for defeat was strong as my desire to win. I was taught that way. It was the impetus that caused me to prepare and prepare until I couldn't lose.

◆

In the Hutchinson household, we were all competitors. Haldon, my older brother, was the same way. We went at each other constantly. I just wanted to beat him as often as I could. Haldon was actually a good basketball player. He ended up playing collegiate ball at Niagara University and then returned to the Toronto area where he started at Humber College. But when we were kids, I didn't care if he was Michael Jordan. I was going to beat him. I genuinely believed that I could be a better basketball player than Haldon. I thought I was the man. I always tried hard. I felt inside that I was better. I always had that belief in myself. But I never beat my older brother in basketball.

He put me in my place every time. He was bigger, more physical, and better than me at everything. It made me want to fight so much more to win—and that drive carried over when I played with my friends.

When you have brothers around you—and my friends were like brothers—it brings out all the competitiveness you have inside. That's how it always was with us. No one in our circle would tolerate losing. We'd compete over the smallest, dumbest things. Who could crumple up a piece of paper and toss it into a garbage can? Who could eat sunflower seeds the fastest? Regardless of how meaningless the task was, we competed—which is something we'd continue doing as grown men, three decades on.

We found joy in those youthful games as we grew up in a rapidly expanding suburb northwest of Toronto. But when it came to football, we shared another level of passion entirely. This was the game that captured our imaginations more than any other.

The patchy field behind Arnott Charlton was our Old Trafford, our Bernabéu—our very own field of dreams. It was where we practised what we'd witnessed on weekly satellite broadcasts of the Premier League or La Liga.

We were so attached to the pitch that when we were in our early teens, a few of us went to Home Depot and rented a lawn roller. We pushed that massive barrel back and forth along the lumpy field as though we were preparing the pitch for an actual World Cup match. We tried to make sure that there were no bumps along the way, which is an impossible task when dealing with the rough, arid patches of a schoolyard. We spent hours on it, trying to get it right.

We carried soccer nets from my house a few blocks away, which we had made by hand with my father in the garage. I'd picked up a hammer (some say for the first and final time) and nailed the pieces together alongside Dad for the makeshift World Cup tournament that we ran each year.

It was a three-on-three tournament that we organized with the kids in our neighbourhood. We were all pretty much the same age, maybe a couple of years between the eldest and youngest in the tournament. We looked forward to it each summer. There was even an entrance fee—each team pooling together cash for the winner's pot. Our home was the headquarters for the World Cup organizers.

We divided ourselves along ethnic lines for the tournament. In Brampton, on its way to becoming one of the world's most multicultural cities, it was never difficult to fill a squad. There were teams from Jamaica, Spain, Portugal, Ghana, among many others. Alex played for the Italians. I was a skinny, undersized striker for Trinidad.

Any kids without compatriots were placed in a hodgepodge group that reflected Canada itself. No one wore that title with pride. In our adolescent world, playing football for Canada carried little weight. We didn't dream of wearing red and white, representing our nation against the world. There wasn't enough inherent pride in the nation's football history to warrant such a fantasy.

At that time, it was difficult to imagine something that we had such minimal exposure to. Some of us might have known about Canada's 1986 appearance at the World Cup—the only time a Canadian team had ever appeared in the globe's most revered tournament. But we were only toddlers when coach Tony Waiters had led a scrappy Canadian team through a historic qualifying round and earned a trip to Mexico to compete for international sport's grandest prize. Canada had failed to qualify ever since, so competing for our own country was not something we dreamed about.

Across the country, hockey was still the sport of our national identity—the frozen game that Canadians had dominated for nearly a century. It was the sport Canada was famous for, our cultural touchstone in the world. We were the birthplace of Wayne Gretzky, king of the cold climate sport, which relatively few nations actually play. Hockey was a monochromatic sport, which—especially in the 1990s—made little room for newcomers. In other words, it was a sport for wealthy white kids. For the kids who were never asked where they were *really* from, because it was assumed that they were from *here*. But rapidly growing Brampton was a place where an increasing majority had deep cultural roots elsewhere. And so our passion was found both home and away, with a unique sense of identity rooted in both where we were now and where we had come from. And the sport of "elsewhere"—the global game so many young people in the Toronto area inherited a love for from their parents who'd made Canada home—was football.

So within our group of friends competing to be champions of the world, we played proudly for the nations of our parents. This was the World Cup of Brampton's own. It was as intense and serious as the actual World Cup could possibly be.

In one of the most memorable tournaments, Trinidad played Jamaica in the final. It was me, my cousin Kevin, and our friend Dwayne against a couple of our friends and this ringer they brought in, who was about five years older than the rest of us, basically a grown man. But we held on and won the World Cup for Trinidad. We celebrated as though we were actually hoisting that gold trophy, the most gorgeous prize in sport—two humans holding up the globe, like hands hoisting a football. We spent our winnings at the local Beckers convenience store like proper soccer stars, lavishly and irresponsibly on things we didn't need, like sour keys, Oh Henry! bars, and sunflower seeds.

When I lay in bed at night, my imagination carried me to only one beautiful dream. One day, I'd play in a real World Cup—as near impossible as that seemed.

2

Local Stars and Satellites

Football is my father's game. Dalton Hutchinson passed it on to me. He grew up playing football in Trinidad; he learned to play on rough grassless lots near the mountains in Port of Spain. There was no glamour in the game, aside from what his imagination could conjure. Like most of the kids he played with, he didn't even own soccer boots. They wore regular runners, if they were lucky, or played in their bare feet. There were few examples of the fame and luxury that football could offer to entice him to dream of something grander. He played the game because it was part of who he was. It captured his imagination and his passion. It was where he felt most at home in the world, the way that many young people feel when they fall madly in love with a sport for the first time. It consumes them.

Growing up, he was always one of the best players in his region— something he'd remind us of often. He was proud of the football he'd played on that small island in the West Indies that he called home, tucked off the coast of Venezuela. When he was young, my father's biggest dream was to one day represent his country at the World Cup.

It was a dream that he'd never have the opportunity to fulfill but one that he'd never fully abandon.

◆

My parents grew up in the same neighbourhood in Port of Spain, but my mother, Myrtle, rarely saw my father play when they first starting dating as teenagers. Her mother was very strict and didn't let her hang out near soccer fields. But he always talked a big game, and whenever he got together with friends in the decades to come, they'd tell stories of those glory days playing soccer together back in Trinidad.

Trinidad and Tobago gained independence from Britain in 1962, in an era of great optimism and pride. A booming oil industry helped underpin the economy in the nascent republic in the 1960s. Port of Spain, the capital, expanded rapidly. But it was also a time of great uncertainty. While the oil industry flourished, there was a great disparity between those who reaped the economic benefits and those who didn't. Though there would always remain a strong sense of identity with the islands, many young people started to look for opportunities elsewhere—particularly in the United Kingdom, the United States, and Canada.

My mother was one of those people. In 1974 when she was twenty-one years old, she flew from Port of Spain to Toronto, following her older brother and sister who had already migrated to Canada. The country had welcoming immigration policies in the 1960s and 1970s, which led to an influx of new Canadians. Like other newcomers, my mother's family was searching for a better life with more opportunities than they could find in Trinidad and Tobago. Mom returned to Port of Spain later that year and married my father, who was twenty-five at the time. Three months later, in 1975, they both moved to Toronto to start their new life together. For my parents, that meant leaving behind many members of their family and close friends who remained in Port of Spain. But they would never really leave Trinidad behind. The country—its culture, its rhythm—would always be part of who they were. Trinidad was family; Trinidad was home. My parents would pass on that sense of identity to their children.

A few years later, my mother's older brother and sister both moved out of Toronto to a quiet suburb northwest of the city. In the mid-nineteenth century, Brampton had been a small village around a four-corner downtown surrounded by farmland and woods. It remained relatively small through the next century, slowly expanding into a town and then a city. In the 1850s, Brampton's population was just fifty people. A century later, a little more than eight thousand people called the town home. But then in the early 1960s, the population more than doubled. And through the '70s, more than 100,000 people moved to Brampton, as affordable houses swallowed up the farmland that once surrounded it.

At first, Brampton didn't interest my mother. It seemed too far away from where they'd settled in Toronto. Even though nearly 150,000 people lived in Brampton at the time, it still seemed like a bit of backwater nearly forty-five minutes away from Canada's largest city, then home to just shy of three million people. But Haldon was born in 1978 and was already running after every ball he could get his little hands on. It made sense for my parents to be close to their relatives as young parents. The houses were much, much cheaper, as well as more spacious with larger backyards. The quiet wide streets and parks of Brampton's new subdivisions were an ideal place to raise kids. There was no question it was a safer place for young kids in a less congested suburb than the bustling, busy streets of the city.

In the early 1980s, my parents moved to 104 Winterfold Drive, a light-brown brick semidetached split-level house, about a ten second sprint from the wide field that sat behind Arnott Charlton Public

School. The house on Winterfold would be our home for the next quarter century. I was born soon after we moved in, on February 8, 1983. My little sister, Toyaa, was born six years later in 1989. Brampton grew up around us, expanding with new subdivisions year after year.

Our parents were very proud of their Trinidadian roots and made sure to pass on that culture to us children. It was about a connection to family and community, and we were lucky to have a strong bond with both as we grew up in Brampton. My mother was one of eleven children—two boys and nine girls—and eventually many of her siblings came to live in the Toronto area too. And there was a strong West Indian community in Brampton, which meant we enjoyed many of the same cultural events and celebrations my parents had growing up in Port of Spain.

Our home was always filled with incredible West Indian food—the best jerk chicken and roti around. If you passed the house on Winterfold at the time, you'd likely have heard calypso and soca music pumping from the windows. Every Christmas, we went to Parang shows, which is a traditional gathering to sing Christmas songs unique to Trinidad, accompanied by horns, steel drums, and other percussion instruments. It was always a vibrant party. Every summer, we attended Caribana in Toronto—one of the biggest annual celebrations of Caribbean culture in the world; it's based on traditional Carnival celebrations, known for its colourful costumes, music, and dancing. When I was young, I never enjoyed trekking with my family to the crowded streets of Toronto, where I could barely hear anyone around me speak. But I came to understand its importance—and the beautiful, unique nature of our culture. Caribana commemorates the abolition of slavery in the British colonies in the nineteenth century. There is a lot of important history within the exuberant festival.

◆

While all of these traditions underpinned my youth, it was football that most connected me to my West Indian heritage. More specifically, it was watching a group of middle-aged men play on a soccer field near the Toronto International Airport on Sunday mornings.

Haldon and I were among the young spectators always in attendance to cheer for their fathers as they fought through the competitive world of over-forty recreational football. My father's team was made up of West Indian players, mostly from Trinidad, with a few Jamaican and Guyanese players to fill out the roster. Most of the teams in the league were made up of players from the West Indian diaspora. There was a sense of shared history as these men, these fathers, battled as if the World Cup was on the line every Sunday—willing to risk life and limb in aging bodies to finish each play. They got into small shoving and shouting matches after each aggressive tackle, each perceived insult. They ran systems and set plays. They whooped and hollered after each goal. They played with pride and passion.

Dad was always the best player on the pitch—the team's "superstar," he would say with a wry smile. Though his youth was well behind him, he was still an athletic, speedy striker. He averaged a couple of goals each game. When his team needed a goal, Dad was there to weave through the other dads and play the hero. Haldon and I would run up and down the sidelines, kicking balls with the other children while our fathers played. To us, at the time, this was some of the finest football we could imagine. They played for the glory of post-game beers and league bragging rights. They played because the passion they'd found on the pitch as boys never faded, even as they became men with busy lives, balancing families and jobs. Every Sunday, they returned to the joy they'd felt as kids.

Although time erased his opportunity to play football professionally or at the international level, it never diminished my father's passion for playing. It also didn't mute his self-assurance in football.

Dad spent too much of his time as a student of the beautiful game, studying its easy secrets and marvelous complexities, to not pass on his vision for how the game should be played. And in his children, he found captive students. Instead of fading with age, Dad's dream of representing his country on the international stage just shifted. If he couldn't play for his country, he was determined that his children would have the opportunity to play for theirs.

Haldon inherited our father's athletic genes and competitiveness. And of course, soccer was the first sport my father made sure his eldest son played. But when Haldon first started playing, my father didn't know how to navigate the ins and outs of minor soccer in Canada. There wasn't a road map for finding your way to the national program. And Haldon didn't have the benefit that I had of an older brother to go first, navigating the landscape of skill development and organized youth soccer well before many of today's well-known travel teams and development programs existed. It was a new world for my parents, raising a young family in a strange new place.

I loved soccer from the moment I touched a ball, which is to say from the moment conscious memory of my life begins. I learned to hold myself up on two feet and then almost immediately learned how to kick a ball. Soccer captivated my young imagination in a way that other sports didn't. It was pure joy—like the first time you taste chocolate, or get a smile back from a girl you like. It was that, but every time I played. The ball connected with my feet in a way that made it seem as though the laws of physics mandated the connection. It's the kind of thing you can feel in your soul. And once you feel it, you know that you can never let it go.

So every opportunity I had, I was outside kicking the ball around the backyard with my father. We spent hours together just playing in the backyard, and in the winter, our basement transformed into a tiny indoor pitch. My dad was just as passionate about teaching me the game as I was about learning it. He showed me everything he knew: how to kick, how to dribble, how to control the ball, how to understand the game. How to harness my love for the game and turn it into a life.

◆

I first joined a local competitive rep team run by the Brampton Youth Soccer Club when I was six years old. Dad joined the team as an assistant coach, and he was my coach, in some capacity, for the next decade.

At that time, soccer was on a decline from what had been an unprecedented surge in youth participation that followed Canada's first and only appearance at the World Cup in 1986. There were more than 1,600 youth participants in the program that year, a number that dipped in the years that followed as the excitement of that World Cup appearance in Mexico faded. The year I started playing club soccer, in 1989, Canada was unable to get past Guatemala in a home-and-away series to qualify for the Concacaf Championship—the regional FIFA championship tournament for North America, Central America, and the Caribbean, from which the two top teams earned a spot at the 1990 World Cup in Italy. The disappointing outcome helped deflate local interest in Canada's presence on the international football stage.

As I ran across the patchy pitch with my Brampton Braves teammates at Century Gardens Recreation Centre in the heart of Brampton, a few blocks from my house, I didn't have a Canadian reference point to emulate. Even though their run was an inspiring and historic moment in Canadian sports, I was too young to find heroes in the 1986 World Cup team. We didn't talk about the Canadian national team at all, to be honest. That team didn't get nearly enough recognition or respect for what they accomplished. We wouldn't have been able to name most of the players on the team.

And professional soccer in Europe wasn't as accessible in the early '90s as it is today. I caught the odd La Liga or Premier League game at friends' houses, but it wasn't something we followed very closely. It was difficult to find examples of what great football really looked like. So my passion formed elsewhere.

Back then, I wouldn't have been able to describe it. But looking back, it's clear. It was simply the love that I felt playing with my friends on the street or at the park, every day. It was the feel of the ball at my feet as I ran, the looks of friends staring as I passed them, and the rush of scoring one last goal before dinner. And it was watching my father and his friends chase the ghosts of old dreams on a field near the airport—the feelings of pride and excitement as we ran up and down the sidelines, following the champions of our world.

At the time, the enormous global reach of the game was still hard for me to comprehend. Our world was Brampton. Home internet was just a concept in the early '90s, and even when it did take off, it would be years before we didn't have to listen to a high-pitched dial-up sound each time we connected—or lost that connection whenever a sibling picked up a landline telephone.

But satellite television changed everything for me. My parents didn't have a lot of extra money to spend on luxuries, but in the mid-'90s, my father decided that the one extravagance they'd stretch for was access to international football. And so, through the miracle of a giant dish contraption attached to our roof, we were suddenly able to access programming from the best European leagues—and my imagination took off.

Every Saturday and Sunday morning, I would wake up early to watch the Premier League, which was founded in 1992 to modernize and monetize England's First Division, capitalizing on England's rich football history in an increasingly globalized world. I sat mesmerized in our living room, watching as much soccer as I could before heading to the backyard to copy the smallest details of the majesty I'd just witnessed. There wasn't a specific team that my father supported, but there was one player we couldn't miss: Dwight Yorke.

When it came to football, Yorke—who was born and raised in Tobago—was the pride of the West Indies. As he established himself as one of the most dynamic forwards in the Premier League, Yorke also starred for the Trinidad and Tobago national team. He'd earn seventy-two caps playing for the Soca Warriors, as the national team was known. Yorke played alongside his friend and Trinidadian legend Russell Latapy in the 1989 Concacaf Championship, narrowly missing a berth in the World Cup by a single point. While Canada didn't even qualify for the tournament, Trinidad and Tobago's electrifying run through the Concacaf Championship became the stuff of national sporting legend in the Caribbean two-island republic, with the team being dubbed the Strike Squad.

Yorke's path to professional football stardom began with Aston Villa, where he played for eight seasons, establishing himself as one of the league's most prolific scorers, but he didn't have the kind of high profile exposure players at more popular clubs received. Then after a controversial transfer to Manchester United in 1998, Yorke's fame took off. There was a lot of talk about him going to Manchester. That was when I really started to follow him. Obviously, the Trinidadian connection was a big reason for that. Before Yorke, I had heard of very few players coming out of the West Indies to play top-tier football. My father made sure that I knew about Russell Latapy, but he'd played most of his club career in Portugal and had just transferred to Scotland at the time and joined Hibernian FC in the Scottish Premier League. None of that carried the esteem that came with playing at Old Trafford.

In his first season, Yorke helped lead the Red Devils to its first Treble—winning the Premier League, FA Cup, and UEFA Champions

League. In one of the most celebrated seasons in the team's history—playing alongside United icons Andy Cole, David Beckham, Paul Scholes, and Roy Keane—Yorke became the league's top goal scorer and was named Premier League Player of the Season.

It was huge. I had spent so much time hearing stories from my father about playing football back in Trinidad, and then I witnessed a player who shared my heritage become one of the most dominant players in the world. Yorke became the model for the kind of player I hoped to be. I loved his game. His first touch was just smooth. He was elegant on the pitch. He was from my world, a product of my culture. And he had conquered football. Because of that connection, the dream that my father passed on to me seemed much less far away.

Like him, I wanted to play for Manchester United one day. And like him, I hoped to play for my family's homeland, Trinidad and Tobago. My parents both still had passports from the country, which meant that I was eligible. For a long time, I only thought about one day representing Trinidad, like my father had dreamed of doing when he was young. Back then, the idea of playing for Canada didn't even enter my mind. As a kid, I couldn't quite comprehend the complex beauty of the Canadian dream I was experiencing. My family was from two places at once, which was a beautiful part of our experience—and that of so many others—who came to make Canada home.

3

Control the Machine

Our house at 104 Winterfold was a central hub in the neighbourhood. It was the home on the street that all the other kids came to. So, of course, 104 Winterfold took a beating. There were always kids over, ripping up around our backyard or bouncing off the walls inside. There were balls all over our house; it didn't seem to matter what room. The basement is where most of the action happened. It was a training ground and a battleground, where sandlot grudges carried over in one-on-one clashes. We absolutely destroyed it with games of indoor basketball and soccer.

For my parents, the constant mess, the patched-up drywall, the random kids who stopped by and made themselves at home—it was all worth it. To them, sports were a way to help their kids apply themselves and navigate the challenges of growing up. As long as we were staying out of trouble and they knew where we were, my parents could live with the chaos.

It was probably good that they kept a close eye on us, because I had a temper that could have gotten me in a lot of trouble elsewhere. I used to get in fights with Haldon all the time, over the stupidest stuff.

Once, after a game of basketball in our basement, I got a little too heated after my brother dunked on me on the mini net attached to the wall. (We had graduated from the Fisher-Price net.) I'm pretty sure it was the game-winning point, and I took exception to the way he'd won. I was a terrible loser. That day, I was so angry that I stormed upstairs and grabbed a butter knife from the kitchen. I stormed back down the stairs and pointed it at Haldon. I was ready to defend my honour with that dull blade. Of course, he wasn't scared of his little brother and his ineffective butter spreader. He just laughed at me, kicking off another chapter in our ongoing sibling war.

◆

I was very confident in my ability at that age. It wasn't so much that I was cocky—in fact, I was a pretty mild-mannered kid outside sports— but I was furiously competitive and knew that I could take over any game that I was playing. I knew that I could, and as I said, I wasn't particularly gracious about losing. The context didn't matter, whether it was a club game or pickup on the schoolyard. This often frustrated friends like Alex, Mike, and Kevin, because I'd play nonchalantly until the next goal was set to be the winner. Then I'd kick into another gear to make sure my team won the game. This kind of gamesmanship always annoyed my friends, but it was my way of playing mind games before I even knew what mind games were.

But even though I excelled amongst my cohort, there was still so much for me to learn in the game. I doubt that anyone watching who really knew football would have believed that I could one day be a professional player. I was tall and skilled for my age, but that didn't really mean much beyond Brampton.

I was still very skinny—and I suffered from asthma. I remember rough nights when I struggled to breathe. And summer days when I was suddenly gasping, scrambling for my puffer. The condition worried my mother so much that for a time she thought I might not be able to play soccer at all. I had to sleep with a breathing machine and had to put a big mask over my face. My friends joked that it sounded like a lawn mower. It often woke up everyone in the house. Sometimes it would stop working, and I'd wake up gasping for air. My mother would have to rush in to fix the machine.

The asthma was particularly bad in the heat, which really should have been a problem when it came to soccer. My mom tried to keep me from playing, but my father always let me push through. Even if I was struggling to breathe, I didn't want to come off the pitch. And there was never a moment when I had to stop playing. Even in training sessions, I would be fine. I'd take a puffer if I needed it and then just keep on moving. It defied logic. My mom was a spiritual person, so maybe all her prayers paid off. When it came to soccer, I refused to let anything slow me down.

Even if I didn't quite have a vision for the path I wanted to take or even where I hoped to end up, I was very young when I decided that football would be my life. I can't remember exactly how old I was when I first declared my intentions, but I can still remember the moment.

My cousin Kevin, who was almost the same age as me and was one of my closest friends—one of the sandlot guys—often slept over at our house. He was the only friend whom I was allowed to have regular sleepovers with, and that was only because he was family and my mother knew that my uncle, Kevin's dad, would keep us in line.

Whenever he came over or if I went to his house, Kevin would toss and turn through the night while my massive asthma machine whirled like a jet engine. Sometimes, as we lay in bed before falling asleep, we'd talk about our dreams, the way kids often do. One night, after hours of playing at Arnott Charlton, I told Kevin that I was going to play professionally one day. He could have laughed at me. We were close enough to give each other a hard time. But Kevin didn't mock my determination. I was lucky to have a cousin and friend like Kevin. We all need people like that in our lives, who make us believe that our dreams are possible. We lay awake for a while, imagining all the wild things we asked the future to bring, naive to how far away and difficult those expectations were. We fell asleep to the whirling groan of my asthma machine.

I was still too young to see how unlikely my dream was back then. In other words, I was blessed with the ignorance of childhood belief. That's part of the beauty of being young. I didn't know how stacked the odds were against me. All I knew was that Dwight Yorke was a legend—and I was determined to make it, just like he had. I figured that if I kept scoring goals and being the best player on the field, I'd inevitably wind up where I planned to go.

But I wasn't living in a world designed for high performance excellence, the way many young athletes do today. Especially in Brampton, there were very few one-on-one coaches or personal trainers to hire to take us to that next level. Even if we'd had a lot of money, there was only so much that money could have done to advance your status in the game.

What we had was Arnott Charlton and each other. That's how we fostered our imaginations as players. That's how we grew and improved as players. It was a group of friends with a shared passion. It wasn't just that we loved soccer. The game was fundamental to who we were as boys growing up together. It was our religion, a way of life handed down from a previous generation. It was part of our identity. It was our purpose. Every minute we spent together on that field—playing keep up, taking penalties, running through drills—was essential to the opportunities that I'd later have in football. Without those experiences, I'd never have stood a chance. I was very lucky.

That alone would never have been enough though. Without a proper guide, my friends and I would have just been kicking a ball around, trying to copy what we saw on fuzzy satellite channels each weekend. We needed a teacher to show us how to understand the game properly—how to read the fortune of an attack, anticipating exactly where the play was heading before it got there. Real success on the pitch is about much more than reacting to the run of play. It's about knowing where it's going and beating it there. It's about more than the past or present; it's about knowing the future.

For me, that guide was my father.

I played as a striker early on in my rep soccer days, which is of course what I wanted to play—it's what everyone wants to play when they are young. Who doesn't want to be the primary offensive option on a team?

But when I was around twelve years old, Dad convinced me to move back to midfield. It seemed like a counterintuitive request at the time. I was faster than almost everyone we played against and was the team's top scorer. But Dad was always thinking ahead. He said that if I was going to move forward in the sport, I had to focus on controlling and distributing the ball.

"You have to control the machine," he told me.

It was one of many lessons he'd try to teach me as we sat in our van at a field waiting for everyone else to show up.

We were never late. *Never*. Dad was strict about being on time. It was a family rule. We were always early to training, and we'd always stay late. He worried that if we were ever delayed getting to a practice or a game, I'd be benched and would miss valuable playing time. And there was no playing time to spare. We weren't spending all these hours practising and driving all over the place just to sit on the bench because we couldn't get our act together.

◆

Dad worked as a welder, putting in long hard hours and then rushing home to make sure we'd get to our games with plenty of time to spare—often at the pitch an hour beforehand. There would be no one from either team there; we were almost always the very first ones. He turned the extra time we had sitting in the car waiting into an opportunity to teach me more about the game. It was all we spoke about. There was always something more to learn—something big or small from my last game, or something he'd seen in practice. Football is a sport of constant development, and Dad was determined to make sure that I didn't sit back and stop learning, just because I showed talent at the level I was playing at. He knew the reality of how much more I needed to learn if I had any chance of reaching a higher level. I loved the time we spent together, talking through the smallest details of our shared passion.

"Even though you don't have the ball, you have to put yourself in position," he'd tell me. "Look active on the field."

He taught me to think of the game in a more cerebral way than kids my age usually did. There was so much more to football than following the ball and scoring goals, he said. This was by the far the most useful skill my father instilled in me during all those long drives and hours spent waiting for kickoff. He gave me a vision for the game.

"You don't have to play the game with the ball all the time," he'd say. "Just keep moving."

A good coach looks at every player and sees how they move and what they do with the ball and without the ball, Dad would tell me. If a coach saw me getting to the right position on the pitch, they'd take note, even if I didn't get the pass.

"If you don't have the ball, get yourself in a position to receive the ball," he'd say.

It was about knowing how to play the game the right way. Anticipating, instead of reacting. Always thinking several plays ahead, instead of trying to catch up to the run of play.

"They are going to say, 'That kid knows what he is doing,'" Dad said.

"You don't have to score the goals. There are ten players on the field. Just show yourself and keep moving."

Another reason my father had for putting me back on midfield was it meant that I would spend more time with the ball than most players on the team. Even if I would score fewer goals, it was a self-serving move from a development perspective. At midfield, he said, I'd spend at least 50 to 60 percent of the game with the ball. That meant more improvement.

"The more touches you get with the ball, the better you're going to be," he said.

My dad was thinking long term. He instilled a mindset of constant improvement in me. He taught me that greatness is a slow and steady process—always getting better one day, one play at a time, and embracing failure as part of that journey.

In those early years, my father recruited my neighbourhood friends—all the sandlot kids—to fill out the rep team that he helped coach. My friend Mike still swears he wasn't very good at all, but we were close pals so we wanted him on the pitch with us. He was actually a lockdown defender. He chased me around the pitch in practice. Dad knew how to put pieces together, but, again, there was a self-serving method to his coaching. He would set the lineup for our team with my best friend Alex beside me at midfield, because he knew that as soon as Alex touched the ball, he'd look to me and pass it. That way, Dad figured, I would get the ball all the time, and none of the other parents would get upset, because it was Alex who was making sure that I received it. It was his secret plan. I'm still not sure if Alex ever realized.

To his credit, Alex was a very good player. We first met in the first grade, and we bonded over football. We played it at school, in our basements, backyards, and at the sandlot. We played on the same club team and at our elementary school. In middle school, he was the captain of our cohort, while I played up on the senior team. When we were growing up, he was at our house so much he was basically part of our family. Alex was the kind of friend that becomes part of your life as long as you can remember—from your first memories as a kid through the rest of your life. Every step of my life, he's been there.

So if my father was going to handpick a player to put beside me on the pitch to make sure I'd get the ball more often, Alex was the obvious choice.

He was often in the van with us on the road to games, singing along to the calypso music my father played. They were catchy tunes. We spent a lot of time in that van, travelling to tournaments across Ontario. And we had at least two games a week somewhere in the Greater Toronto Area, from the west end of Mississauga, a half hour away, all the way east to Scarborough, which could take an hour and a half, depending on the time of day. On top of that, there were practices all over the city, which could take place early in the morning, right after school, or late in the evening.

It wasn't easy for my father or mother. It was a busy life. But the commitment was never a question for my father. He'd go straight from work, tired after a long day, and he never complained about having to drive us out to these games or to tournaments on the weekends. Today, I can put myself in my father's position. I know now, as a parent, what it means to see your child find and pursue a passion—especially when it's a passion you share. Looking back, I understand just how lucky we were.

4

Soccer City

How was a kid from Brampton in the '90s supposed to find their way in soccer? In the world of football, Canada was a remote island when I was growing up. This is something my brother, Haldon, and I often talk about when we think back to those early days.

So much has changed since we were kids. There was no YouTube to watch highlights from around the world. Today my kids can view pretty much any play they want to watch within a few seconds. They have access to so much more information than kids in our generation did. Our kids can now watch a play and immediately start practising it in their living rooms. We simply didn't have easy access to those reference points to learn from.

And the soccer fields I played on were municipal afterthoughts, sporadically maintained. Often the lines were just grassless strips of dirt, rather than white paint. There was almost always a wide patch of dirt in the area where keepers paced back and forth. Scoring a goal meant chasing after a ball as it rolled well beyond the bare white posts, with no net. We had to travel for more than half an hour to the

outskirts of Toronto to find an indoor soccer facility, where the pitch
felt like concrete covered by a scratchy green carpet.

◆

When I was starting out, we played our home games on a pitch next to
a community centre in Brampton called Century Gardens, which was
just a few minutes from our house. Our biggest rival was a team from
Chinguacousy—a region on the eastern side of Brampton, which was
once its own township before the city swallowed it up. Chinguacousy
played home games at the Victoria Park community centre on the
southeast side of town. We hated Ching like any team would their
regional rivals. They were Manchester City to our United, Chelsea to
our Arsenal. Every match between Brampton and Chinguacousy was
filled with the animosity of a proper derby, a match between local
rivals. In our age group, the teams were consistently the top two in
Ontario at the time.

Iain Hume was Chinguacousy's star player and the best player I'd
ever faced on a soccer field. He and I always battled when our teams
met, each of us scoring multiple goals. At the time, I viewed him as
competition, but Iain would quickly become one of the closest friends
I'd find in the game.

Iain grew up next to Bramalea City Centre, the main mall in the
region that was only about a ten-minute drive from my house. But in
the politics of Brampton, it was on the other side of the highway that
cut through town, which meant he belonged to the Chinguacousy side.
He was actually born in Edinburgh, Scotland, and his parents moved
to Canada when he was very young. They brought their Scottish roots
with them, which meant that soccer was their sport. Just as my
Trinidadian roots laid the foundation for my connection to soccer,
Iain's deep connection to the game grew from his parents' homeland

too. Much like the field at Arnott Charlton, Iain played all his early soccer in the field at Clark Boulevard Public School with his older brother and his father. And as with me and my family, they were always doing something with a soccer ball.

But in Ontario youth soccer in the '90s, the pathways to top-level football just didn't exist. Certainly not the way they did in hockey or baseball. Organized youth soccer was still finding its way. All of our coaches were volunteers, like my father. There weren't the licensed, paid coaches who come out to run academies today. But there were still some players who managed to find their way, players Iain and I would come to look to for inspiration.

Several years before Iain and I started competing against each other, Paul Stalteri rose out of Brampton as one of the top players in Canada. Paul grew up on the west side of the city, and he was five years older than us, so we never really crossed paths in minor league soccer. Like Iain and me, Paul found a skilled counterpart and close friend in Jason Bent, who was eight when he moved to Brampton from Malton, a town to the east, just north of Toronto's international airport.

For younger guys like us, in the small community of Brampton soccer, Paul and Jason were local idols. When Paul was twelve years old, he left Brampton minor soccer to play with a club from Malton. Paul was a stalwart defender and skilled midfielder who became an important mentor throughout my career. But he was still chasing his dream when I was coming through minor soccer. In just a few years, he'd become a beacon for players like me, illuminating how far a Canadian player could go in professional soccer.

I was a fourteen-year-old still trying to find my own path in the game when Jason started his pro career in 1997, joining FSV Zwickau in the second tier of Germany's pro soccer system. That same year, Paul started his professional career with the Toronto Lynx, a new franchise in what was then known as the A-League, a pro soccer league with teams in the United States and Canada. That season, he played alongside Dwayne De Rosario—the two future Canadian soccer icons crossing paths before heading down different professional paths. While De Rosario would stick with the North American game, becoming one of the most celebrated players in Major League Soccer, Stalteri looked to Europe. A scout for Werder Bremen, a storied club in the Bundesliga, the top tier of Germany's professional football system, saw Paul play with the Toronto Lynx and was impressed enough to purchase his rights.

Meanwhile, Jason Bent had returned to North America after one season in Europe, joining the Colorado Rapids in the MLS. He'd also earn thirty-two caps with the Canadian national team in his career.

Paul spent two and a half seasons as a Werder Bremen reserve before making his first appearance with the club in 2000, when he was twenty-four years old. Five years later, Paul transferred from the Bundesliga to the Premier League with Tottenham Hotspur. Paul's influence in Canadian soccer can't be overstated. He became captain of the Canadian national team in 2007, and he was the country's most capped player, with eight-five caps, by the time he retired in 2013. Throughout his career, guys like Iain and me were right behind him, finding inspiration in the against-the-odds path he managed to take.

◆

I was still a striker way back when we had our best rivalries with Ching, so it was always billed as Atiba from Brampton versus Iain from Chinguacousy. Striker versus striker. And for the first few years that we played against each other, Brampton always beat Chinguacousy. The games weren't even close. It would be 4–0 or 7–4—always comfortable wins. It drove Iain nuts. But I was taller and faster than most of the other players, so at that age, it was easy to gain an edge on those advantages alone. I could sprint past most of my opponents and score. But as opponents grew and progressed, it became apparent that raw athletic advantage alone wouldn't be enough to set me apart. Iain continued to improve and continued scoring against us at will. Eventually Ching was beating us, and it was my turn to be driven crazy.

As much as we battled against each other on the pitch, we shared a mutual respect. People would debate over who was the better player, but I think we both understood that we were pushing each other to be better. We benefitted from the competition, as we both started to make names for ourselves in Ontario youth soccer.

When we were about twelve years old, our teams merged; after years of head-to-head rivalry, Iain and I found ourselves on the same team. It was around that time that my father moved me back to midfield, seeing an opportunity for much needed development in my game. Suddenly my biggest rival was playing in front of me. That was when our friendship really grew. Around that time, a coach for the Ontario U-14 provincial team saw me play and invited me to try out. It was an all-star-type travel team that played in special tournaments.

My father drove me to tryouts at Lamport Stadium in Toronto, a concrete facility built in the mid-1970s, just north across the highway from where Toronto FC play at BMO Field today. I was excited and nervous as we drove into Toronto; the buildings looked like they reached the clouds. Everything about the city felt enormous. And the moment felt huge too. It was my first opportunity to show that I belonged with the best of the best in my age group. As I stepped onto the pitch at Lamport, Iain was right there with me.

We were both selected to play for that under-13 squad, so between our club games and the provincial tournaments, Iain and I were together all the time. On those road trips with the Ontario team, we were always roommates. We didn't know then that it was an arrangement that would last for another two decades.

As Iain and I became teenagers, Brampton soccer built a reputation for quality. There had been a bit of cyclical reality when it came to the best teams in the area. If Brampton played well, players from other teams would want to join us. We all wanted to be part of a successful team, and we wanted to practise and play at the highest level we could. And when your team continued to do well, you'd continue to bring in better players.

For some reason, the cohort of players from Brampton born in the early '80s had a level of talent that the area wasn't particularly known for previously. The group that Iain and I came up with—born between 1983 and 1984—had more talented players than the group that came up with Paul and Jason. In fact, most of the players on the provincial teams we would play for were from Brampton. There were a few Scarborough guys and a couple of Woodbridge guys, but almost everyone else came from our clubs.

Why was that? What was going on in Brampton that created this nucleus for soccer in Ontario at the time?

Though football has been played around the world for more than a century, the game was highly localized for most of that time. Soccer has only become truly globalized in the late twentieth century, as the sport was beamed into living rooms around the world from places near and far. That's been a huge benefit for modern players, as well as for the sport itself. It's part of the reason so much talent arose out of places that had never been known for first-class talent.

But in Canada, the country's diversity played the biggest part. Brampton is a rich cultural landscape. Though when my parents first moved to Winterfold, there were mostly white faces on our street, the city was quickly growing into a multicultural hub. Brampton had a population of about 200,000 people in the early 1980s—and it was still predominantly white. But over a few years, more and more people came from around the world to make Canada their home, just like we had. Huge, vibrant West Indian, African, East Asian, Latin, Middle Eastern, and South Asian communities—among so many others—called the city home. It was changing, and a sport popular around the world took hold in the hearts and minds of children like me. What was rising then and what would follow was an inevitability we couldn't yet see.

5

For Country and Beyond

I will always remember the first time I looked around a stadium and saw fans cheering for Canada. That moment changed everything for me.

My father drove my teammates to Toronto to watch a friendly between the men's national team and Jamaica at Varsity Stadium. We were about twelve years old at the time and excited just to be making the trip. There was always a rush that came with any trip downtown. Coming from the suburbs, Toronto felt enormous, busy, and important. Packed into the van, with a steel-drum rhythm floating out the windows, we drove down the Gardiner towards the big city. Skyscrapers rose like giants around the CN Tower. I knew that we were going to a soccer game, but that almost felt secondary to the trip. I didn't know what to expect from a Canadian national team game. I figured that it would be a cool experience.

But walking into the stadium woke something up in me. The place was crowded with fans. There was a feeling of pride in the stands that I'd never experienced before. It was my first time watching a high level soccer match live (beyond my father's rec league games, of course). There were supporters for both teams, which I'd soon learn was commonplace for when Canada played at home, but the energy was incredible. Supporters wore red and white and waved Canadian flags. They banged drums and roared each time a Canadian player executed a quality play. I was enthralled by the action on the field, watching these guys play for Canada—at such a high speed, in such a high intensity game. I felt an immediate love. It was a sense of pride, waking up to what soccer could be like here—at home. In that moment, I knew that this was my future. Though I would always have a strong connection to Trinidad and Tobago, my primary goal was to one day play for my home country.

"I want to be on that pitch, playing for Canada," I thought.

As I neared high school, I was confident about where I stood among my peers on the pitch. I'd represented Ontario for several years at the provincial level and was starting to get noticed by coaches and scouts who could have a huge impact on my future.

But there were still some hard lessons to go through.

When I was fourteen years old, I was called up to play with the under-15 provincial team for some training sessions and in a couple of games at Penn State. It was a chance to show what I was capable of with an older group, and I couldn't pass it up. It was a fun trip, but nothing serious. I was only with the older group for a short spell. But I missed the first month of trials for the under-14 provincial team, my own age group, which would compete in the nation-wide tournament against other provinces. The trials gave the provincial coaches a chance to evaluate players through a series of practices, scrimmages, and friendly matches. This was the group of guys I had come up with, along with Iain. Many of these players were on my club team from Brampton. It was a talented group, but I figured that I had my position at midfield locked up. When I joined them, the team had already started playing together in friendly matches as the coaches narrowed down the roster.

On the last day of trials, all of the players sat in the change room after practice. The coaches walked in with a stack of envelopes, with each player's name on one. They handed them to each of us as we sat there, side by side. A piece of paper inside would let us know whether or not we made the team. You could tell the fate of each player by their expression when they looked inside their envelope.

I opened mine.

My heart raced as I read it. I felt dizzy. I read it again. Everyone around me must have known what the paper said as they saw me sink forward. I read it over and over—as though what I was reading just didn't make sense. I couldn't believe it. I'd been called up to play with the older team—and now I'd been cut from my own age group. I was devastated and embarrassed. It felt like everything I'd worked for was falling apart.

I sat in that change room for a long time after everyone else left.

After a while, my father walked in. He saw me sitting there in tears. He didn't say anything as he sat down beside me. Dad put his arm around my shoulder, as I turned into his chest and cried.

I'd never been more devastated in my life.

It felt even worse because I was very close with most of the players who'd made the team. The provincial team was the highest level that we could play at our age in Ontario, and I was being left behind. I'd missed my chance to progress and develop my game alongside them.

I couldn't get over it.

I was hard on myself for not making the squad. I was discouraged. I felt like I wasn't good enough. It felt like everything I'd worked for was over. I'd put so much work into being the best, and I didn't want to keep pushing anymore.

It took me a long time to get past that feeling. It was personal to me. My family saw it every day as I moped around the house. I just wasn't myself. For months, they worried that I was going to quit soccer completely. Haldon tried to encourage me. He could see that not making that provincial team destroyed me. He'd never seen me like that before. Through it all, my parents stayed on top of me. They pushed me through it. This was just a bump in the road for me, they said.

"You had everything that it takes to make this team," Dad said. "You were the best centre midfielder."

Since I'd first started playing the game, my father had told me to believe in myself. All of the work that we put in meant nothing if I wasn't convinced that I could achieve what I set out to do. Belief was so important. Without it, I had nothing.

"You're just going to have to work harder," Dad said. "Don't let this beat you up too much. Know what your strengths are."

It seems so small now, but it was enormous back then. This was my first taste of real adversity, and I can still feel the dejection when I think of it today.

Of course, there would be much more to come in my soccer journey, but the feeling of not making that provincial team never left me. In a way, it was a good thing. It helped me to continue to push, to refuse to give up. Up to that point, things had worked out for me the way I expected. This was my first setback in football—and there would be many to come.

Eventually I came to my senses. I had worked too hard to let one setback derail it all. Instead of wallowing with my wounded pride, I needed to turn that feeling into determination.

After those months of dejection, I learned to work with the disappointment hanging over me. I doubled the amount of time I spent running through drills in the backyard. I worked to be even faster on the pitch. I spent more time studying the game. I had to find ways to adapt and become a more complete player. I was determined to return to camp for the provincial squad and prove that the coaches had made a mistake—a *very* big mistake.

I learned a lot about myself that year. It was a pivotal time in my life during which I had to decide what I wanted to become in this sport. I had learned that nothing was guaranteed; I would always have to earn my place on whatever team I played for. I knew, too, that I would have to give everything I had playing soccer to really make something of myself in the game. I'd always practised hard because I loved to play and learn. It was easy for me, and that made it easy to improve. But as a teenager, I discovered the game had become something more. I had to prepare for the obstacles ahead.

All the lessons my father had instilled in me had prepared me to face greater opponents than I was used to. At each new level I reached, I would have to learn quickly. I had to prove that I could adapt. That was as important as anything. By the time I was fourteen, my father's vision started to make sense to me. I understood what it meant to dictate the pace of the game, defending our half while setting our attack in motion. Moving back at a young age helped me learn the game in a way that I likely wouldn't have been able to as a striker exploiting less talented defenders. Rather than only scoring goals, I learned how to play the game in a more complete way.

I returned to the provincial team trials the next year with something to prove. This time, there would be no doubt: the central midfield position belonged to me. I made the team, putting that chapter behind me, but storing away the disappointment so I'd always remember how it felt and, more importantly, what I'd learned from it.

Playing full-time with the Ontario provincial team broadened my horizons in the sport. It was the first year that my father wasn't directly involved in a team I played for.

"I know you are in good hands now," he'd joke.

With Ontario, we travelled to tournaments in faraway places like France and Holland. I realized on those trips just how far ahead European programs were than what we had in Canada. It was a completely different world. The European clubs we competed against were run like professional organizations. They had money pumping in, and they played on top-level pitches. Rather than being an afterthought in the sporting landscape, football was at the top. It was a brief taste of Europe but enough to make me even more determined to find my way overseas.

Back home, I played well and established myself as one of the top young players in Canada. When I was sixteen, I was invited to join the youth national team. I compared myself to the players around me, and I realized that I was one of the better players in the program. There were a lot of good players and few great players, but I was right up there with them.

Iain Hume had been with me every step of the way, with the provincial team and then with the youth national team. When we were sixteen, he was the first from our cohort to make the move overseas. He left to join the youth ranks of the Tranmere Rovers, a lower division pro club in Birkenhead, in northwest England. Iain's move made me think more about the possibility that lay before me. We'd played at the same level for so long and had entered the national team development program at the same time. Now he was crossing the Atlantic, chasing his dream in Europe.

"Maybe I have a chance," I thought.

6

The Mighty Ducks
of Notre Dame

By the time I could get a driver's licence, I was playing with the Ontario provincial team and the youth national team, while beginning my search for a path to Europe. It was easy to lose track of where I was in life—a sixteen-year-old kid in the tenth grade. I attended Notre Dame, a Catholic school just a few minutes north, across a busy thoroughfare, from where we lived. To me, school was a mandatory distraction from my real pursuit in life. It's not something I'm proud to admit, but if I'm being honest, I didn't have much time for class. I only had one focus.

I was lucky to have a group of close friends I had grown up with who always had my back. As much fun as we had together, these guys were always looking out for me. And, of course, they kept me humble.

One day, Mike came over to my house after class to help me with some math homework that I had told him I was struggling with. The truth was that I just didn't want to do it. I asked him to fill out the answers for me.

"If I fill these in for you, you're never going to learn," Mike said.

"I don't care," I told him. "I'm going to be a pro!"

Mike wasn't having it. "You're going to need this one day," he scolded.

That set me off. It felt like he was doubting me—like he was saying out loud what I didn't want to admit I was feeling myself. For a kid from Canada, my goals were outsized and nearly impossible. Europe was a long way away. I'd worked as hard as I possibly could to improve as a player, but that still might not have been enough.

If there was one thing I knew, it was that Mike and the friends I'd grown up with would always believe in me, even if I found it hard to believe in myself. These were the guys that I spent every day with throughout my childhood, guys who probably knew me better than I knew myself.

The same competitiveness that had dominated our childhood stayed with us into our teenage years. Whether we were playing dominoes in the cafeteria at Notre Dame, rallying in table tennis, or trying to outwit each other in chess. We played a card game called manipulation, our name for crazy eights. We were obsessed with it in high school. We'd play each game for a loonie. But no one was willing to let another person win, so whenever a game got to the point where one person had the final card, we'd team up on that person so the game wouldn't end. Then we'd stab each other in the back, trying to win. Cheating was common; if you didn't get caught, that was on the losers. And we'd do anything to avoid being the loser. The competitiveness got intense. We had a competition problem.

Of course, nothing brought the competition out of us like *FIFA*. We likely spent more hours playing the classic EA Sports video game than we did actually playing at Arnott Charlton. We were always at one of our houses—my house, Alex's house, Kev's house, or Mike's house. We'd all gather in the living room or basement, taking our turns. Kevin was always in charge of drafting the tournament, creating a bracket and laying out who would play whom. *FIFA* was serious business. Anyone who played the game with a group of their buddies will understand what I'm talking about. To this day, as grown men, we still have *FIFA* tournaments whenever we get together. We take it as seriously now as we did when we were kids.

I love that through all these years, the rivalry in us has never faded. As grown men, we'd keep it going. One year, when we were in our late twenties, we rented a cottage and set up a series of challenges, spending our entire weekend competing in an Olympics-style event. We played *FIFA*, lawn bowling, bocce, a basketball H-O-R-S-E competition, and rock paper scissors. I played against Mike in rock paper scissors, going double or nothing and working my way down into a hole that I refused to die in. I kept playing all weekend, until we were even by the time we left on Sunday.

Today, when I'm back home in Canada, we all gather at my parents' house in Brampton—we call it the Hutchinson Farm—and we play a game called internationals. It's a game of keep up, and any person who mishandles the ball and causes it to touch the ground is immediately out. They play it like we used to play the manipulation card game: everyone just kicks the ball directly at me, instead of passing it around as they try to get me out on each touch. It's as if we're kids again; the competitiveness is exactly the same. I refuse to let them beat me—and to this day, the sandlot crew never has.

Those gatherings always feel like a passage through time. That's the thing about our childhood and teenage years: they hold an outsized place in our memories. Back when we were small, every moment felt so big. And as the years pass and we collect more memories, those big moments from our youth stay with us.

Whenever I'm back with this core group of childhood friends, one of the memories that always comes up is the time we pieced together a team of players from our high school and travelled to Florida to take on some of the top teams in the United States. It's a moment of high school glory that has been told and retold, endlessly, to the point that it's almost mythical. And after all these years, it's still one of my most cherished memories from a life in the game.

In the tenth grade, around the time I was playing on the Ontario provincial team and playing with the youth national team, I agreed to play for Notre Dame's varsity soccer team. We were a ramshackle bunch. There was a wide range of ability on the team—many of the sandlot crew, many from the Brampton Braves. We had guys who played high level club ball and guys who had only ever played at the house league level. A few guys might not have ever played the game before.

Before the season started, a few of us sat in science class together and we came up with the idea to convince our coach to let us organize a team trip. We had our eye on an Olympic development program tournament in Cocoa Beach, Florida. The tournament would include good club teams and state teams. A high school team from Canada really had no business being there, especially because soccer was not considered one of our school's major sports—like basketball, hockey, or even gridiron football. For a Canadian high school, we had a pretty good team, but we certainly were not at the same level as American high school teams. At first, it was just a wild idea, but we wouldn't let it go. We did our research and figured that if we could raise enough money to fund the trip, maybe we'd be able to go. We worked out a Hail Mary proposal to present to our coach, Ferdinando Tantalo. To our surprise, Coach Tantalo was all in on the idea.

For a group of teenage boys, it was the trip of a lifetime.

There were about twenty of us on the team. We rented two twelve-passenger vans and packed ten guys into each for the two-day drive to Florida. There was only the coach and a teacher driving us. Just imagine how many fights there were in those vans. It was constant. All the time, proper fights—full fists, with guys being pulled apart across the seats. It was chaos.

The drive down alone is an amazing memory. We bruised and bonded like crazy. We drove for fifteen hours straight to Atlanta, where we all stayed at a house owned by a relative of one of our team-mates, all twenty of us. We spent one night there and drove to Florida the next morning.

No one at the tournament expected us to do well, us included, with our wide range of ability on the team. We were like the Mighty Ducks of Notre Dame. None of the other teams in the tournament thought we belonged there, let alone that we actually had a chance to win. They had a point. We lost two of our games, 6–1 and 7–1, in the group stages, which was pretty demoralizing. But somehow we managed to squeak through the first round.

In the second round, things started to click for us. Our ragtag bunch surprised everyone by making it through each elimination round, even though each team we played was more physical and athletic than we were. Our underdog status really drove me; I felt as good as I ever had on a pitch. Even though our opponents were some of the top young players in the States, I knew that I could outplay them. It kind of put an exclamation point on my aspirations. It pushed me closer to my goal. I was ready to go overseas.

Somehow, inexplicably, we reached the tournament final against a team that had absolutely demolished us in the group stage. They were cocky and made a big show of it, too, laughing throughout the blowout—the perfect villains.

Their centre mid was their top player, which set up a head-to-head battle between us. He was an absolute prick. He started trash-talking before the kickoff and never shut up. I wasn't having it. We'd developed some confidence as the underdog reaching the final, and I had something to prove.

We went at it all through the first half, trash-talking constantly. This guy was on my ass all game, talking non-stop. It was beyond annoying. He kept pissing me off—he was pissing everyone on our team off.

"You guys are shit," he said.

I let him get under my skin; I'd just had enough. "I guarantee you we are going to win this game," I told him.

But we were down 2–0 at the break.

"Alright, this tournament is done," their midfielder chirped.

I was furious. There was no way I could let us lose this game. I came out in the second half with a fire that'd I never played with before. I'd been in intense, competitive games, of course, but I'd always kept my head, remained calm, and tried to make thoughtful plays. But this game took me back to our World Cup tournaments on that patchy field at Arnott Charlton. This game was for a different kind of pride, playing alongside some of my best friends for what would likely be one of the last times. This was for the bond we'd forged over those years together, chasing our beautiful dreams. This was about pride in where we'd come from and where we were heading. I likely never would have been on the verge of playing for the national team and possibly playing in Europe, had it not been for the endless, unforgettable childhood days we spent together. So this was for us.

And also *screw that guy*.

I scored early in the second half to put us within one. The battle raged on, along with the chirping and hard fouls, as the clocked ticked up. When there were only a couple minutes to go, I received the ball back in our third of the field and attacked. It was as though I was nine years old again, playing with an extra gear at Century Gardens.

I carved out an opening as I neared the area and drilled the ball past their keeper.

Tie game. Our team went wild on the pitch. I stared down their best player to make sure he knew.

But I wasn't done.

We kept the pressure on, and with almost no time left, the other team was called for a foul, just above the area on the right side.

Prior to the game, we'd worked on our plan for free kicks in practice. We decided that if a free kick was on the right side, we would take two touches. The first player would line up to kick but just nudge the ball to the left, while my cousin, Kevin, charged in and fired a shot. He was the only left foot we had who could strike a ball.

So, as planned, Kevin lined up to take the free kick. With the ball on that corner, he was set up nicely to bend a left footer around their wall of players. But I had other plans. From the sidelines, my teammates watched me walk over to Kevin, wondering what the hell I was doing. I was feeling too good in this game to not take this attempt, even though I'm right footed.

Kevin had already lined up his shot. He'd thought out exactly how he planned to curl the ball over their line of defenders into the corner of the net. He looked surprised when I walked up to him.

"I'm going to take it," I said.

"What do you mean?" Kevin was baffled by the interruption. Normally I wouldn't step into another player's territory like that. But Kevin was my cousin, so I wasn't worried about how he would react.

"I'm going to take care of it," I said. "Leave it to me."

I'd never attempted a free kick with my left foot before, but I was flying high on competitive adrenaline. After the brief moment of bafflement, Kevin didn't protest. He nodded at me; we knew the play.

"Take the shot." He smiled.

I took a few steps back on his right side. Kevin lined up as if he were the one who would strike the ball. He rushed forward, but instead of kicking the ball, he tapped a gentle pass in my direction. I drove forward with a single stride and shot the ball with my left foot—my weak leg. The ball curled around their wall of defenders and ripped past their diving keeper into the back corner of the goal.

We were up 3–2.

Our players rushed from the sidelines while the other team hung their heads. I took a long look at their midfielder, making sure he knew that a high school team from Canada had just taken his club of American all-stars.

A few moments later, the ref blew out three long blasts and the game was over. We piled onto each other, celebrating as if we'd won the biggest tournament on Earth. At that moment, we had. It was the only moment that mattered. We were the champions, winning a tournament we had no business winning—and we would never forget it.

To this day, I often tell my kids about this experience, trying to show that sometimes the will to win is all you need. Regardless of the challenge, even when you're out-matched and out-skilled, never give up on yourself.

Part II

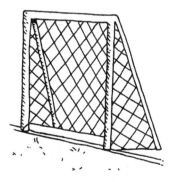

7

Departures

The first time my parents drove me to Toronto Pearson International Airport, helped me unload my bags from our van, and walked me to the security line, my mother cried. It wasn't that her eyes welled, as she tried to hold back tears. It wasn't a lump in her throat, as she choked back her emotion. My mother full-out cried, wet face and all, overcome by the mix of pride, joy, and apprehension as she watched the baby she had raised into a near-adult walk forward into an unknown future, as her role as caregiver and protector lessened. As my parents walked back through the airport's atrium to the van we'd travelled in together for more than a decade, I disappeared through security to catch a flight to Italy.

Mom cried for days after that. It was the beginning of countless comings and goings in the years to come, but it was the only time she came to the airport to see me off. She would say her goodbyes at home. Even now, she can't bear to see me off at the departure gate. That's when she knows, she says, "This is it, he's leaving again." It's a mom thing.

Dad was always the opposite. He was happy to see me go that first time in the fall of 2001, when I was about to turn eighteen years old. My mother had wanted me to focus on postsecondary opportunities— like Haldon had, with basketball. But my father convinced her that this was the path I needed to follow. "Leave this one to me," he said.

He knew that I was ready and that this was my shot. I had to take it. The window for me to find an opportunity to play professionally in Europe was already closing. I'd exhausted every possible avenue in Canadian soccer, proving myself at every level I'd played. I'd grown as a player with Brampton Youth Soccer, then Chinguacousy, and finally the Woodbridge Strikers. I'd represented the province and was playing with the youth national team. But as I reached the end of high school, I still felt behind. My buddy Iain had been playing for a club in England for two years. We'd remained close through the Canadian national development program, and from the stories he told, I knew I was missing out. I'd travelled with the provincial team for tournaments in France and Holland, so I had a sense of the quality and professionalism to expect in Europe.

There was a ceiling on what I could achieve in the sport if I remained in North America. I could play professionally in the United Soccer League or the MLS, which was a few years old. But, especially then, the North American professional system was just beginning to try to emulate what had existed in Europe for a century. Reaching my potential as a player required a move across the Atlantic.

So I jumped at the first European opportunity I had. At a tournament with my club team in Woodbridge were two teams from Italy. A scout for Cagliari Calcio, a Seria B team that was represented by its "primavera" junior development team at the tournament, was impressed by my play. He invited me to Sardinia, the large Italian island in the Mediterranean Sea, for what was essentially a trial with the club's youth development team.

It was a dream opportunity. My mother was obviously hesitant to let me go, but my father insisted that I couldn't pass this up. They scrounged up the money to buy my plane ticket and took me to the airport not knowing when I'd return.

As I flew alone above the clouds over the Atlantic, I was nervous but more excited than I'd ever been about an opportunity in soccer.

From the moment I walked off the plane in Sardinia, I was in awe. The island was absolutely stunning—beautiful beaches, lush hills, and the kind of architecture that you'd see on a postcard. I'd never been anywhere like it before. And the people were so welcoming and friendly. I loved being there. It was like a dream—stunning landscape, wonderful people, and some of the best football I'd ever been around.

The majority of the players in the development trial stayed together in Cagliari, the capital of Sardinia; a few of the local players lived at home. We were always together. We'd eat breakfast, lunch, and dinner together; I'd never been in that kind of football environment before. We became friends despite the different worlds we came from.

The club was on another level from anything I'd experienced previously. It was eye-opening to see how professional the organization was—from the facility to the training staff to the catering and everything in between. There was nothing like it in Canada, which had very little investment at any level of soccer, including the national program, at that time. That kind of high standard was lacking in facilities, equipment, food, travel, and accommodations when we'd gather for training camps or head abroad to compete against other nations.

The level of play was also so much higher than I was used to. With such a high quality of instruction, it was much easier than I anticipated to follow the pace and flow of what was expected of me. I learned something new every time I stepped onto the pitch. It was such a gift to be there and take it all in.

And most importantly, the coach loved me.

I was initially only guaranteed to stay for a couple of weeks, but I ended up staying with the club for another two months. The team wanted me to sign a contract as a player with the Cagliari development team. I called home to tell my parents the news. I knew that they had believed in me all along. They'd sacrificed to make sure I had every chance to follow my heart, and I was proud for them to know that I'd found my way. They were thrilled for me, though Mom was predictably mixed about her baby boy staying away from home for so long.

◆

I was ready to settle into life on this ancient island in the Mediterranean. All I needed was the paperwork. I waited for weeks to be handed a contract to sign. Then one day the coach called me into his office. At first, I thought he finally had everything ready for me to sign, but the mood quickly shifted. He was distraught; there were tears in eyes. He told me that he loved me as a player and as a person and that he saw so much potential in my game—but that the team had signed too many foreigners and the league wouldn't allow them to sign me too. There was nothing he could do.

And just like that, it was over. I felt all the hope and anticipation rush away. I was left feeling dejected. All my momentum had been crushed—all the progress in my game, the confidence I'd gained, the hope that had become anticipation, all lost in an instant. I had the same sick feeling in my chest as when I'd been cut from the provincial team a few years earlier. I was still very young, but it felt like time was almost up on my dream. Sardinia had been my chance, and now that chance was gone.

The coach tried to keep me close to the organization, encouraging me to remain in Italy. He set me up with another Italian club, but it was a fourth division team. I trained with them for a short time and was offered a contract to play with the first team, as a regular player. I thought hard about the offer and nearly accepted it. I didn't want to pass up an opportunity to stay in Europe and continue to develop. But something didn't feel right. While I would have received playing time and kept improving, I couldn't decide if that was worth being away from home. The quality of the club was far inferior to what I'd experienced with Cagliari; it was no better than what I could expect from one of the nascent professional leagues in North America. Yes, it was a chance to play in Europe, but I couldn't bring myself to go from nearly signing with a Serie A club to joining a league that was the same level of soccer as back home. That wasn't what I had got on a plane for. I felt like I would have been selling myself short.

So only a few months after I'd left to chase my dream, I boarded a plane and flew back across the Atlantic.

◆

When I returned home, Canada seemed much further away from Italy than an eight-hour flight. As an eighteen-year-old, I remained focused on finding an opportunity to get my foot in the door overseas. I was still a kid with no money to my name, living at home while completing my high school diploma in summer classes because I'd missed so much of the regular school year. Once again, my parents sacrificed to make sure I had every opportunity possible. They bought all of my plane tickets, though Mom stopped driving with us to the airport.

I went to Hungary for a trial with a team there, but it didn't work out. There was interest, nothing more than that. I was starting to feel embarrassed for trying. The rising hope and deflation of rejection was a lot to bear.

I tried out for the Dallas Burn in the MLS but didn't land a spot. Further deflation.

After that, I went to Germany to train with FC Schalke 04, one of the biggest clubs in the Bundesliga. The opportunity came through the Canadian national team's head coach, Holger Osieck, who was from Germany. Osieck could be a hard-ass as a coach, but he was a big proponent of advancing me in the national program. He felt like Schalke was a good fit for me. From a training and development perspective, he was right. I spent several weeks training with the Schalke youth team, and I also trained a few times with the first team to get a feel for what that was like. It was the highest quality football I'd played. I wasn't able to play in any matches because the team was mid-season when I arrived and I wasn't officially with the club. But they were interested in signing me, I was told. They just wanted to see me in a proper game first.

And so it continued, with opportunities rising and then receding like waves, while I stood on the shore, unable to ride them away.

Back home in Canada, I continued training with the youth national team, which gathered every few months and was a much-needed boost for my confidence. Osieck, who was the technical director of the Canadian Soccer Association in addition to being the national team coach, believed that I'd become a key part of the program one day. I'd played with the U-18 team for a couple of years, and I was hopeful to make the leap to the next level.

Iain was already training with the U-20 squad in the lead-up to the qualifiers for the world youth championships, also known as the FIFA U-20 World Cup. If Canada earned a spot, the team would travel to Argentina that summer to play against the best young talent in the world. I wanted to be there.

After training one afternoon, Paul James, the newly appointed coach of the U-20 program, called me into his office. They were giving me a chance to prove myself with the U-20 squad, and I would join the team for the qualifying tournament in Victoria, B.C. At eighteen,

I'd be one of the youngest players on the roster, alongside Iain—who was still only seventeen.

Playing with the U-20 team was an enlightening experience. It was the first time I trained with older players in trials. The roster was pretty much set, and the other players were used to playing with each other. I was a confident young player, but I experienced nerves that were new to me. I didn't know if I would even make the team. It was intimidating to play with guys who were two years older than me, like Chris Pozniak, who would become a key defender for Canada. It was also the first time I played alongside Julian de Guzman, one of the most promising talents Canada had ever produced; he would become a close friend and important mentor to me in my career.

Playing for James added another element of intimidation. He was a great coach but also the toughest I'd ever played for. He was very firm. James didn't take any bullshit. He wanted the game played a certain way and was quick to get on you if you messed up that plan. But that high standard was important for us. We needed to demand the best of ourselves if we wanted to be competitive. If you made a bad pass or were caught out of position, you heard about it. Though James was demanding, he believed in what we were capable of. He started me in important games, even though I was one of the youngest players on the squad. That came with the expectation that I could handle the competition. Despite the pressure in Victoria, James gave me confidence that I belonged, and I rose to the challenge. We qualified as one of the four teams representing Concacaf in Argentina. I'd played well enough to make sure the coaching staff didn't regret the decision to call me up.

It was a rare highlight in a year of dwindling hope.

◆

A short time later, the national U-18 team, which I played for regularly, played in a friendly tournament in Germany. A coach from Schalke planned to attend a match to keep an eye on my progress in the few months since I'd played with them. It was my chance to show them what I was capable of. The understanding was that if I managed to impress them, they'd invite me to stay with the club's youth team on a proper contract.

Before the game, I was more nervous than I'd ever felt playing football before. I was usually a composed player, and I rarely let pressure get to me. But I couldn't get out of my own head. I needed to impress the coach so badly, so I could get back to Europe and play a full season. Of course, I ended up playing one of the worst games of my life. I completely shat the bed. It was an absolute nightmare. I couldn't settle down and play. All game, I could feel the Schalke coach watching me—and I knew that I was blowing my chance. I allowed the pressure to get to me. I looked like a complete amateur.

I never heard from Schalke again. It wasn't even a matter of letting me down gently. There was no debrief on what they'd like to see me work on, like "play the game a bit more physically" or "play the game at a quicker pace." I never heard anything from them, as though I had never even been there. It was harsh.

Looking back, that year—between 2000 and 2001—was one of the most important seasons in my development as a player. I could no longer rely on my skill and athleticism alone. I needed to become a more intelligent player, to read the game and understand how it was played at a higher level. Not in theory, but within the speed of a game. It was abundantly clear how difficult the competition beyond these borders would be. I was fixated on going to Europe. That's where I considered professional football to be—but don't get me wrong, I would have been thrilled to sign with the MLS if a team had wanted me. But none did. That trial with Dallas was the closest I'd get.

I carried a lot of disappointment with me that year. The really frustrating part was that I felt like I had performed well enough to sign with one or two of these clubs. But they didn't see it that way. When you're young, it's so difficult to have a clear perspective. Emotions are rarely proportionate. I remember how sad I was, but I'd been there before. So I kept my head down. I kept pushing. I kept working. I kept trying to trust that I was waiting for the right opportunity.

Beyond the FIFA U-20 World Cup that summer, I had no idea where the dream would take me next, if anywhere at all.

All I could do was believe that it wouldn't end.

8

Delays

As my older teammates on the Canadian men's U-20 squad scrimmaged around me, I was in awe of their pace and vision for the game. I was determined to make my mark with this national squad, but playing alongside teammates who were two years older than me—quite a big jump at that age—showed me how much room I had to improve. It was intimidating but inspiring. Watching a guy like Julian de Guzman, who played with such flair and with incredible vision for the game, proved to me that Canada was capable of producing top level talent. That I could be that top level talent.

It was also eye-opening to see the quality of the guys who were already playing in Europe—players like de Guzman, Michael Klukowski, Tam Nsaliwa, and our captain Terry Dunfield.

"This is the level I want to play at," I told myself. "I need to push myself to stay here."

These players created a new standard for me, pushing me to become a better version of myself. Like anything in life, we need to surround ourselves with people who challenge and inspire us to reach the next level.

I worked hard in practice, hoping to earn time on the pitch even though I'd enter the world championship as a reserve on defence. With more senior players playing midfield, Paul James made me a back. I was okay with the move if it meant that I might play. I just wanted to prove to the coaches and my teammates that I belonged.

"This is where I need to be," I thought.

♦

The trip to Argentina was surreal. I'd never experienced a celebration of the beautiful game like it—the complete flip of what you would have seen in Canada at the time. In Argentina, football was a religion. Even though it was a U-20 tournament, fans had travelled from all over the world to watch their teams play. Everything felt enormous, almost overwhelming. And that was before we even played a game.

Argentina was a wakeup call. In our first match playing in the biggest international tournament in the world, Iraq scored three goals on us in the first half. As a substitute defender—moved back from my usual position at midfield—I watched from the sidelines as we tried and failed to claw ourselves back in the second, losing 3–0. My first opportunity came in the second game, against Germany, after Paul James juggled our lineup. I was on the pitch for every minute of a brutally lopsided 4–0 loss.

We were effectively eliminated after dropping our first two games. But we hoped to return to Canada with something to be proud of, something to build on. Unfortunately, we were playing Brazil, one of the tournament's top ranked teams with players like Kaká and Maicon. The Brazilians had won their first two matches and qualified for the knockout stage. Fewer than 1,500 people scattered across the 38,000-seat Estadio Mario Alberto Kempes in Córdoba—a stadium built for the 1978 World Cup—for our match. Despite our loss to

Germany, Paul put me back in the starting lineup, and I played every minute against Brazil. We played our best match of the tournament but still fell 2–0 to a lacklustre Brazilian team disinterested as they prepared for the round of sixteen.

In three straight losses, we didn't score a single goal. It was an embarrassing outcome. It exposed the gaps in our preparation, a reality for the national team program at the time. There was very little money to go around, which greatly diminished training opportunities. We had a limited pre-tournament schedule, and with many of our players in clubs overseas, the time the squad had together was minimal. The problems went deeper than that though.

◆

Without a strong domestic league to develop players at home, Canada wasn't producing the kind of depth needed to compete on the international stage. At the grassroots level, there was still an enormous need for more advanced programs and experienced coaching. The truth was, across the board, Canada needed more exposure to the top levels of football.

But there was also a lot to be hopeful for.

Iain and I were both young enough to have another shot at the youth world championships in two years. There was a solid core of young talent rising together, hoping to change the narrative around Canadian football. In fact, we were one of the few Canadian teams that had made it to the U-20 World Cup at all.

For my own development, the experience was invaluable. I was in the middle of the first big, important learning curve of my career. The reality was that I wasn't a top guy on that team. Iain was definitely a bigger factor than I was, at that time. There wasn't even room for me to play my natural position. Even though the outcome wasn't a resounding success, the tournament set a new bar for me.

That was the highest point I could reach in our international program, playing with this older group. And I was determined to keep rising. Everything would develop from that point forward, as I pushed step by step from there. Moving up to the men's national team was the next big jump; their game was a lot quicker and more physical. But wherever I went, I resolved to stick with it. I would take some time to adapt and find a way to fit in. I'd get more comfortable. I'd hold my own.

♦

Instead of starting my pro career with a Serie A or Bundesliga club, I landed at Highland Park—which might sound like a storied stadium of a century-old fabled club in the English Football League, but it was a tiny soccer field with bleacher seating for a few dozen people, across the street from a dental office and a Chrysler dealership in an industrial section of Aurora, about an hour north of Toronto.

The York Region Shooters were about four years old when I joined the team. The team played in the upstart Canadian Professional Soccer League—which was the most recent of several attempts to develop a successful homegrown professional league in Canada. While there was a clear need to develop Canadian talent, a league was a challenging business proposition. The landscape for pro soccer in Canada was sparse, though efforts were made. Opportunities were growing, if slowly in fits and starts.

The CPSL had a mission to provide Canadian players a platform to reach higher levels, like the USISL A-League, which by the early 2000s was the second tier of pro soccer in the United States and

Canada. At the top was MLS, which had formed in the mid-'90s and was bleeding money in its early years as it tried to stay afloat.

For six months, shortly after I turned nineteen in 2002, I criss-crossed the Greater Toronto Area with the York Shooters. We travelled to the U.S. and played a series of games against lower-tier professional teams. Several of my teammates were on the youth national team as well, so we had a fun time together. They were good players. But playing semi-pro football in front of smaller crowds than most of our club teams drew, through family and friend connections alone, felt disheartening. But that was where I was. I still believed that I could play in a top-tier league in Europe, and I knew I still had so much to learn.

It was a humbling year, all around. Everywhere we went, I looked around at the sparsely populated stands hoping to see a scout who might take interest in me. But none came. While still hoping for opportunities abroad, in July 2002, I was offered a roster spot with the Toronto Lynx, a USISL A-League team—which was the top tier of pro soccer operating in Canada. The Lynx played out of Centennial Park Stadium in Etobicoke, which sat about 2,500 people. It was a leap up from the York Shooters. We were rivals with the Montreal Impact, the franchise that later became an MLS team. The Vancouver Whitecaps also played in the A-League at the time, and like the Impact, the team name would carry on in the MLS. If I was going to remain in Canada, Toronto seemed like the best option for me. I wanted to get as much playing experience as possible at the highest level I could, where the game is faster and you have to think more and adapt.

"I'm not going to be here long," I told myself when I signed with the Lynx.

Toronto only had four games left in the regular season when I joined, and the team wasn't in position to make the playoffs. I was with the Lynx for less than a month, but I managed to score three goals in that brief stint. I'd adapted well to the quicker pace of play and felt like I'd grown. The league had challenged me, and I knew that I could continue to grow with Toronto, if I remained with them for the following season.

I was at a crossroads.

Should I keep playing with the Lynx and hope to find my way to an MLS club one day? Should I give up and go the college route—prepare myself for the reality of life without soccer? Or should I keep pushing, against the odds?

Part of me was prepared to return to the Lynx for another season, but I knew in my gut that my heart wouldn't have been in it. It wasn't where I wanted to be. Even though I was frustrated, I couldn't let go of my goal of playing overseas. I clung to belief—belief that all the work I had put in would pay off, belief that I could rise to any level if given the chance, belief that this beautiful dream would one day be worth all of the disappointment. So despite the rejections, I remained focused on one thing: I was going to play in Europe. It didn't matter where I found my start. I just needed a chance to prove myself. The rest would take care of itself.

Shortly after the Lynx season wrapped up, I boarded a flight to Sweden for a trial with a club in Allsvenskan, the top tier in Swedish football. The club had shown some interest in me, but after a couple of weeks, the team's coach shared the same old news: the team liked me, but they didn't have any spots available to sign me.

I packed up my boots and flew home.

"Was this finally it?" I wondered. "How much more rejection can I take?"

A few weeks later, my phone rang. It was an agent that had approached me about reaching out to European clubs. Up to that point, he'd only succeeded in helping me rack up travel points—but now he had news.

The coach of the Swedish club I'd trained with had recommended me to the coach of Östers, a traditionally second-tier club in a city called Växjö, which had just earned a promotion to the top-tier Allsvenskan. Östers was looking for a reliable midfielder. Off the reference alone, the team wanted to offer me what was essentially a half-year trial. I'd commit to playing with the club for a year, but if the team didn't like what they saw, they could dump me after six months. It wasn't a contract that you see very often. It was basically designed to give you a brief chance to show what you could do, while giving the team an easy out if they weren't impressed. It seemed risky to sign something with so few guarantees. But, on the other hand, they were saying I had a chance—and a chance was all I needed.

That December, Haldon returned from college for Christmas holidays. I'd gone through a growth spurt while he was away. To him, his little brother suddenly looked like a grown man. We were eye to eye now, no longer sibling rivals. Just proper adult friends.

I told him the news. The contract was signed.

"Haldon," I said, "I'm going to Sweden."

He smiled wide, with pride. In a couple weeks, I'd move to a country I knew next to nothing about, to play professional soccer in a city I couldn't point to on a map, with a name I'd just learned to pronounce.

It wasn't clear where the path to Växjö would take me, but we both knew that I was finally moving in the direction I'd hoped.

I'd lost track of the number of times I'd been rejected by that point. But I'd refused to stop believing. When other people quit, I held on—even when it seemed like I was wasting time clinging to a dream that would never come true. Press towards your goals, even when it seems there is nowhere else to go.

9

Arrivals

Östers IF didn't know what to expect from me when I arrived, and I didn't know what to expect of them. Both sides were blind in the agreement. But the moment I arrived in Växjö, everyone knew that I was the new guy in town. In Europe, it doesn't take long to realize that many people live and die for football. It's everywhere—in cafés, in stores, on street corners. Anywhere you go, you are almost always within earshot of some sort of discussion about the beautiful game. It wasn't any different in Sweden. When I arrived in Växjö after signing my first professional contract with Östers Idrottsförening, the club that had captivated the region's football passions since the 1930s, strangers already knew who I was. Everywhere I went, people recognized me. It was the first time that I had ever received even the smallest amount of public attention for playing soccer. Up to that point, the spring of 2003, I'd received a very modest amount of local and national media coverage because of my participation in the Canadian men's national team development program and the under-20 squad. It was strange because, as far as actual football went, I was as much a stranger to the fans as they were to me, but still somehow they knew who I was.

Växjö was an entirely new world for me. I didn't know anything about the city at all—or about Sweden. But despite the discomfort of being somewhere unfamiliar, it was a beautiful place to live. Växjö is a city of less than 100,000 people, surrounded by lakes and greenery. It's cold in Sweden, but that didn't really bother me. I'd grown up running through the coldest Canadian winters. In that way, Växjö was a lot like home. But in many other ways, it was very different. It's a fascinating place to visit. It's a very old city, so many streets are narrow and made of cobblestone, which makes it feel like history surrounds you. Ancient ruins are scattered across the surrounding landscape—castles, cathedrals, and fortresses that tell stories dating back to the Middle Ages.

The people were kind and welcoming. They knew that I was there to play football and were interested in my story. But many also seemed to be fascinated by the idea of a Canadian coming to Sweden to play soccer. It didn't make sense to them.

"You don't play football in Canada," I was told on several occasions. "You should be playing hockey."

In their minds, I must have been a hockey player, like every Canadian, who stumbled off my skates onto a soccer pitch. To them, Canadians only played one sport. And to be fair, hockey is the sport that Canada is most famous for. Swedish fans were very familiar with that history. The Nordic nation has a prominent hockey culture and has long produced some of the best players in the world. Just as the Swedes know Canada for hockey, any hockey fan in Canada can easily rhyme off a list of the greatest Swedish players to have played in the NHL: Börje Salming, Peter Forsberg, Nicklas Lidström, the Sedin twins, Henrik Lundqvist, Erik Karlsson, and dozens more. But Canadians who aren't soccer fans might be surprised to know that hockey is the second most popular sport in Sweden, behind football. While Zlatan Ibrahimović is famous for being one of the best—and most confident—players in the world, Sweden has also produced world-class talent like Henrik Larsson, Freddie Ljungberg, and the legendary midfielder Nils Liedholm, among many more. But a Swedish football fan couldn't name players who came from Canada, especially at that time.

During my time in Sweden, hundreds and hundreds of times, without exaggeration, I was asked why a Canadian would play soccer. I always found the curiosity of the fans in Växjö amusing.

"You don't play! What are you doing here?" they'd say.

I had to agree with them. "You're right. I know," I'd say. "Many Canadians don't play soccer, but my family is not from Canada. My parents are from Trinidad."

And really that's such an important part of the Canadian soccer tradition. For years, the sport was played primarily by people whose roots in the game came with them from elsewhere. For decades, soccer in Canada was the game of immigrants. And proudly so. Whenever I was asked about the apparent paradox of being a Canadian soccer player, I shared my family's love of soccer that was passed on to me. It's a story that makes me feel immensely fortunate to have grown up as I did—a kid from a West Indian family living in Canada. That I can embrace my deep connection to both places makes me very proud of what Canada represents.

◆

The team put me up in an empty old office building in a unit that had been retrofitted to serve as an apartment. I'm pretty sure it'd previously belonged to a law firm. They made a bedroom and a kitchen out of what had once been an office. And there was no one else living there. I was the only one in the entire building. It was super weird. There was a large cathedral across the street; its bells would ring out first thing in the morning. They woke me up every day. Since the club didn't know what to expect of me, they weren't prepared to put me up in a proper place.

But Östers was everything I hoped it would be. They welcomed me as one of their own. Most of my teammates were young, like me, and we got along very well. Some of the guys were still going back and forth between university while playing for the club. It was great to have a group of teammates in the same stage of life as me. Many of them spoke English, which really helped bridge any cultural barriers we might have had. Really, we'd have been speaking the same language anyway: all we talked about was football, all the time. A couple of the Swedish guys took really good care of me. At first I'd take the city bus to practice, but soon a few of the guys started going out of their way to pick me up on their way to the stadium. I was grateful for their kindness. I didn't want to admit how nervous I was about being in a new place, training with players at a higher level than I was used to. This was my chance to make my dream come true. The stakes felt enormous—my one shot at something I'd dreamed about for so long.

I remember practising my autograph for the first time, worried that I would scribble something illegible for a fan who asked for it. I'd never had to sign something for an audience before, so I hadn't thought about the pressure of such a simple act. I wanted to seem like a proper professional, not some amateur imposter from Canada. It seems ridiculous now, but it was a real concern for me at the time.

I was fortunate to join the team under a very good manager named Leif Widén, who set me up with my makeshift apartment and took me around the city. He showed me all of his favourite places to eat and gave me calling cards so I could use the payphone around the corner from my apartment to call home.

But I had a hard time adjusting to living alone. I'd taken for granted basic responsibilities, like cooking, laundry, and waking up on time. And the creepy isolation of living alone in a converted office building made me feel like the last person alive in some kind of post-apocalyptic future.

It was lonely. Växjö just wasn't home.

Mom and my sister, Toyaa, flew over to visit shortly after I arrived in Sweden to make sure I was settling in. The distance was hard for all of us. Mom worried about me all the time. When she arrived to see how I was coping on my own, it didn't ease her concerns. She opened my fridge and found nothing but a carton of expired milk.

It was Mom's and Toyaa's first time in Europe. They felt the culture shock, too—the feeling of clearly being an outsider, not knowing the language or your surroundings. It was the first time that either of them had watched me play in a proper professional setting. Toyaa was only thirteen years old at the time, and she hadn't really grasped what I was doing in Europe. She'd been dragged to my games her entire life, so watching her older brother play in a match was nothing special. The Östers IF crowd was modest by European standards, but with more than six thousand people in attendance, it was by far the most people that Toyaa had seen screaming and chanting for a team her brother was on. The crowd was crazy.

"Wow," Toyaa thought, as they sat among the roaring Östers supporters. "*This* is what he does. This is pretty cool."

Mom and Toyaa stayed for about a week before they had to go back to Canada. The visit eased some of the tension I was feeling. It felt more like home having them around. Plus, my fridge was full. But that didn't last long.

The distance was probably harder than anything I'd experienced in my life to that point. I was terribly homesick in the first months playing with Östers IF. I had expected a transition period as I adjusted to life on my own, but it was much worse than I'd thought. I missed my family. At home, I was with them all the time. My life was football, friends, and family. I didn't really do anything else.

Although I'd been away from home for short stints before, I wasn't prepared for what it would be like to live on my own somewhere new. There was culture shock, for sure. It was hard to adjust to a place where most people spoke Swedish. I had to learn how to navigate an entirely new city in a new country. I got lost on walks and on public transit, going places I didn't intend to go. It was easy to feel isolated and out of place. It took time to get used to that.

Like many young people living on their own for the first time, there was a big learning curve. Part of the challenge was learning to be professional. Small but important things like going to bed early and waking up on time. My father had hammered the necessity of arriving early for training and for games, so that was never a problem. I was too anxious to risk being late. I had to figure out how to do things on my own.

One of the things I missed the most was a home-cooked meal made by my mother. That was one of the hardest things. It certainly didn't help that I didn't know how to cook anything. The most complicated thing I cooked was pasta with butter. That's all I was making in the beginning. I didn't even use sauce. I was just inexperienced with cooking. I didn't know what to do. It was particularly tough when I'd come home exhausted and hungry after a game and then think, "Oh man, what do I have to eat?"

So I ordered out a *lot*. But Växjö was a really small city, so it didn't take long to run through all of the options. I was always searching for new places to eat. But in Sweden, everything closes early so if you didn't get to a restaurant by six or seven at night, you would be out of luck. I ended up at the local McDonald's far too often.

Back home, Mom probably felt as anxious about me being away as I did. She sent me care packages all the time. She seemed to think that there weren't any grocery stores in Sweden. In the beginning, the care packages she sent me had basic items like cans of tomato sauce and pasta—as if I couldn't buy tomato sauce or pasta in Europe. As the season went on, the care packages evolved. Mom sent me ingredients with instructions so I could make meals on my own, favourites like lasagna and some of the amazing Trinidadian dishes I grew up on. We spent a lot of time on the phone as I fumbled my way through her directions. It took me awhile to get the hang of it, but eventually I mastered a few decent go-to meals.

There is a comfort that comes from the food you grew up on. The right food can carry us through space and time. You take one bite of a favourite dish and feel the memories surrounding you. Suddenly you're sitting at the kitchen table next to your family and friends.

There were a lot of other basic tasks to figure out that I'd simply taken for granted. My bed was never made. The trash only went out when absolutely necessary. I relied entirely on the cleaning supplies my mother had bought on her visit. I don't recall if I ever mopped the floor, or if I owned a vacuum.

Tasks that seemed complicated then are embarrassingly easy when I look back on them. I didn't even know how to wash my own clothes. I turned white clothes pink in the laundry. I'd been living at home my whole life and always relied on my mother to do the laundry. I would call her to make sure that I was doing it right.

Even after getting my correspondence education from Mom, the guys on the team who took me under their wing would often help me out by taking my dirty clothes home with them to get washed. It's incredibly embarrassing to share that today, but it's the truth.

Once, when my friend Alex visited, he was disgusted by how messy my place was.

"How do you live like this?" he asked.

He cleaned up my place and took the trash out. But he couldn't find the building garbage bin, so he dumped a bag in a trash can outside. Someone came by a few hours later and told me to get my trash the hell out of their bin.

If you've ever been homesick before, you might be familiar with that anxious feeling that tightens your chest and settles into your stomach. The intensity rises and fades, but it's always there, lingering inside you. Everything around me felt slightly off—as if I was living in a strange dream that I couldn't wake up from.

There is a six-hour time difference between Växjö and Toronto, which made it difficult to speak regularly with family and friends. It was a bigger challenge at that time than it is today. There was no FaceTime or Zoom, let alone cheap international phone plans. You had to buy a prepaid calling card every time you wanted to make an overseas call. The longer you chatted, the sooner the money on your card would run out and you'd have to head back to a convenience store to load it up again. It was a huge pain compared to how easy it is to connect with people all over the world today. I spent a lot of money on calling cards in those first few months.

The loneliness was so difficult that at times part of me felt like calling it quits and heading home. I'd never thought that I could miss my family and friends that much. It was a constant battle in my mind. I had to talk myself out of leaving several times.

"This is what I've got to do," I told myself. "Things will turn around. I'll get used to it. I'll get comfortable."

I'd left everything behind to take a chance on myself. I had to see that through.

The only place I really felt at ease was on the pitch; regardless of where in the world I was, the space between the lines felt familiar. Football was a portal to home.

◆

My initial hope was to play well with Östers and get noticed by other clubs. Playing in Europe was an opportunity to be seen.

Östers had recently been promoted to the Allsvenskan, the top tier of professional soccer in Sweden. The club wasn't well-known by most standards, and it sat near the bottom of the league rankings. None of that mattered to me. I was in Europe. I'd signed a modest contract, making the equivalent of a little more than $5,000 Canadian per month, but I had my foot in the door of professional football. Östers IF was the perfect place for me at that time because I was able to play every week. It wasn't the biggest club; it didn't have the biggest and best players, so I knew that, with a lot of work, I could get the chance to play a lot of games. That was one of the key factors in my decision to sign with the club. I wanted to spend as much time on the pitch as possible. But the experience ended up being about a lot more than exposure.

The team averaged just over seven thousand fans per game in a stadium that could hold about eight thousand total. I'd never played in front of that many fans in regular club matches before. I loved the football culture that surrounded the place. The fans were so passionate, even though we weren't a top team. It was exhilarating to play in front of stands packed with fans who cared so deeply about the team and the game. The enthusiasm and professionalism within the culture were completely different from what I'd experienced in Canada.

But I was still a very raw player when I arrived in Sweden. A lot of the things that I had done growing up in Canada I couldn't get away with in Europe. I was used to taking the ball and dribbling more than I needed to. I'd take a lot of touches, spending too much time with the ball and not playing as quickly as I should. I lost a lot of balls that way early on with Östers. I couldn't survive playing in Sweden the same way I'd played in Canada. In many ways, it was a different game.

Everything was much faster and more physical. I needed to learn and adjust. I was decent at holding the ball, but I wasn't very good at passing and simply reading the game. I was fortunate to be playing under a very good coach, Yevgeni Kuznetsov. He was great at teaching me the basics of the game at the pro level. He was patient and meticulous, confident that I just needed a bit of time to adjust.

Our roster didn't boast many players who had competed at a very high level. There were a couple of veterans, whom I learned a little bit from, but for the most part my teammates were on the same level that I was. That meant that we didn't win very many games. We floundered near the bottom of the league rankings all season long and finished with only three wins, eight draws, and fifteen losses.

But Kuznetsov played me all the time, and that helped my game enormously. Getting that first team experience was huge for me. The game speed was a lot quicker than I was used to, and the players were a lot faster. I didn't have as much time and space with the ball. With so much in-game action, it didn't take me long to adjust and improve. Playing at that level, along with Kuznetsov's instruction, changed the way I saw the game. It was what my father has always tried to explain to me, but I hadn't experienced club football in Canada. I needed the higher level of league to truly comprehend what Dad had been talking about.

♦

I took advantage of the chance I'd been given. I played every game that season; the team decided to keep me around rather than terminate my contract after a few months. I showed them that I had the quality to belong and led the entire team with six goals. Our fans no longer wondered why I didn't play hockey. Other teams in the league took notice too. I'd viewed that entire anxiety-ridden, homesick season as an extended European tryout. I stuck it out, and it worked. Looking back, I realize how pivotal that first uncertain season in Växjö was for my career. It was a year of growth, personally and professionally. I proved that I could rise to the challenges of professional football—and I even learned how to cook some dishes and eventually how to wash my own damn clothes.

After the first half of the season, the team decided that they were confident enough in my ability that they could get me a proper apartment. It was like a real condo with a proper bedroom, a suitable kitchen, and a big living room. I started to feel a little bit more secure and less like a stranger in a new place. I was making the most of the shot I had been given.

As a team, we had little to celebrate though. We were fighting to stay in the league all season, struggling to get good results. When the season ended in October 2003, we sat thirteenth in the fourteen-team Allsvenskan, in which the bottom three clubs were relegated each season. That meant Östers IF would move down to a second-tier division the following season, to fight for a chance for promotion back to the Allsvenskan. It also meant that my time in Växjö was coming to an end.

By the end of the season, I'd realized that I was one of the better players on the team. Other clubs in the Allsvenskan looked like they could provide better opportunities. As I improved and adapted, I felt as though I wasn't far behind some of the top players in the top clubs. I fought and worked as hard as I could to show myself in every game. Other clubs took notice. For the first time in my young career, another team was willing to put a price on what they saw.

I returned to Canada at the end of my first full season abroad feeling confident, and I was ready to show the national program how much I'd grown.

10

For the North

If I'd learned one thing in my four years in the Canadian national team program, it was that Canada was never given respect. Opponents, officials, fans—and often ourselves—everyone knew that Canada wasn't supposed to be a soccer nation, and so it was assumed that we weren't. Our successes were viewed as upsets, infrequent glitches in the proper order of things.

In November 2002, our U-20 team pulled off a massive upset, beating the U.S. 3–2 to qualify for the 2003 FIFA Youth World Championship in the United Arab Emirates. It was the first time a Canadian men's team at any level had beaten a U.S. national team since the senior team beat the Americans in a World Cup qualifying game in 1957. Despite that victory, we were still widely considered to be much weaker than our Concacaf rivals from Costa Rica, Mexico, and the Americas.

That was a theme for Canadian soccer in the fall of 2003.

Our men's senior team had won the 2000 Gold Cup, one of the most memorable moments in its history. That win was viewed as an outlier. As the next generation, we were also dismissed.

It was a reality I'd come to understand during my time with the U-20 team—a sting that still lingered from our embarrassing last place finish in Argentina. I'd also experienced it in the several games that I'd played with the U-23 team, attempting to qualify for the Olympics, and a few stints as a call-up to the senior national team.

Each opportunity made me better, playing alongside quicker, more talented players at the international level. In those early years, I also developed a sense of pride in Canadian soccer and what I knew it could be. I'd gone from being a kid who dreamed of playing for Trinidad, the country my parents grew up in, to being named joint captain of the Canadian U-20 national team at the FIFA U-20 World Cup.

In the two years since I'd started out playing on the under-20 national team as an eighteen-year-old, our core group of players had spent a lot of time together in camps and international matches. We'd grown as individual players and as a team. The bulk of us had played side by side for three or four years, since we were about sixteen years old. We were a very tight group. Over training camps and international friendlies, I'd begun to emerge as a leader on the pitch—becoming much more vocal, demanding more of myself and my teammates.

At twenty years old, Iain Hume was playing like a seasoned veteran. He'd already played several seasons as a striker with the Tranmere Rovers. Nik Ledgerwood was playing with 1860 Munich in Germany's third tier of professional football. Other core members of our group were playing college soccer, like Josh Simpson, who was at the University of Portland in the NCAA, and keeper Alim Karim, who was playing for Syracuse University.

Most of us had also played with each other before being recruited for the youth national team. We met several times during breaks in club play for international competition ahead of the 2003 Youth World Cup. It was rare that youth national team players were able to spend so much time together, but we'd all committed to being there. You don't see that very often at that age. But this was a special group. We all got along and did everything together, even away from the game. There was a lot of passion among us. And we were tough—we played hard, battling like hell every time we stepped onto the pitch. We were technically sound too. The key for us, though, was that we were just having fun. We didn't expect too much, so we enjoyed ourselves. We had some good players, but we didn't really envision ourselves doing anything that special in the tournament. There was something freeing about playing without the pressure of expectation.

◆

For the 2003 U-20 World Cup, we were placed in a group with Brazil, Czech Republic, and Australia—which put us squarely in the underdog position. Both Brazil and the Czech Republic were well-established contenders. Australia was expected to compete. We were expected to settle into a distant fourth. Outside our team, it seemed like no one thought we had a chance.

We didn't care. We didn't give ourselves much of a chance either, but that didn't mean we felt like we didn't belong. There was a swagger rising in our group that hadn't existed in the same way at the 2001 U-20 World Cup.

Of course, we knew that we were the underdogs. The dismal outcome in Argentina two years earlier had established that. But we had something to prove, and we thrived knowing that other countries wrote us off. We knew that we were better than what our opponents expected of us, and that was all that mattered. All we needed to do was play the way we knew that we could and hope for a bit of luck.

I was certainly a more confident, well-rounded player after a single season in Sweden. Holger Osieck, the head coach of the men's senior team, had seen an improvement in my poise and presence on the pitch coming off my first season with Östers. Ahead of the tournament, he told the press that he was convinced that I had the tools necessary to play in one of Europe's top leagues. It was certainly a confidence booster, particularly coming from Osieck, who didn't often make that kind of bold prediction.

Dale Mitchell, our under-20 coach, looked to Iain and me to lead the team through the qualifying rounds.

"Apart from these two players, the others played to their potential in qualifying play and that's the reason we advanced," Mitchell told the *Toronto Star*. "Hopefully, a couple of the others will shine, and if that happens, anything is possible."

Despite the doubt that hung over us, this group was special; we could feel it. And if you were outside our locker room in Dubai at the U-20 World Cup in 2003, you'd have heard that feeling down the hall.

Usually I wasn't very loud or overly emotional in the locker room, but I'd come out of my shell as a team leader heading to Dubai. It likely had to do with having a season of pro football behind me, as well as my familiarity with all the players on the team. I was growing as a teammate, not just as a player. I was one of the oldest in the group now, a veteran by U-20 standards. I felt responsible for how we performed, in the way that players put in leadership positions should.

Right before we played, I would call the team to the centre of the locker room. Standing in the middle of the pack, I'd break into the Ruff Ryders "Down Bottom"—an explicit anthem that we blared all the time.

It was a way to get everything out of me—to get myself motivated and to get the team motivated. It was part release, part war cry.

"It's for the north!" I'd shout.

"Hey," my teammates would call back.

"It's for the south," I'd go on, a little louder.

"Hey!"

"It's for the east!"

We'd be hyped up now.

"Hey!"

"It's for the west!" I'd holler.

"HEY!"

We could feel the energy rushing through us. Our group had so much of it, and we fed off each other. It was crazy. You wanted to go to war as soon as you stepped onto the pitch after that, because we were so into it. That was the time in my career when I was most vocal. Singing at the top of my lungs with good energy. We were ready for every game we played.

On the pitch, I funnelled all of that energy and excitement into focus. I've been told that I looked almost stoic at times, but the rush was there. I'd learned to keep a calm demeanour on the pitch. I wanted to play with precision, not panic. I wanted to make quick decisions, anticipating how a play might unfold several passes ahead. I needed to be ready to strike as an opportunity unfolded, without putting myself into a precarious position by trying to force a chance that wasn't there.

The national team coaching staff decided to use me in various positions, depending on the competition we faced. They could play me as a centre back, a central midfielder, or an attacking midfielder. Against stronger teams, I was often dropped back to the defensive line to put pressure on our opponent's most dangerous strikers. I didn't question the moves, even though they sometimes felt unorthodox. My father had always taught me to listen to my coaches, so it was never difficult for me to leave the decision-making to them.

We started off slow at the U-20 World Cup, playing far below our potential. We dropped our first game against Brazil 2–0 in front of thirteen thousand people. In our second game, against Australia, Iain—who wore his hair in a dyed red and white mohawk—scored Canada's first goal at the world under-20 championships in more than five hundred minutes of competition. Despite that key moment, we still fell to the Aussies 2–1.

With our second loss, it seemed as though we would fulfill the negative predictions of our performance. Outsiders counted us out as we headed into our final game. The Czech Republic was a much stronger team than the Australian team that had just beaten us. With a win, we'd have a chance to squeak through to the round of sixteen, where the four best third-place teams in the round robin would join the top two teams from each group.

Despite our disappointing start, we refused to quit. We didn't care if everyone else had counted us out. We knew that we were talented, that we were capable of winning. We knew that we were better than we were given credit for. It was time to prove it.

◆

We played a tight game with the Czech Republic in our third match, which was scoreless through the first half and into the second. With less than ten minutes remaining, Iain scored his second goal of the tournament. We held on for a thrilling 1–0 victory, which barely squeaked us into the round of sixteen. We were last among the third-place finishers to qualify.

Once again, we were heavy underdogs. By Canadian standards, we'd already achieved something unexpected. With that win, our team advanced further in the under-20 tournament than any Canadian squad had before. We could have been satisfied with where we sat, but we wanted more. We faced Burkina Faso in that playoff—the only team not to concede a goal in the first round, winning its group with a 2–0–1 record.

We rode the excitement of our win over Czech Republic into our match against Burkina Faso. We had no idea what to expect. Most of us had never even heard of the West African nation before that. But they were a good team. They were strong, intimidating. They tried to out-muscle us.

It was a chippy, hard-fought game with seven yellow cards—four to Burkina Faso and three to us. It was an evenly fought game, though we had a slight edge in controlling the tempo.

The game was scoreless through the first half. But ten minutes into the second, Iain delivered a perfect right cross to Josh Simpson, who took one step into the penalty area and drilled a left-footed shot into the top corner past just beyond the hands of the diving Burkina Faso keeper. We went absolutely crazy, celebrating as if it was the final.

For the remaining thirty minutes, we packed our zone defending a relentless attack. Burkina Faso did everything they could to equalize, but we held our line of defence. In the final moments, Ousseni Zongo nearly scored for Burkina Faso in a last-ditch attempt, but our keeper Alim Karim turned him away. It was a historic 1–0 victory. By far the biggest moment in our generation's tenure with the national team. By getting through the round of sixteen, we'd gone further than any Canadian team at that level at a FIFA men's championship. But back home, our accomplishment received little attention in the press.

I felt that I'd played my best match of the tournament. I felt at ease, on top of the play—comfortable under pressure with a vision for the attack. I was able to dictate the pace of play, making quick decisions on and off the ball, while creating quality chances for my teammates.

We were absolutely buzzing. We had thought we wouldn't get out of the group and now we were in the quarterfinals against Spain. Our confidence was growing. None of us had played in this type of setting before, even those of us who were playing in Europe. It was only an under-20 tournament, but it was still the world stage. I remember thinking, "This might be the furthest I go."

It seemed unlikely that I'd ever play in a World Cup. I wasn't even confident about my future with the men's national team. It was surreal. We soaked in every moment possible.

More than fifteen thousand people came to watch our match at the Mohammed bin Zayed Stadium in Abu Dhabi. I'd only played in front of that many people a handful of times. Spain was led by Andrés Iniesta, an FC Barcelona product who was already touted as one of the world's best young midfielders and was on his way to becoming an icon in Spanish football. Spain's starting eleven all belonged to top clubs, including two other players with Barcelona and one from Real Madrid.

Our starting eleven was made up of four university students, four players from the A-League, and three overseas pro players. Our nerves got the better of us in the first half as we tried to avoid mistakes that we knew the Spaniards could capitalize on. We were shaky, overthinking the game.

Iniesta scored to put Spain ahead in the thirty-fifth minute. You could clearly see the difference in the class of player he was. Iniesta was elegant on the pitch. He seemed to really enjoy playing. He made everything seem effortless, reading two or three plays ahead. He played with unmatched intelligence. We were the same age, but he seemed so mature—so certain of his ability. Our coaches moved me to centre back for that match, so I was able to watch everything that Iniesta did, without being tight next to him. It was remarkable to watch. He wasn't the kind of player who just blew by you; he'd outsmart you and find that killer pass. Of course, I still had to be on my toes, because he was always looking for a sneaky, near-indefensible pass.

We trailed 1–0 at the half, still very much in the game. We carried that nothing-to-lose swagger. We knew who we were playing against. We had some quality, but nothing compared to them. As expected, Spain carried the majority of the possession. In the match, Spain had 59 percent of possession to our 41, but we made them earn every chance they managed. Though we didn't have the ball often, we tried to counterattack whenever we did. We wanted to stay in the game as long as possible. You never want to be in a game thinking that it's already over. We carried that little bit of hope, which had already taken us further than we could have imagined. All we needed to do was cling to it for one more half.

Less than ten minutes into the second half, Iain brought us to life with another miracle, scoring from way out. The goal jolted us back to life. We played like a Canadian underdog team should—with absolutely nothing to lose and a whole lot of respect to earn. Spain suddenly found themselves in trouble, especially when they were reduced to ten men in the sixty-fifth minute after one of their players picked up a second yellow card on an aggressive shoulder challenge on Sita-Taty Matondo.

We failed to spread them out to create gaps in the Spanish defence. Still, we played strong, surprising the Spanish when we found our chances. Just before the end of regulation time, Iain was given a free kick. He fired a near-perfect shot that zipped past their diving keeper—but hit the post. I can still remember the rush of elation when the ball disappeared behind their players. Everyone thought it was a goal.

The game was tied at the end of regulation, which put us into a golden goal overtime. All we needed was a single stroke of luck and we would defeat Goliath to advance. Anything seemed possible if we could just find our opportunity.

It wasn't meant to be. Five minutes into extra time, Spain's Javier Arizmendi corralled a ball we failed to clear, darted by two defenders, and tapped in a goal to end the game and our remarkable underdog story.

We were dejected after the 2–1 loss, knowing how close we'd been to pulling off something that had seemed impossible when we'd arrived in the United Arab Emirates nearly three weeks earlier.

Hindsight would offer more clarity, as it does.

Spain went on to lose to Brazil in the final. Considering where we'd started, it was hard to be upset knowing that two of the teams we lost to—one of which we took to extra time—were the best in the world.

The whole run we had in the UAE was unreal; we were on the edge of an appearance in the semifinals. I still get a rush thinking about it today. We'd stepped up onto the world stage and performed in a way that forced others to take notice. Sure, it was at a youth level, but those teams were still the best of the best, and we'd held our own. Our team would be remembered as arguably the best Canadian U-20 team ever. We were a group of talented players rising—some finding their way at home, others starting to make a name for themselves in Europe.

The disappointment that filled our locker room after the loss to Spain was an important moment in our development as a national program. We'd made a lot of noise—inside that locker room and beyond it. We started as an afterthought. We left believing that we could have gone all the way.

At the end of the tournament, I was selected to the U-20 World Cup all-star team as one of the best eleven at the tournament. Iain was also named to the all-star roster as one of four additional players. The honour meant a lot to us. Not only individually but as a statement about our team and what Canada was capable of.

I'd been in the national program for four years at that point. I already had six caps with Canada's U-23 Olympic team and four more with the senior national team, getting in a brief amount of time as a bench player on a squad led by players like Paul Stalteri and Jason de Vos. But that tournament—my last with the U-20 team—was by far the best experience and most success I'd had wearing a Canada jersey. It was the catalyst for the belief that would drive the next two decades of my career repping the maple leaf.

"It's for the north . . ."

Always.

11

Helsingborg

In the year after I'd signed the flimsiest no-guarantee contract in professional soccer, everything had changed.

Östers had been so unsure of my ability that they protected their investment in me with a six-month escape clause. I was the club's Canadian experiment—a skinny, five-foot-eleven, 153-pound Canuck with a return policy. As I was about to turn twenty-one in early 2004, newly relegated Östers looked to cash in on that gamble. My agent had told the team that I wanted to move on, and they respected the request. The Allsvenskan was a great stepping stone in European soccer. But playing in Sweden's second division was not. It wasn't where you wanted to play to make a name for yourself. With the European transfer window open that January, the team looked to move me to a higher tier club for a price. The club owned my rights for another season, but we mutually agreed that it was time for me to move on.

For the first time, I felt truly confident about my chances. I'd developed exponentially during my season with Östers, and the team had provided invaluable proximity to other European clubs. My performance at the U-20 World Cup widened that exposure. I'd generated enough buzz about my potential that teams around the world were starting to pay attention. There were rumours that I was getting calls from MLS teams like the Los Angeles Galaxy and D.C. United. Even Dallas Burn decided to take another look. My agent told me that he was receiving a lot of interest, and I read about it in a few newspaper articles. There were also calls from a team in Portugal, three in France, three in Germany, and a couple in Denmark.

"A bit of a frenzy," Barry MacLean, my agent at the time, told the Canadian Press. "We've got a lot of interest in him, that's for sure. Probably more than any other Canadian player I've dealt with. . . . The fact that he did so well at the World Cup, that didn't hurt."

But nothing was happening with these clubs—and anything that did happen was only a trial. It was always unclear which of these clubs was actually interested. It made me question what was going on. Was it just talk, or was there truth behind it? I didn't really know what to believe, especially when those conversations didn't turn into anything more than that.

One of the potentially exciting opportunities I had was a trial with the Serie A club Udinese Calcio in Italy that January. It was unusual—you don't often see a player who belongs to one club train with another on a trial. But Östers approved it, because they knew that I wanted to leave, and they wanted to make some money off their investment in me. It was a cool experience. Udinese was coached by Luciano Spalletti, who went on to coach Inter Milan and Napoli, where he won a Serie A title, before being appointed manager of the Italian national team in 2023.

I was a wide-eyed kid in my short time there. Nobody really gave me a serious look. Most of the players didn't even know why I was there training. They were like, "Who is this kid?" I was in Udine for five days and only had a few moments on the pitch with the first team. I spent most of my time training with the reserves and other guys on trial, unlikely to make it through. It didn't feel discouraging because I had finally figured out how these trials worked and how difficult it was to make it through. It was a humbling reminder of how far I needed to climb to reach that level.

After Italy, I travelled to Antalya, Turkey, to work out with Spartak Moscow and Saturn Moscow, which were both training there at the time. I wasn't really comfortable. I wasn't keen to go to Russia; my heart was still set on Europe.

Considering the challenge I'd had trying to catch a break in Europe, it felt good to finally be wanted. But I knew that one decent season on a losing team in Sweden wasn't enough to establish myself as a pro. It was a start, but I was still a long way from where I planned to be.

Several of Östers' opponents in the Allsvenskan also showed interest. It seemed ideal to remain in Sweden, where I was getting comfortable and had earned some recognition. Before the 2004 season began that spring, Östers agreed to a transfer with Helsingborgs IF, a century-old club, which had won the league championship a few years earlier. As one of the top five clubs in the league, it was a place that I had hoped to go to. Östers benefitted from receiving a modest transfer fee of a couple hundred thousand Swedish Kronor (which was a little more than $40,000 Canadian at the time), and I had another opportunity to move through the ranks of European football. The team played out of its namesake Helsingborg, a coastal city on the Øresund, a strait in the Baltic Sea that forms the border between Sweden and Denmark.

From the start, there was a lot more pressure in Helsingborg than I'd faced in Östers. Once again, everyone was aware that I was the new kid in town—but this time, they had higher expectations for me as a player.

Helsingborg was a bigger city than Växjö, nearly double the population. The team's stadium, the Olympia, was much larger, too, with a capacity of around sixteen thousand fans. And it was almost always full. My memory of the home opener that season is still so vivid; the stadium was completely packed and had an amazing atmosphere. That was one of the things I'd loved about playing against Helsingborgs while I was with Östers: there was so much energy in that stadium. Östers always had decent-sized crowds, but this was another level. This was much more of a professional environment.

For the first time, I felt like a professional footballer. I no longer felt like I was clinging to a fantasy. People actually recognized me from my season with Östers. The fans were so passionate. They'd stop me at the park and around town. Having people turn to look at you and ask for an autograph (which I was still trying to get right) was such a new feeling. The fans knew me as a player and not the new Canadian in town, who played soccer instead of hockey.

I was also much more comfortable being abroad than I had been in my first season away from home. The anxiety and culture shock had settled, though it still lingered a bit as those things do. I'd started using MSN Messenger to chat with friends, which was a game changer. It was the beginning of feeling connected to people even when you are oceans apart.

Everyday life was easier, in part because I was getting used to things but I was also growing up. The camaraderie with my teammates was different with this new club; we had a lot of guys in their early twenties and we hung out together a lot, which really helped. The club also took very good care of me. They set me up with a nice place to live and a Honda Civic to drive around town.

One of my teammates, Thando Mngomeni, became like a brother to me. An instant best friend. We were born just a few days apart, albeit on different continents. Thando was South African. He was a very good player and one of the few other internationals on the club. We connected right away. Thando was a funny guy, always cracking jokes. We were very much alike, always laughing together. He was chill. He didn't make any trouble or anything, but he liked to party and have fun. I went out with him a few times but not too much. I've always been an early-to-bed kind of guy. My focus was still very much on proving that I belonged, and I was always concerned about jeopardizing that.

But I loved Thando's energy—I loved how much fun he always seemed to have. He reminded me of my friends back home in Brampton, the sandlot guys I'd grown up with, goofing around and enjoying the smallest moments. Even though Thando and I came from different worlds, we had so much in common. We were together every single day. We'd meet up for breakfast, lunch, and dinner. We'd take the ferry across the channel to Denmark and drive around Copenhagen together. Whenever his friends or my friends came out to visit, we'd all hang out together. He was an instant good friend in the way that someone in university might make while studying abroad—a stranger walks into your life and almost immediately it's as if you've known each other for decades. When you're away from home and you don't have anybody, it gets hard. Thando was the kind of person who helped fill that void.

◆

On the pitch, I struggled through the first few months in Helsingborg. Much of what I loved about the move to Helsingborg also posed challenges. It was a big adjustment—playing with a bigger team and getting more pressure from the fans and stuff like that. There was also more competition for me in the middle, which added another element. In the end, I couldn't play my game the way I wanted to. I didn't score a goal the entire season, which was only one element of my play—but a disappointing one. It was a frustrating, inconsistent season.

At times, I was grateful that I didn't understand Swedish. We had passionate fans who expected a lot from their players. And the press could be harsh. Sometimes I'd see my name in a headline and not know what the rest of the article said. But I could tell that it wasn't good by the rankings they gave each player in the paper after each game. Ignorance was my ally. I didn't know what they were saying, so it couldn't hurt me. I did my best to not worry about it.

Despite our challenges on the pitch, we were led by a very good coach. He did a lot of work with me, trying to help me develop my game. He was very vocal. We met often, talking through the challenges I was having on the pitch, helping me adjust. He sharpened my football IQ, showing me how to read the game better. Despite my disappointment, he remained encouraging. I never doubted that I was valued on the team. I think they saw the work that I put in, despite the challenges. No one wanted more out of me than I did.

After the season, I went straight to work. There were long breaks between seasons in Sweden, so I'd head home for a couple of months, spending Christmas with my family. I didn't take any time off: I hit the gym hard. I needed to have a better season. I knew that I was capable of doing better; for some reason I wasn't able to play at the level I felt I could reach. In my mind, I needed to get stronger and faster. Being lean had always been an advantage for me, but I felt like I'd been outmuscled too many times on the pitch. That's what I put my focus on.

I didn't have an actual trainer—so it was mostly just me and friends, like Alex and Haldon, heading to the LA Fitness near my parents' house every day. They were like my own versions of Mickey Goldmill, pushing me to be better. There were no days off. But I didn't really have a plan, aside from adding muscle. I did a ton of heavy squats, bench presses—all of the typical bulking-up exercises. I wasn't quite Rocky at the end of the off-season, but I was as strong as I'd ever been.

Every winter in Brampton there were money tournaments: teams entered to play five-on-five indoors with a cash prize on the line. These weren't casual men's league friendly matches. These were full-on battles with few rules and big grudges in what was really an underground league. My closest childhood friends always had a team. My brother played with them too. It was essentially the same crew of guys who grew up playing together on the field behind Arnott Charlton. I usually didn't participate, but when I returned that winter, they convinced me to join them. It was risky, because as a pro player I'd have a target on my back. Missing time as a professional because of an injury from playing in some money tournament back home was an objectively dumb risk. I don't know what I was thinking.

Even with five players per side, the space in these indoor set-ups was super tight. There was hardly any room to manoeuvre before an opponent was on you, often with a hard tackle. The matches were reckless. It wasn't a lot of money on the line—probably only a couple hundred for each player on the winning team. But the minute there was cash involved, things got intense. In reality, it was more about pride than anything, and there were plenty of egos on display.

Everyone knew that I was playing professionally, and a target was on my back. Players went after me, trying to knock me down a peg. I was on the receiving end of some dangerous plays, but I didn't back down. The competition was as heated as any match I'd played in Sweden or with the national team. I never witnessed any fists being thrown, but it got close several times. The refereeing was terrible, so players took liberties all over the pitch. Some of the tackles were unbelievable. Guys would get more pissed off each play, until it turned into a shoving match.

It was ridiculous in hindsight, but at the time I didn't care. I was back home playing with my boys. The passion we shared had never left us. It was as if we were kids again, chasing after a ball for hours without a care in the world beyond the match we'd invented that day. There was something rejuvenating about a homecoming and old friends, connecting the past and present. I was reminded why this game became so addictive in the first place. As always, with our group, it was impossible to take any form of competition easy. So, of course, we went all the way to the finals. Thankfully no one from the Canadian national team or Helsingborgs found out about it. They wouldn't have been happy. I could have killed my whole career.

But damn, it was so much fun.

When I returned to Sweden at the end of January, I was considerably stronger than when I'd left. There were no trials with other clubs or rumours of a transfer this time. I was committed to Helsingborgs and determined to prove that my struggles in the first season with the club were behind me. Sweden's climate is like Canada's, so our winter training camps were held indoors or within a dome. I must have carried some of the rhythm and intensity I'd found playing alongside my friends in that money tournament, because everything seemed to click for me right away.

My second season in Helsingborgs was much different than the first. I started off a very good run through our exhibition matches, and that momentum carried me into the season. Our team as a whole was much better that season. We brought in a few new players who made the team stronger and had a really good start to the campaign. I scored my first goal in our first game of the 2005 season, which was a big relief.

We came out flying and managed to stay near the top of the table through most of the year. When a team is playing well, when everything is clicking, players have more confidence, and the fans really get behind you. Everyone seems to step up their game. It makes everything about the game feel easier. I followed up my first goal with several more early on, which made me so much more at ease.

In my first season, I'd been more of a holding midfielder, focusing on the defensive end, but I'd always been more of a box-to-box midfielder—using my speed to attack and defend. In my second season, I found my rhythm in that more natural role. After my first goal, I kept pushing for more, and it worked. I kept finding the back of the net. Everything was much more relaxed for me. I finished with six goals, which wasn't an earth-shattering amount but pretty decent for a midfielder.

I covered more ground and played a more versatile game. The work I had put in at the gym probably had a lot to do with my surge; my newly acquired muscle helped me feel confident with the ball and more consistent in my play. I knew I had an important impact in each game I played. Now when I saw my name in a newspaper headline, I felt confident that I wasn't being trashed. The fans certainly seemed much more appreciative of my play.

Despite our strong start, we trailed off from the top of the table as the season went on to finish sixth in the league. But it was a big leap up from our tenth place finish the previous year. I finished as one of the top players in the club, leading the team with combined goals and assists, with six and five. Considering my performance the year before, I couldn't have hoped for a better outcome. It was the best season I'd played in Sweden—and it was my last.

12

Copenhagen

Ståle Solbakken was at home in Norway watching a Helsingborgs match on a Swedish television channel the first time he saw me play. One of the most celebrated players in Norwegian history, Solbakken was in the early years of a managerial career that would only widen his legacy in Scandinavian football. He was in the midst of his first coaching stint, with Hamarkameratene—the Hamar Comrades—in a small town on the shore of Norway's largest lake, Mjøsa. Solbakken was impressed by my speed and tactical sense in the match he watched. His interest grew after a Norwegian agent called him to ask if he'd seen me play. After that, Solbakken came to Sweden to attend a Helsingborgs game in person. Thankfully I didn't screw up terribly in that game, and he remained impressed.

In late 2005, Solbakken and I both faced crossroads in our careers. A few years earlier, he had been one of Norway's top players in the middle of a promising career in the Danish Superliga. After helping push FC Copenhagen to the top of the table, he suffered a heart attack during a training session in March 2001. Solbakken was only thirty-three years old at the time. Copenhagen went on to win the championship, but Solbakken was forced to retire because of his medical condition. A brilliant tactician, he moved into coaching with Hamarkameratene—also known as HamKam—a second tier club in Norway where he'd spent the first five years of his playing career. Solbakken led HamKam to the top of the league, earning its promotion to Tippeligaen, the top tier of Norwegian football (now known as Eliteserien). Earning a reputation as one of the best young coaches in Scandinavia, Solbakken was soon ready for a new challenge.

After two seasons with Helsingborgs, I was also ready to take another step forward. In three years, I'd gone from being a homesick stranger in Sweden to an established player in the Allsvenskan, generating interest from teams across Europe. My time with Helsingborgs and Östers had been essential—and I was grateful to what both clubs and the league had given me. I had arrived as a raw player and quickly learned that I wouldn't be able to get by on my athleticism alone. I understood the gap between where I was and where I hoped to be as a player. At twenty-two years old, I felt like I was ready to try something new. There was no certainty as to how long my career would last, so I always felt a sense of urgency. I'd proven that I was a top level player in the Allsvenskan. Now I needed to see how far I could go.

There was one year left on my three-year deal with Helsingborgs, but I was intrigued by the outside interest and Helsingborgs was interested in getting a return on its investment in me. It seemed a move would benefit both parties. Two interested clubs were located right across the Øresund in Denmark—Brøndby IF and FC Copenhagen, the top two teams in the Danish Superliga and widely viewed as the best in Scandinavia at the time. Brøndby IF were the reigning league champions, while Copenhagen was leading the league into the winter break of the 2005–06 season. (The Danish Superliga season runs much longer than the Swedish Allsvenskan: Allsvenskan

runs April to November, while Superliga spans July to May.) In exposure and competition, either club would be a jump up from the
Allsvenskan. I was excited about what might lay ahead. As much as I
liked being in Helsingborgs, I had to be true to myself and my goals.

When Ståle Solbakken signed on as the head coach of FC Copenhagen mid-season on January 1, 2006, his first move was to sign me.

He reached out shortly after he signed and asked to meet. You can
see Denmark from Helsingborg. It's about a twenty-minute ferry
ride, so I took a trip across the Øresund to meet with Solbakken, not
entirely sure what to expect. He looked a bit like an athletic Michael
Stipe, the lead singer of R.E.M., and he spoke perfect English with
a Norwegian accent. Solbakken told me how he had been impressed
watching me play on Swedish television. He liked the versatility in my
game and felt that I'd fit perfectly into his vision for Copenhagen,
which he laid out convincingly. We were aligned in our vision for the
game. What Solbakken planned to build in Copenhagen excited me.
I left our meeting ready to buy whatever he was selling.

I took the ferry back convinced that I was ready to make a permanent move across the channel. But I still had another year on my
second contract with Helsingborgs. Our preseason had already
started. During training, I confided in a few of my teammates who
had spent time playing in the Danish Superliga. Each of them told me
that I needed to leave. Copenhagen was one of the biggest clubs in
Scandinavia. Parken Stadium, FC Copenhagen's decade-old home,
held more than 38,000 fans for home games. It was by far the largest,
most magnificent facility that I'd ever played regular matches in. A
few years earlier more than sixty thousand screaming fans had packed
into Parken for a Michael Jackson concert, setting the stadium's
attendance record. But on any given match day, FC Copenhagen fans
could match the passion of any global superstar concert that swept
through. I'd never experienced anything like that.

I made one more trip to visit the city, walking the cobblestone streets of Copenhagen. It was a beautiful city. I loved everything about it. The city, the team, the opportunity—everything drew me to Copenhagen. But the biggest factor was Solbakken. I always felt that the best way to join a club was to have the coach behind you. You never want to join a team on a decision made by the manager alone. The coach deploys the strategy, the coach decides who plays—it's the coach who, in so many ways, dictates the success you find with a club. When it comes to playing time, it's the coach who decides your fate. I learned early on in my career to make sure that I was part of the coach's vision before joining a team. Solbakken made it clear that he wanted me in Copenhagen. And there was no doubt in my mind that I was ready to make the move.

A few days later, Copenhagen secured my transfer from Helsing-borgs for around 1.1 million Euros (or $1.3 million U.S. at the time). Leaving Sweden was bittersweet. It was my first home away from home—the place where I'd first felt the pang of homesickness and learned to move through it. It was where I'd learned to separate whites and darks in the laundry, and how to cook my mother's lasagna. In only three years, I'd gone from being a skinny unknown in Canada to earning the attention of some of the region's biggest clubs. But more than that, I'd gone from being a boy chasing a dream into a man firmly living it. I knew that there was still so much for me to learn about the game I loved, but I recognized how far I'd come. And I would never forget Sweden for showing me just how far I could go.

♦

I was introduced at Parken in my No. 13 FC Copenhagen jersey, as the Lions' newest addition at midfield later that January. I signed a four-year deal with the club, which would keep me in Denmark until 2010 when I'd be in the prime of my athletic ability. Any chance I had to advance my career in Europe further would come through Copenhagen.

In Denmark, everything was bigger—the stage, the attention, the possibilities, and, of course, the potential for failure. There was pressure from the start, with the media in Denmark touting me as the team's million-euro acquisition, with the expectation that I would be one of the team's new stars. It was an intimidating prospect on a team with veteran stars in Marcus Allbäck and Michael Silberbauer, a young Danish midfielder who was a local hero and one of the best players in the league. The Danish Football Association only allowed three non-EU players to be on the field for a club at the same time, which meant that I'd be expected to perform if I was going to hold one of those spots.

But just like when I first arrived in Sweden, I faced a big learning curve in the Danish Superliga. Several of my teammates and opponents had played in the Premier League and for top-tier European teams. In Sweden, there weren't many players who had played at very high levels. I was still a young player with plenty to learn. In Copenhagen, there were several veterans who had played at a level I could still only dream of reaching.

While I'd learned to make plays at a faster pace in Sweden, my transition to Denmark required a big jump in my tactical understanding of the game. After three years in Sweden, I was still pretty raw. I'd still take the ball and try to out-sprint defenders or dribble through them, as I always had. I lost the ball far too often, sacrificing possession. My game was still geared towards individual finesse rather than the cohesive movement of the whole. After I had adapted to the pace of play in Sweden, my speed and versatility allowed me to maintain the edge that got me noticed by coaches like Ståle Solbakken. But in the Danish Superliga, that wouldn't be enough.

Solbakken was a strategic mastermind. From our earliest discussions and training sessions, I understood what he needed from me. He recognized my strengths and weaknesses, with a view to turn me into a more complete player. He was a direct and precise teacher. He'd give the team instructions in Norwegian, which were easily understood by my Danish teammates, because the languages of the neighbouring countries are similar. I was usually able to pick up on his instructions as he directed players to specific positions and showed us how he wanted us to move. But Solbakken always took time to make sure that I understood, repeating his instructions in English. There was no ambiguity about how he wanted me to play, and I appreciated his approach to the game.

Under Solbakken, I learned to play the game at a quicker pace. Not in terms of my physical speed, but in the way I executed tactically. He wanted quick touches, maintaining team possession while attacking in a controlled and purposeful way.

We were racing for a league title from the moment I arrived. It was an entirely new football experience for me. It was professional to a degree I'd only imagined. It was the first city I'd played where there were two major teams in town—Copenhagen and our rivals, Brøndby IF. We faced them in my very first match. It was a Royal League match, a tournament that ran within the Superliga season. It meant that there were extra bragging rights on the line, as teams hoped to add the prize to their mantle. We were away at Brøndby, which had the second largest stadium in Denmark, next to ours.

I'd always watched derby games on TV when I was young, seeing famous rivals like Inter Milan and AC Milan face off against each other. I'd dreamed of playing in something that big one day, but I had no comprehension of what it would actually be like. It's one of those things you can't appreciate properly from a distance. You have to feel the stadium shake around you.

The thirty thousand fans at Brøndby Stadium made sure we felt every minute of it. It was a cold, wet February night in the west end of

Copenhagen. Fans launched smoke bombs from the stands, and you could barely see the pitch during the match. It was wild.

Something changes for players when you reach a game with so much hype around it, like that one had. You can tell what it means to the players on those nights—from the intensity in the locker room as you prepare to the way you feed off the mania roaring in the stands. The battles on the pitch carry that much more intensity too.

Brøndby started the match with a flurry of chances, dominating the pace of play. But we quickly adjusted into a compact midfield, asserting ourselves. We narrowly missed scoring on two free kicks from André Bergdølmo, our veteran defender. A few minutes later, I found myself in an open position and took a shot that sailed just over the bar, as I looked up in disbelief. I was that close to starting my Copenhagen career with a goal. We scored twice in the second half and hung on for a 2–1 win, which kept us in the running to defend the Royal League trophy that Copenhagen had won the season before. It was a game easily forgotten in the history books; for me, it was a memory that I'll never forget. All the smoke and the damp chill—the madness of that packed stadium, the rush of a near goal. My dream of professional soccer, fully realized—I was there.

Denmark's passion for football was on a different level than anything I'd been part of before. Maybe it was the sheer volume of fans at every game. Playing in front of almost forty thousand raucous fans on a regular basis does something to your psyche. The celebrations inside Parken were monumental: it was as though every goal scored was glorious and meaningful. It made every game feel like the most important match you've ever played in. And the place our club held in the heart of the city was immediately apparent. In Sweden, I'd grown used to being recognized as a player away from the pitch. But in Denmark, we were treated like celebrities. It seemed like everybody in the city loved football. For a player in his early twenties, it's a pretty incredible experience. The city was gorgeous. The restaurants were outstanding. The nightlife was wild, though I didn't go out very often. It really was a young footballer's dream. There were plenty of possible distractions. I was making a decent salary for a twenty-four-year-old, with local fame in a world-class city. But my life was football. I didn't really date and rarely partied. If I wasn't playing football, I was thinking about it. At that time in my life, my passion was singular.

◆

Unlike my first season with Helsingborgs, I was able to make an impact right away with Copenhagen. Solbakken looked to use me in a variety of different midfield roles, showing me how to become a more versatile player. He liked that I was an open-minded, active player who was willing to adapt. I had a decent understanding of the game and was eager to learn. He believed that I had the ability to play all over the pitch and shield the ball effectively.

Solbakken felt that our opponents underestimated my ability, and he took advantage of their oversight by using me in ways that could exploit it. I was undersized but fit, which allowed me to surprise opponents with bursts of speed at opportune moments. He was confident in my abilities to both attack and defend, which made me a key part of his system. It meant that regardless of what kind of game we were in, I served a purpose. If we were dominating the ball against a weaker Danish side, I was used on the attack. Playing against a more talented club—as we soon would—I fit into a more defensive strategy. In either approach, Solbakken felt that he could trust me tactically. My lean physique and fitness allowed me to play full matches without losing speed.

That April, we won the Royal League with a 1–0 win over Lillestrøm at Parken, with Razak Pimpong scoring the winner in the eighty-ninth minute. It was a huge victory—and I got to raise my first professional trophy. And it was only the start. We sat atop the table all season and were on course to win the Danish Superliga championship.

Being part of a winning campaign is so satisfying. I'd never experienced it before. To be celebrated across the city—to feel that widespread, shared appreciation for what your group has accomplished—there is nothing like it. We secured the Superliga championship in early May and celebrated winning the double at Parken, with our fans going wild in the stands. It was incredible to see what the championship meant to them and to the city of Copenhagen.

On the pitch, I embraced my teammates like old friends I'd conquered the world with. I gave Solbakken a big hug too. I finally understood what it felt like. I'd known these men for half a season, but we would share this victory forever. That's the thing about winning. It lives with you and the people you share it with. It creates a lifelong connection that can't be taken away. Flags fly forever, as they say. Beyond banners, though, there is a bond that forms among players who have endured the grind of a season together and come out on top.

Decades on, you can gather in the same place and feel that rush return. There is nothing like it.

Nothing in my career to that point had matched the absolute joy of winning a title. That experience alone was enough to have made the move to Copenhagen worthwhile. It was just the beginning though. Within a few months, I'd be running across the pitch at Old Trafford, living a version of my boyhood dreams in the Champions League.

Part III

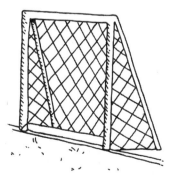

13

Champions League

There are moments in our lives when the past and present connect in a surreal way—when it is as though you're watching the now unfold through the eyes of some younger version of you.

That's how I felt as I watched the 2006–07 Champions League draw. At the same time that I sat in my condo watching television in Denmark, I was a boy in Canada feeling my dreams begin watching football with my dad. The annual competition of the top clubs from across Europe was some of the most exhilarating soccer I'd witnessed.

A day earlier, I'd been part of one of the most exciting upsets in Copenhagen history. In the second leg of our Champions League qualifying match against Ajax, we'd stunned the four-time European champions with a 2–0 win in Amsterdam. We'd dropped the first leg 2–1 a couple of weeks earlier at Parken, and almost no one gave us a chance to beat a powerhouse like Ajax by the two goals needed in our second match to win the qualifier. But in our second match, we'd managed to survive an Ajax onslaught in the first half, with the match scoreless heading into the second. Then what everyone had thought impossible happened. Michael Silberbauer tucked a free kick just inside the post to give us 1–0 in the fifty-ninth minute. Then with less than thirteen minutes to play, one of the Ajax defenders deflected the ball into his own goal off a corner kick. A two-goal margin was enough to carry Copenhagen into the Champions League for the first time in the team's history. We clung to the lead as though our lives were on the line. With ten minutes to go Ajax's Klaas-Jan Huntelaar headed a ball off our crossbar. It was that close.

We held on to the 2–0 lead.

The whistle blew three times, the most wondrous sound I'd ever heard. My teammates rushed the field around me. I was moving, too, rushing with them, embracing—but I felt like I was floating. Weightless. I couldn't believe it. The tournament of the world's best clubs, which I'd watched play out on fuzzy satellite channels as a boy, was suddenly a reality for me as a man. It was the euphoria of a dream coming true.

We returned to Copenhagen as local heroes. The city nearly caved in with joy. Qualifying alone was historic. I didn't think the moment could get any better. But there I was, the very next day, sitting in my condo watching the Champions League group stage draw unfold live in Monaco. Who would we face in the next chapter of this impossible childhood fairy tale?

Group F was announced and there were tears in my eyes.

Copenhagen, Benfica, Celtic—and Manchester United.

In that moment, I was a grown-ass man, a professional football player, and I was a boy watching Man U dance across my television screen. Soon I'd be playing on the same stage as the team I'd always cheered for.

"This is insane," I thought.

I called my family right away.

"Can you believe it?" I asked my parents over the phone. None of us could really. But it was a particularly sweet moment for my father. He had put so much time into this shared journey, fostering my dreams and passing on his passion. My father was never a man of many words, but I could picture the grin on his face over the phone. The smile of a proud father, which I now understand. The wide and endless kind.

My family and friends quickly fixed their schedules and made arrangements to make sure they were in Copenhagen for our home-stand against the Red Devils. For the next two months, it was all I could think about.

♦

Copenhagen's first Champions League run kicked off in mid-September against Benfica, the storied Portuguese club, in front of a wild sold-out crowd of more than forty thousand fans at Parken. The atmosphere at the match was electric, as usual. We managed to keep Benfica from scoring but only generated a few chances and ended in a nil-nil draw.

Two weeks later, I stepped onto the pitch at Celtic Park in Glasgow, a stadium that carries more than a century of football legends and ghosts within its imposing stands. With more than sixty thousand fans packing the largest stadium in Scotland, even being an opponent gives you chills.

Even though we were the Danish champions, we were the under-dogs of our pool. Still, we'd travelled to Glasgow feeling confident. We'd toppled Ajax and held Benfica scoreless. We'd stood up against two of the finest clubs in Europe and proven that we belonged. Solbakken underpinned that confidence. "We have nothing to fear," he told the Danish press before our match.

And Solbakken was right. We played valiantly, matching Celtic through most of match, but we were unable to equalize after allowing a late first-half goal. That marker stood through the second, and we fell 1–0.

It was all a set-up for the meeting of my dreams. Two weeks later— Tuesday, October 17, 2006—a rainy day in Manchester.

My family and friends gathered around the television back at home in Brampton, as the skinny soccer-mad boy who used to sit beside them jogged nervously onto the Old Trafford pitch.

When you finally arrive at the places you dream of reaching in life—wherever or whatever they may be—there is an awe that over-comes you. You can feel it from your head to your toes, as your mind tries to process the fact that, indeed, you are now there. I'll use the word again, because it's the only way to capture this feeling: it was surreal. Absolutely, astoundingly, beautifully surreal. Everything about Old Trafford was as I'd imagined it to be.

I remember walking out of the tunnel in our royal-blue Carlsberg kits, next to Man United in their red AIG kits, each player holding the hand of a child who accompanied us onto the pitch. It was over-whelming. At that moment, I felt more like the child whose hand I held than a professional football player. With 72,000 fans in the stands, I'd never experienced anything like it. The stadium was huge, and I felt so small. On the other side of the pitch stood Wayne Rooney, Louis Saha, and Cristiano Ronaldo among a roster of the world's top players. The presence that these guys had was incredible. They stood on top of the soccer world. These were guys that I'd been watching play on television for years. Even the players who were my age. When I was playing in Sweden and Denmark, I watched their games all the time.

My god, it was overwhelming. I felt so many emotions. I was ner-vous as hell. But I was also so excited to be there. It was as if I had suddenly burst through my childhood TV screen into a match I'd been watching.

Back home, my father watched alongside our family; a dream that he'd carried since childhood was coming true. I knew he was proud. Knowing that everyone I loved was watching on television added another emotion that underscored it all, and it also made me more nervous.

I tried to settle down as the match began. Solbakken played me on the outside. He was excellent at using a strong midfield to contain an opponent's attack, especially during away matches where teams usually carried the momentum in front of raucous supporters. He hoped to make use of my speed to neutralize any attacks on the outside flank. I don't know if it was a successful strategy or not. The game was a blur. It felt like the ninety-minute match went by in twenty minutes.

I never did settle down. As I sprinted around that damp pitch, I felt like I couldn't play my game—everything was happening so fast around me. It was intimidating seeing all these guys on the other side. It didn't feel real. While I'd learned to control my emotions in pro games, this was much more pressure than I'd ever experienced before. I was overwhelmed. It was hard for me to stay calm, which is what I needed to be to play my best. I rushed every play I was involved in.

It was a big lesson for me. I needed to learn how to play my game regardless of who was on the other side of the pitch, or which renowned pitch we were on that day. If I wanted to play professional football, I had to believe that I belonged at every level—and back it up with my game. I was a confident player, but in many ways that match in Old Trafford revealed to me that parts of me still doubted my ability and questioned whether I belonged on the pitch at all.

◆

As the game sped around me, I didn't play the way I would have liked to. At one point, I did manage to win a ball off Darren Fletcher and thread a pass through two Man U defenders to Marcus Allbäck, who spun it into a blistering shot that was stopped by a diving Edwin van der Sar. But that was little consolation. It was one of only three attempts on target that we managed in the match, compared to Manchester United's ten. Our keeper, Jesper Christiansen, made several miraculous saves that kept the score more modest than it could have been. But there was only so much he could do. Just before the end of the first half, Paul Scholes scored on a brilliant strike from well outside the box to put us down one. John O'Shea put United up 2–0 early in the second off a corner from Ronaldo—and then Kieran Richardson finished us off in the eighty-second minute.

We had no chance. Despite my frustration in my own play, I didn't want the game to end. The boy in me enjoyed every fleeting moment of it. The match ended, and I stepped back into the real world, trying to process what I'd just experienced.

That match at Old Trafford still feels like it was more dream than reality.

It was good that we had travelled to Man U first. When Manchester United came to Parken for our second match, the nerves were gone. It was a damp, cold day with the temperature hovering around freezing. The perfect conditions for Nordic football.

Playing host to a team like Man U was different than visiting them at Old Trafford. They are goliaths standing in your home. And Parken was the kind of stadium that can engulf its guests. And our 40,000 fans made their 72,000 seem tame.

In that wide blue sea of a crowd sat my family. Mom, Dad, and

Haldon were in the VIP seats reserved for family. Toyaa couldn't make the trip because she had school. (My mother was very strict about that, especially with her. At least one of her babies was going to be an academic.) Alex was there too—somewhere. There weren't enough family seats available, so he was relegated to the top of the stadium, tucked behind a pillar. I gave him the tickets, assuming they'd be good seats, but I didn't know where they were. "You couldn't have given me worse tickets," Alex told me after the game. "I was in the clouds!" I don't think he ever forgave me.

If there was one match that my family and friends couldn't afford to miss, it was this one. Playing at Old Trafford was a milestone, but facing Man U at home was a step beyond it. I still had a sense of awe as we lined up against Manchester, but the nerves were gone. We were home now, and that meant something to us. In Copenhagen, it was impossible for it not to.

Our team was special that season. When I look back on my career, it was a roster that I always consider to be one of the best teams I played for. That's coloured by big moments, of course, but also by the collective personality of that group. We were a team that fought for every game. We carried a lot of confidence and believed in each other. There was a winning culture in the group. We were all focused on the same goal: to win. Solbakken made sure that we were well prepared for every game with a tactical plan.

We did everything we could to be ready for that game, spending a full week training and perfecting specific tactics before United arrived in Copenhagen.

At the time, Man U dominated pretty much every team they played. We would have been embarrassed with our 3–0 loss in our first meeting if such a beating wasn't a regular occurrence for teams visiting Old Trafford. But we had more hope now. We allowed ourselves to believe.

If I'm being honest, I don't think we truly expected to win that game, but we were going to give it everything we had, because we had nothing to lose.

When a team allows itself to be unburdened from expectation and to play with a relentless pride—a pride that reverberates across the stadium, among the fans who share it—that's when something special happens.

The game was a battle with both sides playing tight defence and thwarting each other's attacks. United had much more possession of the ball than we did, but we didn't give up many chances and generated our own in transition. We played toe to toe with their superstars through the first half. The game was scoreless heading into the second half, and we knew anything could happen.

But United seemed to remember who they were in the second half and dominated through the first twenty-five minutes. We lost individual battles and broke down tactically—and against a team like Manchester United, giving up the slightest opportunity dismantles you. Off some quality transitional play, United generated several good chances to take the lead, but Christiansen turned them aside. Wayne Rooney nearly headed in a cross, and John O'Shea shot wide on a clear chance in front. Our best opportunity came off a cross that I managed to get my head on, but it was stopped by van der Sar. Solbakken moved me to the left midfield position in the second half, shifting his tactics to accommodate a more aggressive offence, effectively using me as a second striker. Despite the move, we just couldn't generate many quality chances. As the second half ticked on, we seemed unlikely to get our first Champions League goal.

Then it happened.

Off a set piece, I followed a Lars Jacobsen corner kick, as it looped towards the United goal and leaped just as it reached the packed crowd. Somehow I managed to get my head on it. The ball ricocheted off a United defender but rolled to Marcus Allbäck a few metres from the goal. Marcus swung at it, sending the ball on a crazy spin around the Man U keeper and into the back of the net.

I don't know if I'd ever jumped that high out of pure joy in my life.

Copenhagen: 1

Manchester United: 0

We mobbed each other in shock and joy. I jumped and jumped and jumped. I couldn't control it. It was the first Champions League goal for the franchise. Parken shook. Somewhere among the mob, my family was watching the impossible happen.

It was the seventy-third minute. There was still seventeen minutes plus injury time to play—an eternity. If we could somehow hold on, it would be the biggest win in team history. And so we clung to that lead with everything we had.

Even amid the adrenaline, it was impossible to forget who we were playing. I had to make sure that I left this game with something to remember it by. Because of Solbakken's move to put me into a striker role in the second half, I spent more time up against Man U's defenders. During a brief stoppage, with about ten minutes remaining, I asked United's legendary centre back Rio Ferdinand if we could exchange jerseys at the end of the match.

Christiansen made one more spectacular save, challenging Paul Scholes on a wide-open chance late in the match. That sealed it. When the whistle blew a few minutes later, history was complete.

Parken erupted. It felt like we'd won the Champions League final. It was a moment that would live on in team lore for decades to come. For our team, it was evidence of what we already knew about ourselves and what we were capable of. We were giant killers. For me, it was the fulfillment of a dream. Absolutely surreal. For my father, it was another kind of special. I could see the joy on his face. When I embraced my parents, I knew it was a moment that he would never forget.

I made sure of it by running over to Ferdinand and pulling off my jersey. He did the same and handed it to me. I'm not sure what he did with mine. I doubt he left Parken with it—and if he did, I'm sure it was quickly given away. There was no way he was going to keep it.

I gave away Ferdinand's jersey too. It was hung in my parents' basement where Dad and I used to watch United play.

14

Reality Check

For weeks after defeating Manchester United, it felt like there was a constant celebration in Copenhagen. We were already well-known around the city, but this was another level entirely. Even the Danish Superliga championship that we'd won the previous spring didn't carry the same kind of mania as our upset victory did.

It was a remarkable feeling—to be recognized and celebrated as heroes in our city.

The exuberance was somewhat muted later that November when we fell 3–1 to Benfica in Lisbon, effectively ending any hope we had of entering the knockout phase. Our final match at home against Celtic on December 6 was really just a formality. The Scots were already through, so the match carried little weight for them. But with our fate decided, we wanted to put on a show for our fans to cap off what had been a historic autumn for the club. With our draw against Benfica and our victory over United, we remained undefeated at Parken in Champions League play. We intended to keep that unblemished record at home. Parken was packed for that final Champions

League match, and the fans roared as loud as they had against United. The energy hadn't subsided. I could feel it as we lined up for the kick-off, and that energy carried me. Solbakken moved me up to forward alongside Allbäck, running with a four-four-two lineup—four defenders and midfielders behind a two-man forward line.

Less than two minutes into the match, I tossed a throw-up to Allbäck and broke towards the centre of the pitch above the box. The former Aston Villa striker returned the ball to me as I cut towards the edge of the box from the right side. The ball bobbled and bounced off a defender's stomach right into my path as I cut through the inside of the box, alone with the keeper, who rushed at me. In that moment, I knew it was my time. My momentum carried me to the right, and the keeper dove with me, forcing me into a tough angle. I struck the ball with my left, lifting it just over the keeper's legs, placing it in the right corner of the goal.

The stadium went wild. I turned and stretched my arms out wide, like the wings of a bird, charging towards my teammates at midfield.

"I just scored in the Champions League," I thought, as my teammates mobbed me. "What's going on?"

It was unbelievable. I went crazier than I ever had after scoring a goal in my life. It was a celebration that had lived in my mind for years—pretending to score in my backyard or knocking in a winner at Arnott Charlton. I'd heard the words cried out and the rush of the crowd in my mind so many times before: "Atiba Hutchinson scores!"

It took me a long time to settle down as the match carried on. I probably never really did. I was way too high to drift back down to the earth. Jesper Grønkjaær, a former winger for Chelsea, scored our second goal with a volley from eight feet out in the twenty-seventh minute. Early in the second half, Allbäck put Celtic away. We'd finish with a 3–1 win, keeping our no-loss Champions League record at Parken alive. We celebrated the win with our fans in the stadium, lingering long after the final whistle blew. It was a season that Copenhagen fans would never forget. And as long as I live, I'll never forget it either. It remains as dreamlike today as it did then.

◆

We went into the winter break that season leading the Superliga standings, suffering only one loss in league play through the fall. As reigning champs, we were the favourites to finish at the top of the league once again.

I flew home that Christmas feeling as proud and accomplished as ever. I couldn't walk down a street in Copenhagen without being recognized. I felt the heat of the spotlight. In the Danish press, I was heralded as one of Copenhagen FC's key players. The fans were incredible, but it still astonished me that anyone would want to have a photo taken with me.

I'd just finished the most successful year of my career. Since joining Copenhagen, I'd played a key role with the club and raised a championship trophy, played in the Champions League, beaten the club of my childhood dreams, and even scored a goal in one of the most prestigious tournaments on the planet. As the plane touched down in Toronto that December day, I was as famous as I could have possibly dreamed—in Denmark.

If I'd allowed the attention in Scandinavia to get to my head, Canada quickly put me back in my place. Going home was always a lesson in humility. There is nothing quite like leaving a city where you can't even pay for a meal and returning to where you grew up— and almost no one knows your name. Walking through the airport, no one looked my way. At customs, I had to explain what Copenhagen FC was. I could walk through a packed mall during the Christmas shopping rush and no one looked at me twice.

That winter was the first time I realized how starkly different the two worlds were. I wasn't upset about not being recognized. The anonymity was a nice change from Denmark, and I truly didn't expect anyone to know who I was. But the contrast was so obvious, it was impossible not to notice. Several of our Champions League matches had been broadcast on television in Canada, but it felt as if only my family and friends had watched.

I enjoyed another quiet Christmas with Mom, Dad, Haldon, and Toyaa. I spent time with the boys—now grown men embarking on careers—all of us still marvelling like little kids about what the past year had brought. It was a wonderful feeling. We hit the gym and looked ahead, as I wondered where else this unlikely career could take me. This time I avoided playing with the guys in the money tournaments though.

♦

Although the public at large didn't seem to be paying attention, the Canadian soccer community certainly was. There were passionate soccer fans, of course. The Voyageurs, a small but dedicated group of supporters, followed the men's national team fervently. But we were still an afterthought in the Concacaf and not a thought at all on the wider international stage. In Canada, it often felt as though we existed in a tiny bubble with that dedicated fanbase and journalists who followed the sport.

In January 2007, I was nominated as the men's player of the year by the Canadian Soccer Association for the first time. I was up for the honour alongside my national teammates Paul Stalteri, Tomasz Radzinski, Martin Nash, Adrian Serioux, and Dwayne De Rosario. Stalteri was playing for Tottenham, and Radzinski was playing for

Fulham in the Premier League at the time, but both were as anonymous in Canada as the rest of us. De Rosario, Nash, and Serioux were all playing professional soccer in North America. Nash played for the Vancouver Whitecaps, and Serioux was with Dallas FC, both in the USL. De Rosario was starring for Houston Dynamo in the MLS, the former San Jose Earthquake team, which had just won the league championship in its first season in its new Texan home. The MLS was still establishing itself as the top league in the United States at the time. In Canada, professional soccer was still struggling to take hold. Toronto FC would begin its inaugural season in the MLS that spring. I was excited by the potential of an MLS club in Toronto, though it didn't distract me from my goal of continuing to rise through the European ranks. I thought about the possibility of one day playing in the region where I grew up, but only in the distant future—perhaps as a way to close out my career, being able to play in front of my family and friends regularly. It was a hopeful time for professional soccer in Canada, but there remained a long way to go. The Whitecaps wouldn't join the league for another four years, in 2011. The Montreal Impact would join a season later in 2012.

The nomination for player of the year was a big deal for me. The award was voted on by fans and journalists, with the votes weighted fifty-fifty. It suggested that even though it felt like few people were taking notice of my career in Europe, the people who knew the game were. De Rosario won the honour in the end—his second in a row—a well-deserved tribute to my national team midfield counterpart, the most dynamic scorer Canada had ever produced who remains our country's leading scorer in men's football.

◆

When I returned to Copenhagen after the winter break, our club continued with our same momentum. The energy around the team had yet to dissipate. It was incredible.

We were a strong and deep club, especially at midfield. Solbakken had a wealth of talent to work with. Our captain, Tobias Linderoth, held the central midfield position and was a stalwart defender as well as being a set-piece specialist. When I was acquired by Copenhagen, Solbakken envisioned me playing alongside Linderoth in the middle, with an aim to further lock down that defensive side of our game. But the club had also acquired Danish star Jesper Grønkjær the previous summer, who complemented my offensive instincts. Solbakken had come to rethink how I was best used in his plan. He felt that I excelled in a freer role, without being restricted to central midfield. "He thrives without restrictions and is offensively minded," Solbakken told the Danish press that winter, comparing me to Arsenal's Tomáš Rosický. He wanted to use my speed to push forward on the attack. He saw me as a ball-playing, offensive midfielder who could find space on our attack, while turning quickly to challenge defensively in transition.

I thrived under Solbakken's vision, as my game continued to evolve. I scored seven goals that season, adding a potent attack led by Marcus Allbäck and Fredrik Berglund, who led the club with eighteen tallies each. Under Solbakken, I felt free to attack, almost as I had when I was a kid playing striker. And while I was used on the attack, I continued to think of my game in a complete way, as I'd grown up understanding it. The defensive side of my position was still very important to me. I believed that I actually played my best games when I touched the ball the least, which probably seems counterintuitive. I prided myself on being positionally aware.

This was an essential time in my development as a player. I was thrilled to be where I was, but when reporters asked me about my long-term goals, I was always honest. That winter, when I was asked that question, my answer was muted by the quality of play I'd witnessed around me during our matches in the Champions League.

"I'll never be good enough to play for Manchester United," I said. "So I take things as they come."

And as things were coming, they were going very well. Copenhagen—the club and the city—was everything I could have hoped for. We surged through the winter months into spring atop the table, well on our way to securing a second straight Danish Superliga championship.

But even though everything seemed to be going well, I knew that I had a lot of room for improvement. So I focused on how I could reach the level of play that I hoped to achieve; I didn't want to grow overly satisfied with the considerable improvement I'd made. I was still adapting to the speed of the European game at its top tier. I was celebrated for my quickness on and off the ball, but I was very self-critical about how quickly I reacted when the ball hit my feet. It wasn't an issue of speed so much as it was an issue of reaction. I needed to learn to think faster when I had the ball—to make quicker decisions and release the ball sooner, which is what I mean about spending less time with the ball. The ball moves much faster than I can run, so our attack was much more efficient when I was quick to get rid of it and help move the offence forward.

In May, we secured the league championship with a 1–0 victory over Brøndby, in our rivals' stadium across town. Once again, we were kings in Copenhagen. Within a year, I'd been part of two championships, a joy that would never grow old. We celebrated as hard as you might think, standing on top of our world. But just over a week later, we lost to Odense Boldklub in the Danish Cup final (the country's annual knockout cup, much like England's FA Cup) and failed to secure the coveted double.

It was the beginning of my time with Copenhagen FC and I was excited for what the coming years would bring. There were whispers that other clubs were interested in acquiring me, but for the first time, I had no desire to move on. I was still growing as a player. And in that season of my life, I felt that Copenhagen was exactly where I needed to be.

I was learning that with every height comes a levelling-off. It had been the most exciting and fulfilling year of my career. With the accolades I was starting to receive—the respect of fans, a semblance of fame, honours for my play—came the humbling truths. Though I was well-known in Denmark, most people at home knew nothing of me. And though I was playing the best football of my life, I was acutely aware that I was still nowhere near as good as I hoped to be. Part of me wondered if I'd reached the ceiling of my career—but I remained determined to push further and reach greater heights.

15

Own Goals

First goals live with you. They never fade. You can remember the feeling of that moment, seeing the mesh beyond the posts wave with impact and hearing the volume in the stadium rise or fall depending on whether they view you as a hero or the opposition.

My first Gold Cup goal as a member of the Canadian men's national team was another story entirely.

The tournament for the most coveted prize in Concacaf takes place every two years, featuring teams from across North America, Central America, and the Caribbean. Alongside the 1986 World Cup qualification, Canada's first and only Gold Cup victory in 2000 was one of the biggest moments in the history of our men's national team. I played in my first competition as a twenty-year-old substitute player in the 2003 Gold Cup in Mexico, playing sparse second-half minutes. We finished last in our group with Costa Rica and Cuba.

By 2005, I had a much more established role with the team, starting at midfield. I was twenty-two years old with eleven international caps to my name. My good friend Iain Hume also played an important role with the program. He'd turn twenty-two later that year, and had already had ten caps. We were a relatively young team, led by twenty-five-year-old Kevin McKenna and twenty-seven-year-old Dwayne De Rosario up front—and Jim Brennan, who was one of our oldest players at twenty-eight. De Rosario and McKenna both had more than two dozen caps to their name. Brennan held the most with thirty-eight.

Despite being ranked eighty-fifth in the world at the time, we were a collection of quality players who should have been able to compete. But we played sloppy and undisciplined football. We were also the victims of terrible officiating, which had come to feel standard whenever Canada was on the pitch. In our first match against Costa Rica, I was one of five Canadian players to receive a yellow card. Kevin McKenna, one of our top defenders, was suspended for a match after being ejected for collecting two yellows. The Costa Ricans, who were given a single yellow, beat us 1–0. That meant that the next game against the United States was a must-win for us.

We met our rivals at Qwest Field in Seattle that July, hoping to upset the Americans. We did alright through the first half, opening the second with the game still scoreless.

A couple minutes into the second, I managed to get my head on a ball, sending it just beyond the scrambling keeper's reach and bouncing across the line and rolling into the back corner of the net.

1–0.

The fans at Qwest Field erupted, a sound I'll never forget. But if you happened to be a Canadian fan watching at home, you probably remained seated.

"Another disastrous goal for Canada," the play-by-play man declared. "We see this time and time again. And it's happened here."

The official scoresheet recorded the moment for posterity—the game's first, scored for the United States.

Atiba Hutchinson (48' OG).

OG as in own goal. As in, while trying to clear a cross into the box from U.S. midfielder John O'Brien, I headed the ball past the outstretched hands of Canadian keeper Greg Sutton into our own net.

I was mortified. We ended up losing the match 2–0, after Landon Donovan scored on a header in the ninetieth minute to put us away for good. The Americans outclassed us in the match, having complete control offensively and outshooting us 13–5. The loss extended a winless streak against the U.S. to eleven games, with six loses and five draws. On top of that, we'd been completely shut out in five straight meetings.

"I thought maybe if I get my head on it, it goes for a corner," I told reporters, who wondered what I was thinking when I'd decided to put the ball in our own damn goal.

As the U.S. celebrated their victory, O'Brien made light of the play that handed the Americans the lead.

"It worked out great," he said. "It was fun to see it in the back of the net."

My teammates did their best to console me after the goal, but they knew there was nothing anyone could really say. That kind of game-altering mistake hangs over any player. I knew enough not to let the goal affect my confidence. Mistakes happen. But I was dejected after the match. I felt that I'd let my team and country down.

One of the things I love about sports is the constant parallel to life. Own goals happen all the time in life—so much that the phrase is euphemism for screwing up in some unnecessary way, whether on the job, in a relationship, or anything else, really. The key is always to pick yourself up and keep playing the game. Leave your own goals behind you.

A few days later, we played Cuba in our final group stage match. With two losses, we needed to win by at least three goals to have any chance of moving on to the quarterfinals. In the national team's previous eighty matches, we'd only scored three or more goals four times—twice against Belize, and once against Switzerland and Libya. Once again, we were technically the underdogs—Cuba was ranked seventieth in the world—but we were the dominant team that day. We had multiple chances to score in the first half, but we couldn't convert, missing the goal on several attempts. Once again, the officiating was brutal. I picked up another yellow card at the end of the first half.

Finally, our striker Ali Gerba found the net in the sixty-ninth minute, converting a sharp pass across the area. Knowing that we needed to win by such a wide margin, we piled on the attack as the second half ticked on. We generated multiple chances, pushing frantically for another goal. Frank Yallop, our coach, was tossed out of the game with less than ten minutes remaining for criticizing one of the officials.

I found my redemption with three minutes left in regulation. With a brief opening, I stepped into a wicked shot from well beyond the box that found its way past the Cuban keeper. My teammates embraced me as I yelled out in excitement and relief for my first Gold Cup goal that wasn't on my own team. There was little time to celebrate though. We pressed through the final three minutes trying to generate another goal that would put us in a position to qualify. Instead, Cuba broke the shutout in the ninetieth minute, deflating any hope we had.

We'd failed to get out of the first round for the second Gold Cup in a row.

It was a demoralizing result.

Since I'd debuted with the national team at twenty years old, Canada had been an afterthought on the international stage. No one feared us. That bothered me. It bothered all of us. We knew that we were better than our opponents gave us credit for, but sometimes it felt like a forgone conclusion that we'd never be given the respect we were fighting for. The assumption that Canada wasn't a soccer nation felt impossible to escape.

The frustration certainly mounted in those early years with the national team. It seemed like we couldn't achieve what we collectively believed we could. We had talent and chemistry. But we couldn't find the results we hoped for.

In 2007, it finally felt like everything was about to change.

Coming off the wildest year of my career—a long-term, well-paying pro contract, two league championships, the Champions League—I joined the Canadian national team for another run at the Gold Cup. I was by then an established player with the national team. In four years with the senior team, I'd collected twenty-seven caps and scored three goals, doing my best to answer the call to return home during the international windows in our seasons in Sweden and Denmark. In Europe, the necessity of my commitment to the national team was often questioned—something that would occur frequently throughout my career. Across the pond, Canadian soccer was still sniffed at. I was considered an anomaly from the land of hockey players. No one would ever question an Italian's or Spaniard's commitment to play for their national team. But a Canadian? What was the point of taking an eight-hour flight to play for a country where so few people cared that you were there at all? I always shook my head at that argument. I was proud to be Canadian and honoured to represent the country, whether people were paying attention or not. I was proud of my teammates and the quality of what I knew soccer could become in my homeland.

There was a lot to be excited about. By 2007, our team was heralded as one of the most promising rosters we'd fielded in years. Over the past four years, despite disappointing results, we'd grown as a consistent core of players who were developing together as well as in our professional careers. Something special was stirring in Canadian soccer, though the results didn't necessarily show it and it often felt like few people beyond our group were paying attention. We were led by guys like Paul Stalteri, Ali Gerba, Dwayne De Rosario, and Julian de Guzman, among a group of accomplished players mostly in our early to mid-twenties. Our veteran keeper Pat Onstad was our oldest player at thirty-nine. Greg Sutton, our other keeper, was the second oldest at thirty. The future looked promising.

Stephen Hart had taken over as interim head coach of the national team, after Yallop resigned in 2006. Hart was a Trinidadian who immigrated to Canada to study at Saint Mary's University in Halifax and ended up making the country his permanent home. He brought his passion for soccer with him from the island, much like my father had. Even though Hart was just an interim coach at the time, he made a big impact. He was very relaxed and encouraged us to express ourselves as players. He wanted us to go out, enjoy the game, and play some good football. That might sound basic, but it was a refreshing message as a player. We had a good team, and Hart wanted us to be confident in that. He was focused on making sure we played a good brand of football—with smart passing, speed, and possession. We shifted our focus to playing an attacking style of football.

Under Hart, we felt free on the pitch. We had fun and enjoyed playing together. We were a very diverse team, with players coming from all different backgrounds. That brought a unique sense of personality and character, which was a strength of our national program. We embraced that side of ourselves as a group in 2007.

Our experiences as professional players also played into that. Julian de Guzman was playing in Spain, after starting his career in Germany. Stalteri was still with Tottenham Hotspur in the Premier League. Iain Hume was now with Leicester City in the English Football League, the second tier of English football. De Rosario was one of the top players in MLS with the Houston Dynamo. Several of the players had experience playing in the Netherlands, Belgium, Scotland, and the Czech Republic. Sutton, Chris Pozniak, Adam Braz, and Marco Reda were all members of the inaugural Toronto FC roster. That collective education brought a lot of unique perspectives and abilities to our team. Playing a much freer style of football allowed us to embrace that mix and create something special.

◆

This was a pivotal time in Canadian soccer. Things were starting to change as we embraced our identity as a team. Part of that identity was being fed up with the lack of respect from our opponents and the international soccer community. We had a shared sense of what our goals were as a team. We wanted to win and prove what Canada was capable of.

At twenty-four, I was still a young player. But after three years playing professionally overseas, I was much more confident. I'd won championships and played alongside and against some of the best in the world. I knew that I was one of the better players on our team, which I felt came with a lot of responsibility. I don't know how other Canadian players around me looked at it, but I really felt like I was emerging as one of the guys on the roster that others could look up to, especially with my previous role as captain of the U-20 team. I wasn't a very vocal leader, but I tried to set an example in how I trained and played. I worked very hard in practice. That work ethic has always been important to me. I wanted to set a high standard for myself and my teammates.

But if I considered myself to be a leader at that time, I still had a lot to learn about the role. I wasn't always as tactful as I should have been. Sometimes, in the heat of the moment, you'd hear me yell on the pitch out of frustration—often at myself, but also at my teammates.

As the years went on and I matured as a player, I became a much more vocal leader. And, I think, a better one. As a veteran, I'd always try to be encouraging, knowing that younger players looked up to me.

Of course, I'd still show frustration on the pitch or in training, but I was much more careful about how I expressed it. If I did anything to the detriment of my teammates, I wasn't really leading at all.

◆

The 2007 Gold Cup is probably the most memorable moment of frustration in my career—and it was directed at objectively terrible refereeing that screwed us out of a chance to win the trophy.

We opened group play with a thrilling 2–1 win over Costa Rica in Miami, led by two goals from my midfield partner Julian de Guzman, who was later named player of the tournament.

Guadeloupe stunned us in the second game, as we fell 2–1 to the tiny island nation. But we rebounded in our third match against Haiti with a 2–0 win on two De Rosario goals.

Up to that point, the tournament had been one of my best wearing No. 13 for Canada. I played in the middle alongside de Guzman, whom I had great chemistry with. Stalteri, our captain, felt that with us side by side, we were as dominant a midfield as he'd ever seen Canada have. I was getting into my prime, and in those few games, I helped control the pace, played a strong box-to-box game, and really showed my teammates what I was all about as a player. If there was a tournament in which I really asserted myself in that on-the-pitch leadership role, this was it.

We rolled over Guatemala 3–0 in the quarterfinals, with two goals from Gerba, pushing us to the semis, deeper into the Gold Cup than any Canadian team had been since unexpectedly hoisting the trophy in 2000.

That set up a semifinal meeting with the United States at Soldier Field in Chicago. Once again, we were considered the underdogs. On the women's side, the rivalry between Canada and the United

States was as good as it gets, but we hadn't been able to challenge the States the same way. A Canadian men's team hadn't beaten the U.S. since 1985.

We appeared to be on course for another defeat as the Americans dominated play through the first half, rifling several chances at our keeper Pat Onstad. We defended with numbers, swarming the U.S. attack, which helped slow down their assault, but we hardly managed to get the ball out of our end. We were fortunate to head into the break down only 2–0.

In the second half, we were sparked by the energy of Iain Hume, whom Hart sent on for David Nash. In the seventy-sixth minute, as time ticked away on our hope to reach the final, I rushed with the ball from half and passed to Iain with the outside of my foot as he cut to the right side. He let the ball lead him, as defender Carlos Bocanegra rushed, and then swiftly cut in towards the area as the defender stumbled to catch him. He had a fraction of a second to launch a left-footed shot from the top of the box past the reach of keeper Kasey Keller. The ball kissed the left post and into the net. Gerba rushed into the net to collect the ball as I embraced Iain before we sprinted back to half. We trailed by a single goal with fourteen minutes left in regulation. There was hope.

A couple minutes later, Iain kept us alive again, this time on the other side of the field. Off a U.S. corner kick, Landon Donovan managed to get a header right on target. But Iain, standing on the goal line, twisted his right leg up to knock the ball away. The goal would have done us in. Instead we were still alive.

We kept pressing with ten minutes to play, but the Americans defended well against our relentless attack, thwarting all attempts to equalize. In the eighty-eighth minute, Michael Bradley took down de Guzman from behind and was given an immediate red card; we had a man advantage through the final two minutes and stoppage time.

Still, we couldn't generate the chance we needed—until the final moments of the added time. Making a last-ditch effort on the attack, I rushed towards the U.S. goal as Patrice Bernier lobbed a pass towards the box from half. American defender Oguchi Onyewu played the ball with his head, but he failed to clear it. It landed right in front of me just inside the box. I took a few strides and chipped the ball over Keller as he dove towards me. The ball bounced into the bottom right corner of the net.

For a brief moment, I felt the rush of scoring the biggest goal of my life. I was so happy that I had scored a goal. I was young and hadn't scored many goals. Now I'd played the hero and tied the match for Canada.

But almost immediately, it was taken away. Amid my celebration, I turned back to see referee Benito Archundia raising his hand to call the play offside.

I rushed to him. My eyes were popping out of my head. I demanded an explanation. "How!"

Archundia tried to turn away from me, but I put my hands on his chest trying to plead my case. There was a fire inside of me.

The moment the ball touched Onyewu, the play could not have been offside. It was impossible. It was clear to everyone at Soldier Field that the ball had hit a U.S. defender and bounced to my feet, except for the linesman whose job it was to watch the play. There was no reasonable way to misinterpret what had occurred. I couldn't believe it. We had tied the match—the Gold Cup semifinal against a team we hadn't beaten in two decades—and a referee was taking it away from us. It was robbery.

"How!" I demanded.

But Archundia refused to listen. He blew the final whistle almost right after the goal was taken away. Stalteri rushed to him, arms stretched wide, begging him to explain. Archundia just turned and tried to walk away. Stalteri, Onstad, and several other players swarmed around the officiating crew as they tried to leave the pitch, trying to get an answer. Stephen Hart rushed over to pull our players away. Stalteri, our captain, was beside himself.

I simply couldn't believe what had just happened. We walked off the field knowing that something had been stolen from us and that there was nothing we could do about it. Canadian fans watching at home heard broadcaster Gerry Dobson lament the disastrous outcome. "Unbelievable the way it happens time in, time out for the Canadian team," he said. "It's happened again. . . . It's unbelievable the way it happens and it seems to happen time and time again."

I definitely wanted to do more. I think each and every one of us wanted to, because we felt like we had been cheated. I had to hold everything in, because I wanted to go after the guy. The officials knew that they'd made a mistake. There is no way around it. It was objectively the wrong call.

It was infuriating that it had happened in that game, against the United States, against whom we always had a tough match and always ended up on the losing side.

We had played so well in that tournament, and we felt like there was nothing that could stop us. The Americans were winning the game, but they were on the ropes. We were almost there. We had the momentum. And then in the moment we feel like we've finally broken through— the referee calls back the goal. All of a sudden, it was over.

Everybody saw what happened in that moment. We saw it, the Americans saw it, the fans saw it, the officials saw it. There was no question that it was a goal. We'd been screwed, and there was nothing we could do about it.

In other words, we'd been Concacaf-ed—screwed out of a result by officiating. It was a feeling we'd experienced before and would experience again.

16

How Winners Lose

There is no feeling like hoisting a trophy at the end of a marathon campaign. It's the payoff at the end of the long journey. It's what we play for—to fulfill the dream of winning a trophy, of being on the other side of the hard work, the relentless battles, and seeing the passion and obsession that it takes to get that point pay off.

But improvement, growth, character—all those things that are so essential to winning—come with losing.

That's a lesson learned over time, not one that you can comprehend right away. For me, one of the most important seasons of growth in my career came *after* winning two back-to-back league championships with Copenhagen—in a season in which we won nothing at all.

Returning to Denmark after the disappointment of the Gold Cup loss to the United States in the summer of 2007, I was hoping to continue what I'd started in my first two seasons with Copenhagen.

I'd flourished under Solbakken's guidance. He'd brought me in with a vision to play me as a defensive midfielder, but that strategy soon switched. I played a box-to-box style of midfield, used at both ends of the pitch. But often Solbakken moved me into more of an attacking role. He praised that versatility in my game. As I've said, Solbakken viewed me as a player who could defend and attack, which meant I was useful to his tactics regardless of the circumstances. If we were outgunned against Manchester United, I could lock down defensively. In the Danish Superliga, where we often dominated, I could be used effectively in our attack. Solbakken felt that he could trust me tactically in either situation—and it helped that my speed made me effective at both ends. He liked that I was open-minded and eager to learn. I was also calm under pressure, but I had an edge when we needed it. Solbakken also felt that I was a brave player—that I had a healthy respect for our opposition, but I wasn't afraid. It was a good mix, he said.

"The attacking ace who has seen the most significant development under his Norwegian coach is Atiba Hutchinson," the Danish newspaper *Ekstra Bladet* declared in its preview for our upcoming season.

"Yes, it's quite a change," I told the paper, noting that only a few years earlier I was playing central defence with the national team. "I didn't expect to be a striker when I came to Copenhagen, but it's been perfectly fine. Usually, players move further back on the field as they age, right?" I joked.

Looking back, I think that part of Solbakken's strategy in using me as more of an offensive player was that he felt I was still too inexperienced for a defensive midfield position. It's a role that requires a veteran presence, essentially acting as the cornerstone of the team. It carries lots of responsibility. You're in a position where you can't lose many balls. You've got to keep your team in possession of the ball by making the right passes. You're the main point of transition from the defence to pushing forward—a link from the defenders to the attack. There is very little room for error. If you lose the ball there, right in the middle of the pitch, it can be very costly. There were many times in my career when I lost balls in a bad part of the pitch, and it led directly to a goal against us. But if you play the position right, you can really dictate the way the game is played.

The more you play that position, the more you learn. It's something that requires experience and a high football IQ. In my first couple years in Copenhagen, I was fortunate to play alongside and learn from Tobias Linderoth, the Swedish veteran, who was our rock in the middle. He was a player who kept it very simple. He was calm and precise. Linderoth didn't waste much time dribbling. He'd see his pass and know what was happening around him. He played it quick and got into position to receive it again—and do the same thing again, keeping the ball moving from side to side.

I knew that I wasn't there yet, but I was developing at a rapid pace.

Along with the guidance of Solbakken and the example of Linderoth, there were so many experienced guys to learn from on that Copenhagen roster. Several of our veterans had played for some of the top clubs in Europe. Linderoth and Marcus Allbäck had both played in the Premier League and for the Swedish national team in the World Cup and done very well. They were strong leaders who brought that pedigree with them. They shared a winner's mentality—they wanted to win at all costs. I was fortunate to have mentors like them. It was like having coaches on the pitch with me, leading by example.

Linderoth was our captain. He had so much hunger in him. He wanted to win every ball and hated losing. And he was very vocal about it, which worked because all of our guys bought into the same mentality. That was something I didn't have on other teams. There was this collective refusal to accept anything less than a win. Everybody would push each other to be better and not accept losing. It was a mentality that I wasn't used to, but I loved it. I experienced the outcome of it as we hoisted back-to-back trophies. This was what it took to be a champion. Talent alone would never be enough.

I had always been competitive, but in Canada there wasn't the same winner's mentality. The culture wasn't the same. At that time, I was in a honeymoon phase of my career. I just loved playing football. I looked forward to every game. I wanted to win, but the competitiveness my teammates carried was on another level entirely. With everything they did, they always wanted to be better. They never settled. If things didn't go well in a training session, we'd be on each other, pushing to be better the next time. It was about always demanding more from yourself.

It wasn't about pouting or trying to drag your teammates down. That's a key distinction. There were going to be losses. We knew that. But the point was moving forward, doing what you can to be better and more prepared.

We put a lot of time into getting all the details right. Everybody bought into Solbakken's tactical game plan. With every loss, we prepared to be better the next time around—always looking to improve.

There were many things that I took with me from my time in Copenhagen, but the one thing that really altered me as a player and leader was that: the visceral desire to win everything that I took part in.

Everyone in the locker room spoke English, except maybe one or two players, so it was easy to connect and really feel part of the group. I was always good at handling the different personalities in the dressing room. I felt comfortable socializing with everyone on the roster, which isn't always the case when it comes to professional football, where there are usually some big personalities in the room. From the moment I joined Copenhagen, I'd felt accepted. There was a real camaraderie in our group. The experience taught me something important about the makeup of a team that wins championships. We couldn't win as a bunch of individuals, and if we didn't connect off the pitch, it would be hard to connect on it. Copenhagen taught me the importance of that unforced cohesion among teammates.

Of course, it's easy to connect with your teammates when you're winning games and raising trophies. The real challenge comes when things aren't going well.

After those first two seasons in Denmark, we carried a hangover into the 2007–08 season. That June, Linderoth left Copenhagen for Galatasaray in the Turkish Süper Lig. Our offence wilted, and we seemed to regress in every area of our game. It happens with a quality club sometimes. From the start of the season that July, we struggled to catch our rhythm. We were used to being a team that could go runs, winning six or seven games straight and creating comfortable gaps between us and the teams behind us. But we never really hit our form that season. Nothing clicked.

It was disappointing because at the time we were the biggest team in Denmark, with the biggest fanbase, and we expected to win every year. Anything less wasn't acceptable to us. It wasn't meant to be that year. We finished third in Superliga, and we had a dreadful showing in the UEFA Cup, finishing fourth in our group and failing to advance to the knockout stage. Our fans were rightfully critical of our play.

We were critical too. When we would lose a game, it was complete silence in the change room. No talking at all. Everybody had their heads down, pissed. We wanted to get back out there and be ready for the next round. In the past, we'd found a way—but that season, we couldn't.

Our disappointment when the season wrapped up in spring 2008 was as palpable and formative as our joy when we won the title a year earlier. In Copenhagen, we knew that a losing season had to be answered for. There would be heavy expectations when we returned to Parken that summer, and we were determined to meet them. It was the winning mindset of a team that understood what it took to win a championship. Our struggles that season had made that strength of that mentality clear to me. I'd experienced what losing felt like for a winning team. I knew that we would put in the work to make sure we didn't feel it again.

That summer, as I returned home to try to help Canada qualify for the World Cup for the first time in more than two decades, I knew that I needed to bring that winning mindset with me.

17

Away at Home

When I was a young player, my goal was to make it to the World Cup—but in a far-off-in-the-distance kind of way. It was one of my bucket list goals, and I still had the comfort of time.

My early ideas about playing for Trinidad and Tobago had long faded through my years with Canada's youth national team. My experience at the U-20 World Cup in Dubai ensured that I would never walk away from the red and white. I loved playing for my country, and I hated to lose. Both of those truths fuelled my passion for the national team. But in my early twenties, I was still learning about the fleeting nature of time. I was still rising, and I had no sense of an end on my horizon.

I didn't really consider the fact that I was only three years old the last time Canada qualified for the World Cup—or that that appearance was the only time Canada had ever made it. When something never happens, it's easy to ignore its absence. As my time with the national team went on, I started to understand how rare these opportunities were—and what it meant to miss out.

Making it to the World Cup is a complicated multi-stage process with teams competing in regional qualification tournaments to earn a spot in the final tournament. That process begins a full two years before the World Cup takes place. In Concacaf, we played in a qualification tournament with a preliminary round and group stages, which culminated in the final round. The Hexagonal—as the final round is known—includes the top six teams from each of the Concacaf group stages competing for one of three World Cup berths for the region.

In 2004—vying for a position in the 2006 World Cup in Germany—we made it through the group stage easily, beating Belize in a two-game home-and-away series. At the time, Canada was ranked tenth in Concacaf and ninety-fifth in the world. We were one of twenty-four teams to move into the group stage, in which we played Costa Rica, Guatemala, and Honduras. We finished last in the group, snuffing out any hope of heading to Germany.

It was a brutal result: we earned only five points in our six matches and suffered a minus-four goal differential. It was another frustration on a long list.

As disappointing as failing to qualify for the World Cup was, the naivety of youth allowed me to look ahead to the possibility of the 2010 World Cup in South Africa. But I noticed something then among my veteran teammates—a feeling that I would come to recognize too well as I drifted closer to the end of my career. They were frustrated knowing that their time was slipping away.

When we didn't qualify for the World Cup, I could see what that disappointment meant on a veteran player's face. It's heartbreaking for them. I saw guys who had taken their last kick at a lifelong dream, realizing it wouldn't happen. When I was first part of a Canadian team that failed to qualify, it was apparent how much it hurt. It resonated with me.

"That could be me at some point," I thought.

♦

Despite being robbed in the 2007 Gold Cup, our national team felt good about our chance to reach the World Cup in South Africa in 2010. We had a lot to be optimistic about. Over the previous eighteen months, we'd become a cohesive group with a bit of flair.

Though we didn't have a lot of depth, we had all kinds of options on the attack, between Gerba, Hume, Radzinski, and Rob Friend up front. I'd line up alongside De Rosario and de Guzman; we were widely viewed as the strongest midfield presences the men's team had ever had.

We were lucky to still have strong veterans in guys like Stalteri and De Rosario—guys I'd known forever and will always look up to. There was a lot of banter and fun, because we knew each other so well. It was a great environment. Stalteri and De Rosario were like proper big brothers to me. They took me under their wings and guided me when I was a young player. I'd played alongside them ever since I'd come up with the national team, and they looked out for me, giving me guidance and advice.

And de Guzman—Jules—is only two years older than me, but I always looked up to him like he was one of the older guys. Jules was there when I first started playing with the under-20s at age eighteen. He went to Europe when he was really young, so he'd tell me stories about playing overseas and what it takes to stay there. "It's hard out there," he'd warn me. "You have to have thick skin." Jules was a big part of why I wanted to be there. He gave me honest advice. He reminded me that, above all, I had to believe in myself. Not only say that I did, but really know that I belonged. Nothing was going to be given to me, he said.

For years and years and years, Jules and I played together. Sometimes DeRo would join us as an attacking midfielder, or to the left or right. Both Jules and DeRo were hungry. You could see that they were playing for their lives. They didn't want anyone to take their positions. Every time they went onto the pitch, you could see that hunger. They kept high standards, training as if every session was their last. They had the fight in them.

Jules would win balls, tackle everywhere, and was very good on the ball. There was a lot of flair and style in his game. It was amazing to see the work ethic he had even as a twenty-year-old. He was like a natural captain—very vocal, always communicating. He was like a little pit bull.

And Dwayne had so much style in his game. You could see how much he enjoyed playing and expressing himself. He taught me to remember why I played. You want to play well, you want to fight, you want to win—but enjoy yourself. It's a game. Do your thing and show everybody what you're made of.

I loved those guys like family.

But even though it was a great group and a good environment, I think we'd all admit that, at the time, we didn't hold high expectations for the men's national team. It was fun to get together for training sessions and games, but there wasn't much of that win-at-all-costs passion beyond it. We had a strong bond and a great time, on and off the pitch. Training sessions were filled with laughter and banter. If you did something funny or stupid on the pitch, like tripping over a ball, you were going to hear about it. It often felt like a vacation more than an intense training camp, which meant that we lacked structure and professionalism. We were too comfortable with losing. The confidence wasn't there, and to be honest, neither was the commitment. We didn't feel like a team that could go up against any team and win games. We'd go out there, play the game, and hope for the best.

At the same time, it infuriated us that we didn't get any respect on the international stage. We talked about it all the time. We knew the

shit we would take when we went back to our clubs after an embarrassing outing with Canada. There were times when we couldn't even beat
El Salvador back in the day. Our European teammates had never even
heard of some of the countries we'd lose to. They couldn't understand
why we'd waste our time playing for a country that wasn't any good.
We'd hear it constantly: "Man, Canada's so shit."

I hated being told that my country was terrible soccer and that I
shouldn't care about representing it. That only deepened my determination to prove them wrong and fuelled my frustration when we didn't.

On top of that there was a constant lack of respect within Concacaf
itself. Being cheated out of the Gold Cup final was one thing, but I
saw a constant imbalance in the way our matches were officiated. We
dealt with that for years. Especially in an environment like Central
America. It felt like we were not only playing against the other team
but also their wild fans and the referees—who would absolutely
obliterate us. They gave us no respect. I felt as if Concacaf didn't
want Canada to excel or reach the last round of the Hex. It was hard
to make things happen. It seemed like every call went against us. It
was frustrating and common. When you're a bigger club, you get
more calls. I saw it in Europe too. Clubs that were considered smaller
rarely seemed to get those advantageous calls that can dictate the way
a game goes. Because of that, the smaller teams struggle for that
rhythm to get into the flow of things. I felt that a lot playing with
Canada. I'd want to explode on the pitch with frustration. I'd finish a
game feeling as if we'd been cheated, but I'd try to leave it behind.
Then in the next match, I'd be trying to control the pace—but the
refs would just screw us. It was hard not to lose my head. It can
become a problem, because players lose focus. The referees become
the main focus, instead of trying to get a result in the game.

If it had been a one-time thing, it would have stung, but it wouldn't
have been so infuriating. But it was the same thing over and over and

over. I had to learn to keep as calm as possible, because if you go to the referee and do something you're not supposed to do, it can result in a ten to fifteen game suspension.

We also often felt deflated anytime we played a home match. It was one thing to not be given any respect from our opponents, but it was another thing to receive little support at home. We hosted World Cup qualifying games where there was practically nobody in the stands—or they'd be packed with fans for the other team. Whenever we played a team like Honduras, it felt like we were playing in their home stadium—even though the game was happening in Toronto or Montreal. Three-quarters of the fans were cheering for the other team. A lot of those fans travelled from abroad to be at the game, but a lot of them were homegrown. They were supporting their country of origin or their parents'. In a way, it was a sign of Canada's strength—a hugely diverse population, with people passionate about supporting the places they were proud to come from. I grew up the same way, feeling that proud connection with Trinidad through my parents. That diversity was part of our strength as a team.

But when you're playing at home and all you can see is a sea of blue jerseys and Honduran flags and wild cheers for your opponent—it's demoralizing.

It often felt like we were playing for our country, but our country wasn't behind us. It was always hard. That pressure to perform for a packed stadium of fans cheering for us was never there. Aside from a small group of dedicated supporters and our families, it seemed like no one noticed. There was no expectation, no pressure. It was hard to feel the weight of representing your country in a match when your country didn't even know you were playing. Regardless of what we did, nobody really cared.

All of those factors combined to create an environment that didn't have an urgency to win. In Copenhagen, I had learned about that urgency—and what a team culture built on it could achieve. I understood what we were lacking.

At the 2007 Gold Cup, we had found that passion. We played with the kind of expectation that is needed to win big games. We showed that we deserved the respect that we craved. It was a flicker of what we could be. And the anger over how it ended stayed with us. We carried that feeling into the qualification tournament for the 2010 World Cup.

Dale Mitchell—a familiar face who had coached us during our surprising run at the 2003 FIFA Youth Championship—had taken over as head coach following Stephen Hart's interim tenure. It was a tough position for Dale to be in, because we'd had such success under Hart in 2007.

That August, we entered the third round of the World Cup qualifier alongside Honduras, Jamaica, and Mexico. We would play each team in the group twice, home and away, with the top two teams advancing to the Hexagonal.

More than 22,000 people packed into the brand-new BMO Field for our first match against Jamaica. It was a great turnout for our opponents. When we looked around the stadium, it was a sea of yellow. The majority of the fans had come out to cheer for Jamaica in what felt like an away game for us in the shadow of the Toronto skyline. We drew the Jamaicans 1–1, fortunate to sneak away with a point in our invaded house. Two weeks later in Montreal, there were thirteen thousand fans in the stands for our match at Saputo Stadium against Honduras, who seemed to have the home-crowd advantage. Despite the deflating presence of so many Honduran fans, we managed to strike first, with Adrian Serioux scoring in the fourth minute. We had all the momentum, until Tomasz Radzinski was bodychecked off the field into advertising boards by a Honduran defender. There was no foul called on the play. Radzinski cut his finger in the collision. He was treated on the sidelines while play continued. We ended up playing down a man for seven minutes, until Iain Hume was brought in as a replacement. A few of us didn't even realize Radzinski wasn't on the pitch. We never got back into the game. This time we fell 2–1.

It felt like the momentum we had carried out of the 2007 Gold Cup had deflated. A few days later in Chiapas—in front of 27,000 boisterous fans—we lost 2–1 to Mexico. We followed that match with a trip to Honduras in mid-October, where we were met by an army of 36,000 fans ready to tell us exactly what they thought of Canadian soccer. We'd hear chants like "This isn't hockey" over and over again, amid much more aggressive jeers and the constant beat of drums. It was a wild environment, exactly as football should have. The Hondurans beat us 3–1. Without a win in four matches, we were effectively eliminated from World Cup contention. We finished with a 2–2 draw to Mexico in Edmonton—our best showing of the group stage—and then travelled to Kingston for a 3–0 loss to Jamaica.

And just like that, another World Cup slipped out of reach.

18

For the Stars

One day when I explain to my kids how I met their mother, I'll have to give them a history lesson on the ancient days of Myspace.

Like most people in 2008—and really ever since—much of my social life was maintained online. MSN Messenger had been my go-to for staying connected with all of the friends I missed back home. The rise of social networking made life much easier for a young person like me living abroad; luckily the long-distance calling card days were over for the most part. But it was Myspace that changed my life. If you aren't familiar, Myspace was one of the early social networking sites in the 2000s; people could share photos and videos and connect over shared interests. Once upon a time, it was a big deal.

By 2008, I was enjoying life in Copenhagen as a single pro athlete in his mid-twenties in a beautiful city. I had good buddies for team-mates; we would spend our time hanging out at each other's flats, visiting unique places in Scandinavia, or hitting up nice restaurants. (I was much more of a foodie than when I'd first arrived in Europe and barely knew how to turn on a stove.) I was making decent money for someone my age—not life-changing money, but enough that I was able to buy my mother a Lexus as a gift and help fund some long-needed repairs around the house for my dad, after receiving my signing bonus with Copenhagen. I wasn't driving a fancy sports car or spending wild amounts of money on lavish vacations, but I was certainly much better off than I'd been back when I was playing with the York Region Shooters.

My parents taught me the value of a dollar growing up. "It's not how much you make, but how much you save," they told me. That resonated when I first earned a little bit of money and has served me well ever since.

One area in which I allowed myself to indulge was sneakers. I've always been a passionate collector of footwear. One of the newspapers in Copenhagen even wrote a feature about my obsession, calling me a "sneaker freak." A reporter tagged along with me as I hit some of my favourite stores in the city to add to my collection. I was never one for flashy kicks; I preferred classic Nikes, usually variations of white. Copenhagen had some great shops on Strøget, the city's main commercial thoroughfare and one of Europe's longest pedestrian streets.

I was no longer an uncomfortable kid feeling like an outsider in a new place. In two years, I'd come to love life in Copenhagen. I lived in an area called Frederiksberg, a beautiful neighbourhood with lots of green space, a few minutes from where the team trained. It was a friendly and relaxed city, much calmer than the constant rush of Toronto. I liked the pace of life, and it was easy to feel content. The city was especially nice in the summer when the parks and streets were full of life.

It also helped that in Copenhagen people knew who I was. The recognition felt nice. It wasn't over the top, but it was constant. That feeling of being welcomed and respected went a long way to make me feel at home.

Of course, not everyone in the city cared about football. A lot of people had no clue who I was. Like Sarah.

When I'd first arrived in Copenhagen a couple of years earlier, I somehow came across Sarah on a Myspace page. I can't even remember how exactly, but I know that I was the one who added her as a friend.

She was beautiful, smart, and interesting—as far as I could tell from Myspace. At first neither of us said anything, but then we exchanged a few messages and some friendly banter. It was only a passing interaction. We remained digital acquaintances who had never met in real life—very typical of that era. We chatted every once in a while, but it was nothing serious. Though we both lived in Copenhagen, it was two years before we met in person. We'd started chatting a bit more frequently that year, during my third season in Copenhagen. Finally, we decided to get together for dinner.

Sarah invited me over to her place, because she loved to cook.

"Is there anything you can't eat?" she asked before I came over.

"No," I said. "Absolutely not."

I don't know why I lied.

Based on that false information, Sarah went ahead and made one of her favourite dishes, which was made with peanut butter and was very spicy. When I arrived, Sarah had dinner all laid out and told me she'd made an African stew—and told me what was in it.

"Oh," I said. "I can't eat that. I'm allergic to peanuts."

"That would have been nice to know," she replied.

Great start.

I ate bread and we drank some excellent wine. Despite my dietary restrictions, we had a wonderful night. When I was about to leave, I offered to take Sarah's dogs out for a quick walk so she wouldn't have to. It was a cold rainy night, and I figured it would be a gentlemanly way to make up for all the work she put into the meal I couldn't eat. Of course, I didn't mention that I'm also allergic to dogs. A past girlfriend of mine had dogs, so I knew I could put up with a little sneezing.

Sarah had a tiny Bichon Frise named Peanut, and a mixed breed named Nomi. They seemed well trained and nice enough, so I was pretty confident that this was a zero risk proposition. It wasn't the first time I'd walked a dog. Sarah told me that the Bichon would just walk beside me and didn't need a leash. No problem, I thought.

After a couple minutes outside with the pups, it appeared to be an easy win for me. But then I glanced behind me and the Bichon was gone. I completely lost sight of the little bastard.

A called for him, but he didn't come. He didn't bark. It was silent. I started to panic.

"I'm on my first date with her," I thought. "And I lose her dog?"

I called for Peanut, but he didn't respond. There was no sign of him anywhere.

I called Sarah, panicked. She came out and we both ran down her street shouting for the dog to come back. After a couple minutes, I was sure the dog was gone. But she let out two loud whistles, and suddenly Peanut came trotting back, delighted as ever.

The miracle was just enough to land me a second date. This time, we went to the theater to watch the movie *Ice Age*. Afterwards we went to a pub nearby and played air hockey. I was all in right away.

Sarah was fascinating. Both of her parents grew up in Iran and as adults moved to Denmark, where Sarah and her brother were born. Their family moved a lot as she was growing up. Her father ran a Persian carpet company, a business that took him to the United States for several years, Iran for a few more, and then back to Denmark. Sarah spent time in all three countries in her youth, before settling in Copenhagen to study.

She didn't know anything about football, which meant she wasn't impressed by the championships we'd won or my appearance in the

Champions League. She'd never even been to a game before. She'd never set foot in Parken. She was working at a law firm when we first started dating, while studying at university. There was little room in her world for simple games. She was confident but shy and very private—completely disinterested in the fame of a professional athlete.

I fell in love with Sarah right away.

I felt very comfortable with her. I saw her as someone that I could raise a family with. She was warm and thoughtful. She really cares about other people, especially the people whom she is close to. She'll do anything for them. That connected with me, because I'd always kept a tight circle of friends and loved ones who meant the world to me and whom I always tried to take care of. Long-standing relationships are priorities for us both; those kids I ran around the sandlot with playing soccer as a young kid are still my best friends today. We were both family people.

And she was very funny. We laughed a lot together—we just got each other, as though the world was outside our endless inside joke. It was all the small things. That was one of the biggest things.

Though we'd grown up in very different worlds, with different cultural backgrounds, we connected. We understood what it was like to grow up in a country where you are a minority, with a beautiful family history and culture from elsewhere. I fell for Persian food with the same passion I had for West Indian dishes. Her family made some of the best food I'd ever tasted. More importantly, we shared similar views about the world—a desire to see it, experience it, and understand it. She spoke three languages—English, Danish, and Farsi—and was curious to learn more. She thought about the world in ways that I hadn't. She cared about injustice, poverty, and all the imbalances designed to keep distance between those who benefit and those who suffer. Sarah opened my eyes to so many things.

Sarah and I fit together in a way that I'd never experienced before—the way that people who are meant to be together do. We moved in together almost right off the bat, during my third full year in Denmark in the 2008–09 season.

We met when I was very focused on finding the next stage of my career. I was a laid-back person when it came to being with people, quiet and easy to get along with. But I was very serious about my career, my continued development as a player, and, increasingly as I got older, being in the best physical condition possible. Every decision I made factored in how it impacted my ultimate goal of winning club championships on the pro level and showing the world what Canada was capable of on the international stage.

I sacrificed a lot of the fun that friends my age in Copenhagen and back home were able to experience, as they enjoyed carefree twenty-something days, still young and not tied down with responsibility. It was a prime era in their lives; they were trying to get a feel for life, experience things. I missed out on many memorable moments. Maybe not "missed out"—I chose to use those years of my life differently. I'd sacrificed a lot of time with friends to go live in hotel rooms across Europe, trying to find a place to pursue my dream. I'd missed out on many of the normal things that people my age did. I didn't have a normal high school graduation, because I needed to make up classes in the summer due to all the time I'd missed with soccer. I didn't go off to university and experience living on campus around students; I wasn't able to make those friends that all the buddies I grew up with had. I didn't regret those decisions, but I knew what I'd missed. I left everything behind to take my chance. I was focused on what I really wanted to do.

Back home, my friends often tried to get me to go out to a party or club when I'd visit, but I always resisted. I didn't go to any parties; I didn't drink at all until I was 25 and even then it was minimal. During periods of my career I'd commit to sacrifices like not drinking for an entire year, just to set goals for my health and to see them through. The first party I went to was when I was twenty-two or twenty-three in Europe. And I was nervous. When my teammates went to a club, I might tag along for a bit, but I worried that I would somehow jeopardize my career by putting myself in a bad situation.

Of course, my friends in Brampton loved trying to tempt me into those situations—but they were always very protective of me if they did. One time, after much prodding, I tagged along with the guys to visit a friend studying at the University of Waterloo. We went to one of the local college bars and were having a good time until one of the guys in our group got into a bit of a shoving match. Immediately, even though I had nothing to do with it at all, I was surrounded by my friends as if they were members of the secret service. They ushered me out the door, while our guy was still in the middle of a skirmish. He definitely needed their backup more than I did, but they wouldn't risk me getting involved in a brawl and potentially with the police. Those were the moments when I realized that my life was different. It meant a lot to me that my friends cared so much about protecting me, but it was also a weird feeling. I was just one of the guys, but one wrong move, one innocuous accident could mean the end of my career. I felt like I was constantly in bubble wrap.

The year that I met Sarah, my group of close friends from Brampton decided to take a guys trip to Cuba. We were chilling at a resort, and the guys wanted to head into Havana, rent some mopeds, and explore the city. I decided to tag along; I've always loved seeing new places. Spending time with the guys was always a great break, forgetting about football for a while and having some fun. We wouldn't do anything crazy, just simple fun—like renting motorized bikes in a city we weren't familiar with. We had no clue of what we were doing, which was part of the adventure. While touring around, we took a right turn onto a street that was much busier than we expected. I tried to turn quickly to avoid traffic, but the handlebars on my moped locked up and the bike toppled, throwing me into the street. Thankfully, the cars coming towards me slammed on their brakes. It could have been game over. Traffic stopped all around us as my friends hopped off their bikes and ran to me, worried I'd been seriously injured. I was worried too. It took me several moments on the pavement to catch my breath. Luckily, I'd avoided anything more than a few scrapes and bruises. Spooked and embarrassed, I pulled the bike up off the street, and we rode on, while the citizens in traffic were probably shaking their heads at the idiot tourist who nearly killed himself.

It was an incident we all remember well, because everyone immediately thought about my career. Riding a moped was something that I probably shouldn't have been doing, but I did it anyway. The fact that I was the one who took a tumble was a sobering reminder of what was at stake. Of course, anyone getting hurt would have been terrible. But if I'd fallen at an awkward angle, a knee or ankle injury would have had enormous ramifications on my soccer career. My livelihood and my dreams could have been over in a split second. I hated that I had to worry about these things, but that was my reality. I had to be conscious of ordinary things in a way that most people in their mid-twenties aren't. I had to think about potential outcomes of situations, like getting hurt doing something fun but dumb with friends, or being in a club when a fight broke out. I had to worry about protecting my image and my health. I had to avoid indulgences like alcohol and late nights. I had to take it easy even when adventures with my best friends called. That was the last time I rode a moped. One warning from the universe was enough for me.

◆

While shopping for sneakers on Strøget that day, the journalist asked me if I had any role models. There were many people that I looked up to, but only one came to mind as the person who had the blueprint I'd been following.

"People who are ambitious and give everything to achieve their goals," I told her. "For example, my father, who has always worked hard to make the most of life. He played football himself back in Trinidad, where my parents are from, and is very proud of me—but never satisfied. He pushes me to always move forward. To reach for the stars."

For years I'd been reaching—looking ahead to what height I could reach next. During that season in Copenhagen, as I turned twenty-six, I realized how my life was transforming and all the aspects that had already changed. My youth was behind me now. I'd been in Europe for five years. I'd found a way to make a great living playing professional soccer. I'd played on some of the grandest stages and against some of the best football players in the world. I'd held my own. I lived in a beautiful city where strangers knew my name. My entire world had expanded. I'd travelled the globe, playing the game I loved. I'd experienced cultures that I'd known nothing about. I'd visited some of the most gorgeous cities in the world. I'd witnessed the harsh realities of poverty in places we'd visited with the national team.

Now I'd met a brilliant woman and I could see my future unfolding with her. I'd experienced so much more than I knew to hope for when I had set out on this unlikely journey. I was partway through a beautiful dream.

I was happy with where I was in my life, but I also knew that the job wasn't complete. I owed it to everyone who had supported me on my journey to keep pushing forward and to never be satisfied. I owed it to myself for all the work and sacrifice I'd put in to get this far. I couldn't become complacent.

There were still so many stars left to reach.

19

Parken's Roar

Nearly two decades after beating Manchester United in the 2006 Champions League, we returned to Parken.

We were middle-aged men now, nearly all retired and settled into life on the far side of our careers as players. But as we gathered side by side and our names were read out for the fans, Parken felt the same as it had when we were young men.

In 2023, Copenhagen drew Manchester United in the Champions League, meeting the club for the first time since our win. Our old team was invited back to Parken to celebrate the occasion. I wasn't sure what to expect of the reunion. I assumed that there would be guys well past their playing days, maybe a bit overweight, looking tired and old. But my teammates looked like outlines of their former selves—still fit and healthy, still vibrant. Everyone had been taking care of themselves. Our veteran star Marcus Allbäck, now fifty, looked like he'd hardly aged. We could have put on kits and run back out on that field. Guys like Lars Jacobsen, Michael Silberbauer, Martin Bergvold, Oscar Wendt, William Kvist—I swear Scandinavians age better than most. It certainly didn't feel like seventeen years had passed since we had been in the locker room and on the pitch together every day. My close friend Razak Pimpong, the Ghanaian forward, embraced me as we soaked in the scene under the lights. We were each still part of the game in some way. It never leaves you.

We returned to that chapter in our life to celebrate the past and herald a new era for the Lions. Once again, Copenhagen had drawn Manchester United in the Champions League, and so the 2023 roster would make the same attempt we had seventeen years earlier at Parken. It was incredible to witness how much that moment in the team's history had meant to such a passionate, dedicated fanbase. When a team like Copenhagen defeats a giant like United, it becomes part of history. I love that about football. It's possible for the team you support to cross borders and leagues and levels to conquer leviathans.

And so for a moment we travelled back in time and felt the glory of that place again. We hovered somewhere between the present and past, experiencing that magic. It gave me chills.

So much had happened since then. We'd rebounded from our one frustrating season, refusing to accept losing. We returned to the Danish Superliga championship again in 2008–09—the season Sarah and I got together—and added the Danish Cup to our trophy case.

It had been the most exciting and rewarding time in my career. I made lasting bonds with world-class teammates. Zanka, a Danish defender who was just seventeen when he joined FCK in 2007, had become like a younger brother to me. His full name is Mathias Jorgensen, but he's been known Zanka throughout his career. (He got the nickname from character in the movie *Cool Runnings* played by Doug E. Doug.) Though he was born and raised in Denmark, Zanka has Gambian roots. We connected as two of the few Black players with the club, and just seemed to really get each other. We've remained close friends ever since, regardless of where we played. It's those kinds of friendships that you come to realize are as valuable as anything you might accomplish over the course of a career.

With a single season remaining on my four-year contract with Copenhagen, I was in a position to move forward from the most formative time in my professional career. I'd received interest from clubs beyond Denmark for the past couple years, but I was focused on seeing my commitment to Copenhagen through to the end. I was playing at the highest level of my career, and I was continuing to improve. Ståle Solbakken had taught me so much, alongside my teammates. There is no education in sport quite like playing for a team that wins championships. It was the most professional environment I'd ever experienced. I understood what it meant to be part of a winning culture. Nothing could be more valuable than that. And then it was time to reach further.

At the time, Copenhagen didn't look to cash in on players through transfer fees. They were happy to let players go on a free transfer once their contracts were up. Copenhagen was very good at bringing in cheap players or signing players who didn't have a contract. They were always looking to find talent to stay atop the Danish Superliga table and win the league every year, and they wanted to keep their players as long as possible. That was good for players like me. It also meant that I'd have an opportunity to collect more of a signing bonus from a prospective club, as the team wouldn't have to pay Copenhagen a fee as well.

My contract would end with the 2009–10 season. Going into my final year, everyone had a feeling this would be it. Copenhagen made me an offer to extend my contract, but they knew that I was interested in taking the next step. It was an amicable decision. I owed Copenhagen so much, and they were grateful for what I'd become to them. Solbakken was particularly supportive of my looming departure, like a teacher proud to see a student move on to the next chapter of his journey.

That season ended up being my most successful year on the pitch. I was reaching my prime as a player, taking on more responsibility as a defensive player and setting up our attack. I was a much more consistent player than when I'd arrived. I could control the game and have a big impact in helping the team play at the level we demanded.

There were rumours of interest from teams in England, but nothing came of it. I had talks with Lille in France's Ligue, but nothing concrete happened. There was serious interest from Trabzonspor, a team in the Turkish Süper Lig. At the time, veteran players often went to that league for a big paycheque, but I wasn't ready to make that move. I knew almost nothing about Turkey, aside from the good experiences I'd heard about from teammates who had played there. It seemed like a faraway, foreign place to me at the time. I wanted to remain in Europe, and I had visions of playing for one of the continent's traditionally bigger clubs.

We entertained two offers from teams in the German Bundesliga, which I was very interested in. Then one day, halfway through my final season with Copenhagen, I received a call from Fred Rutten— the venerable coach of Philips Sport Vereniging. Along with Ajax, PSV was one of the top clubs in the Eredivisie, the Netherlands' professional league. It was a world-famous club with a championship pedigree. To say that I was shocked would be an understatement. Rutten told me that the club was interested in signing me. I couldn't believe that they had even thought of me.

Though I was confident in my ability and had a goal to land with a team on the level of PSV, I felt nervous. This was a massive club. Was this opportunity actually real? It was what I'd dreamed of. If you had told me when I was a kid that I would have the chance to play for PSV, I would have lost my mind. Of course, my biggest dream had been to play in the Premier League—but the Eredivisie was world-class and PSV was its equivalent of Man United in Holland. It was even more surprising that Rutten himself had called me. That was so important to me throughout my career: knowing that I had a coach who wanted me to play within his system was so valuable. That was why Copenhagen had worked out as such a good fit for me.

In my nervous, incredulous excitement, I quickly agreed to a three-year contract worth significantly more money than I'd ever made. It came with a large signing bonus. For the first time in my professional career, I'd reached a life-changing opportunity financially.

Sarah and I had been together for about a year. She had just started studying business management at Copenhagen Business School and was committed to seeing that through. Now I was asking her to uproot our life and move to Holland. Sarah knew what this meant to me and for our life together. We agreed that she'd remain in Copenhagen for half a year after I left, so she could finish what she'd started. We weren't sure how the move to Holland would affect her journey, but she was willing to make the sacrifice. It would be the first of many she would make in our life together—an act of love and support that I'd never be able to fully repay or show proper gratitude for.

With half a year remaining in my contract with Copenhagen, I had one last chance to show the club, the fans, and the city what it all meant to me.

We established our dominance early in the season and never let up. By March 2010, after a six-match winning streak, we sat comfortably atop the table once again and looked to secure our second-straight league championship—a fourth in five seasons. Though I was often asked about my looming future with PSV, which would begin on July 1, I was focused on making sure we hoisted another trophy in Copenhagen.

"Right now it's all about winning another championship," I told reporters, as they pressed me about my future.

I scored only three goals that season but added four assists, while playing the most complete, consistent football of my career. I controlled the pace of play in the middle and was central in leading our attack through entire matches. I was playing the kind of football that Solbakken had envisioned when he first took a chance on an unpolished Canadian four and a half years earlier. He spoke often of how proud he was of me and what he believed I could accomplish at PSV when I moved into the next chapter of my life.

On May 5, we defeated HB Køge 4–0 to secure the championship, celebrating as if it was our first. There is no feeling like winning a championship. It never gets old. Copenhagen taught me that.

As a player, you spend the preseason busting your ass to get fit, and then you grind through a season with ups and downs, injuries and exhaustion, own goals and victorious goals, brutal moments and unforgettable ones. You gain your form and lose your form, and you fight to find it again. You give everything you have. And at the end of it all, to win a championship—well, it's one of the most gratifying feelings in the world. You don't have any lingering questions running through your mind; the closure is complete. It was all worth it.

That's the spirit of winning. There is nothing like it for a player, and there is nothing like it for a fan. Over the years, I would hear so often from Copenhagen fans who told me what that era meant to them. Defeating Man United in that single game at Parken was a lifetime memory for so many. When you're part of a community like that, football means something. It's more than a sport; it's a community, a family. It's the feeling of being part of something unique, beloved, and special. Yes, football takes people's minds off the world for a while. It's an escape. But it's also a constant—something you can rely on, something you are a part of. At the end of it all, whether you defeat a giant or hoist a trophy, you look around a roaring stadium and understand what it's all for.

I was far from being an old man when I returned to Copenhagen with my old teammates in 2023, but it was a moment to look back on my life thus far, reliving what had made the journey so special. We lined up on the sideline of the pitch as our names were announced over the speakers at Parken. I wasn't expecting the cheers after my name was called.

Copenhagen was where I'd really grown into the player and person I'd hoped to become. It was where I lined up against my childhood dreams, learned how to be a champion, and found the love who would become my family. It was the beginning of everything I'd hope to find as a player and as a man. Everything I learned in Copenhagen allowed for the journey of the next two decades of my life—the winning franchise, learning what that takes, and being able to bring that to the rest of my career and the Canadian national program. It was irreplaceable.

I clapped along with the fans as they cheered for our old team, returning the appreciation to them. But there was no way to really show my endless gratitude.

That night in Copenhagen, we watched the young players battle United with the same passion and vigor we once had. We listened to the same roar that seemed to carry on, never-ending, from years before. It was a wild match, tied at three with a few minutes remaining when Copenhagen scored to take a 4–3 lead over their world-famous opponents. When the final whistle blew on the Copenhagen upset, we celebrated up in the stands, just as we had those years before on the field. It was a new glorious moment in the club's life, as our own echoed amid Parken's roar.

Part IV

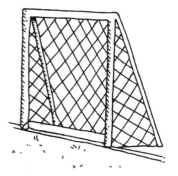

20

Ups and Downs

That night in 2023 brought home to me the incomparable feeling of being part of a team—and part of a community. When you win, you win for and with the people around you, not only the guys in the lineup and in the organization. It is no exaggeration to say that the fans are part of the team (just as opposing fans can be part of *their* team and bring their energy to bear against you). When I left Copenhagen in 2010, the years ahead gave me a powerful sense of the other side of the story. You can truly win only as part of a team, but there are highs and lows you can face only on your own.

There were incredible highs in wait for me. I will never forget looking out at the bright lights and the sea of faces from the stage of the Circus Building in Copenhagen, clutching a trophy of a footballer backflipping into a bicycle kick, trying to comprehend how I'd gotten there. In front of a massive, glitzy crowd, which included Franz Beckenbauer, one of the greatest players in the game's history, I accepted the award of Danish Superliga Player of the Year.

That was November, already several months into my first season with PSV Eindhoven. When I left Parken for the last time, it never crossed my mind that I'd be considered for an honour like this. The league's top player? It didn't seem real—but I was so happy.

I flew back to Copenhagen to accept the award at the annual Danish Football Association award show. It felt like a storybook way to officially cap my FCK era and begin my journey with PSV. I stood on stage in a black tux with a black dress shirt, which Sarah had helped me decide on. I was nervous on stage—call it joyfully overwhelmed. Thrilled but barely aware of the ovation as I walked out onto the stage.

"Is this really for me? Am I dreaming?"

My heart raced; I felt like a kid about to give a speech in front of his fifth grade class. I was comfortable with people but not with being the centre of attention. In a match, you don't have time to think about the fact that, really, you are performing on a giant stage. There are nerves, sure—but a different kind. The nerves I feel before a game are the kind that ramp up into adrenaline. It's about performance—wanting to play as best I can, knowing that opportunity is moments away. It's all focus and excitement, before the flow that sets in the moment the ball begins to move. An awards stage is so different; every eye was on me awaiting my word. If I was a professional orator, perhaps I'd feel something closer to how I feel stepping onto a pitch. But instead I just felt out of place and a little embarrassed.

"Really? For me?"

Four years earlier when Solbakken had first called me, very few people in Denmark knew my name. Now I was the first Canadian to be honoured as the league's top player. I was at a loss for words—though I know I managed to say something and I wasn't laughed off the stage. I also didn't suddenly wake up from a dream, feeling foolish. I thanked my family, my girlfriend, and all the Danish fans. To applause from the audience and under the shining lights, I walked off the stage clutching that trophy with as much exhilaration as I'd felt holding any trophy in my life.

I embraced Sarah as I returned to my seat. She was still living at our place in Copenhagen, with our two pups, while completing a semester at Copenhagen Business School. Soon she'd join me in Holland where we would begin our life together in earnest. In that moment, I felt like the most fortunate man in the world.

◆

More good fortune was in store only a few weeks later. In December 2010, I was named the Canadian men's player of the year for the first time. That fall, I'd made my fiftieth appearance with the national team, in a 2–2 draw with Ukraine. Playing for the national team meant as much to me as my career in Europe, so being recognized within the country, for what I'd done with the national team and as a pro abroad, was very meaningful for me.

This moment in my life meant much more to me than an honour for a well-played season. It was a reflection on how far I'd come—and how impossible it still seemed. I could have easily given up on Europe all those years before. It would have been the practical move—to play soccer at a Canadian university, get my degree, maybe bounce around the North American ranks before moving on. Keep the game close, but never try to achieve the dream. It would have saved me so much time and frustration.

But at twenty-seven, I could look back with the clarity of hindsight.

I was becoming the player that I'd always strived to be. It was a matter of time and experience. I was a much smarter player, seeing the game in the way that I'd marvelled at while watching Champions

League matches on my television as a kid, as well as later in pro train-ing camps as I did everything in my power to find a way to Europe.

As my career with PSV started, I realized how essential every step along the way had been—even the most frustrating parts. It was all part of my extended football education. My career to that point had been a giant learning curve.

I took what I had learned about the game from my father as a child—my foundation as a player—and added the experience of training with the youth national team. When I flew to Europe, over and over, essentially knocking on doors hoping a club would take me in, I was still so raw. Everywhere I went, I was so open to learning from experienced coaches and players who had achieved so much.

My first couple seasons in Sweden were really an apprenticeship, learning the trade in a professional environment, gaining knowledge through experience. And in that way, I kept playing and learning, playing and learning.

I didn't have the type of training that a lot of the European play-ers around me had from an early age. They were much more refined at a much younger age. So I was just all ears, all the time. I wanted to absorb everything I could.

In Copenhagen, I was like a graduate student—more advanced than when I'd first arrived, but still learning about the game from veteran teammates and under Solbakken's careful direction. By the time I left, I was a four-time champion who understood what it took for a team to remain atop the table and secure a title. I was a more complete player, winning balls, making quick decisions, doing the right things on defence, and creating attacking positions to help my team. I finally felt like I was in good form. The entire time, I had been fine-tuning my game.

There were times when I'd wonder whether I'd taken the right path or how things might have turned out differently had what I'd hoped for actually happened. What if a big club like Udinese or PSV had picked me up right away? It certainly would have been more glamorous. It might have generated more attention back home. I might have felt like I'd accomplished my dream much sooner.

But what would I have lost? What opportunities to grow as a player would I have missed out on? What if I'd earned my chance with a big club but rarely played? What if the coach hadn't viewed me as a player he could use and left me lingering on the sidelines or buried in a position I wasn't suited for?

There were so many scenarios that could have unfolded, which at the time I might have preferred. But looking back, I realized how essential each step in my long journey to that point had been.

I needed my father to show me how to love and respect the game. I needed my friends and Arnott Charlton to find my passion and learn how to believe in dreams. I needed Brampton minor soccer to understand commitment, and the national team development program to learn where I stood among my peers and to learn from the best in our country. The rejection of all those early trials—with Cagliari, Schalke, and all the others—to find my way to Sweden. I needed Östers to get to Helsingborgs. And Helsingborgs to cross the Øresund to Denmark. I needed to go to Copenhagen to become a champion and to prove I could play alongside the biggest names in the world.

Every move that I'd made was the perfect step for me. Each place I wound up taught me something that I needed to know and became a memory I'd always cherish. Each was an essential element in my continuing education as a footballer. I don't think I'd have it any other way if I had the choice.

Through it all, the most important thing I'd come to understand was the importance of being open to people who can help you. It was a lesson my father had taught me—play the game as much as you can while you can, and never stop listening or searching for ways to get better at it.

Part of that meant going to teams where I knew that I would play, rather than where I'd be a bench player getting in twenty minutes here and there. I always wanted to be on a team that wanted to use me, with a coach who saw me working in their system. There is no substitute for actual playing time, especially when you are young. You might sign with a big club, but if you're on the bench, what good does it do you? Of course, there are beneficial aspects—like training sessions, world-class teammates, and the environment of a professional club. But I'm convinced that there is nothing better to grow as a player than to play games, week in and week out. It's like logging flight hours as a pilot. A player can only learn so much on the sidelines.

Still, playing time is only part of the equation. How you approach that playing time is just as essential. Every single week, I tried to grow as a player. It was never about trying to be the best or prove that I belonged. I wanted that, of course, but my primary focus was improvement. I wanted to evolve as a player.

My philosophy was simple: learn every day—and be better than yesterday.

If I walked away from a training session or game without having learned something, I'd wasted an opportunity to grow as a player. I was determined to never let that happen.

Without each step along the way, I believe I would never have been granted the honour of being named Superliga Player of the Year or the Canadian men's player of the year. And I likely wouldn't have been in a position to impress Fred Rutten during our match against PSV in the UEFA Europa League a year earlier, leading to the team sending me an offer I couldn't refuse. I wouldn't have been the player I was when I made the move to Holland.

For me, PSV was the high level I strived to reach in my career. But as with every other step in my journey, I viewed it as yet another opportunity to learn and grow.

And right away, once again, I knew that I had a lot to learn.

◆

From the moment I arrived in Eindhoven, I was nervous. PSV was a big club. The leap from Copenhagen to PSV was huge—and I felt the pressure right away. It was a transition from a team that was well-known in Scandinavia to a team that was well-known around the world. I'd be lying to you if I said it wasn't intimidating.

Philips Sport Vereniging—or Philips Sports Union—was a century-old team founded by employees of the Philips electronics company, based in Eindhoven. The city of about a quarter-million people remains a major tech hub today. Over the course of a hundred years, PSV became a dominant force in Dutch football, frequently rivalling Ajax Amsterdam and Rotterdam's Feyenoord as the top club in the Eredivisie, the Netherlands' top level of professional football.

Philips Stadion was a world-class facility with room for 35,000 fans—all of whom knew football intimately. The crowds in the Eindhoven were different than I'd experienced in Copenhagen and Helsingborg. It was a much quieter experience: fans watched each play carefully, and there were fewer wild outbursts and roars coming from above. It was a buttoned-down experience. They were wonderful fans, of course, who really know football. They know when a player is good. They know when a team is good. They can identify the issues when something is off right away. They were intelligent about the game and watched with a critical eye. When I made a mistake, I could feel the eyes of 35,000 people watching me. The quiet was unsettling, like the long pause before a spelling bee judge hits the buzzer when the contestant has missed a silent letter. The PSV fans always knew what action or pass you should have made when you didn't. It seemed to be like that for everyone in Holland—from the coaches to the players to the fans. The whole country focused on the minutiae of the game. They expected to see a quality brand of "total football."

Holland was the birthplace of total football, a tactical approach that became popular in the 1960 and 1970s, particularly under Ajax coach Rinus Michels who led the team to three straight European Cups, the precursor to the Champions League, in the early 1970s. The world really took notice at the 1974 World Cup: the Dutch reached the final with a dazzling, overwhelming attack. The total football concept focused on being versatile and precise. It was about controlling the ball as much as possible, without losing possession. Every move you make with the ball or without the ball is designed to keep the ball away from your opponents. Quite simply, a team can't win a game if it doesn't have the ball.

Players interchanged positions seamlessly during a match, which meant that they needed to be able to play in all areas of the field. This allowed a team to maintain its control and shape on the attack, pressing aggressively—while quickly transitioning to defence as soon as possession was lost. Off the ball, players moved constantly, confusing opponents trying to mark their rapidly changing coverage responsibilities. The defensive line would play very high, near midfield, overwhelming opponents by compressing their field, making it difficult for them to adjust and advance.

I remember thinking, if I ever become a coach, I'm going to teach the way they play in Holland.

In my first PSV training session, the influence of total football was apparent. As a coach, Fred Rutten—a silver-haired dead ringer for

Mad Men's Roger Sterling—stressed the details. His attention to the finest points of the game was on another level, a different degree of intelligence and understanding. In particular, there was enormous focus on passing. Rutten stressed the importance of doing things right on the ball and moving off the ball. He took nothing for granted, and no detail was too small—like passing to the correct foot. He loved to play small-sided games.

The difference with PSV was in those details. At the highest level of the game, it wasn't enough to make a quick decision and move the ball forward or back. It was as important that you passed the ball to your teammate in a way that put them in an optimal position to receive it. In other words, if I was passing the ball to my teammate, it was my responsibility to show him where I wanted him to go with the ball, while also showing him where the pressure was behind him. I needed to be his eyes and set him up to receive the ball in a way that factors in what he himself cannot see. If he had pressure coming on his right side and I passed the ball to his right side, I'd set my team up to lose possession. Instead, I needed to pass the ball to his left side to show him where I wanted him to turn. It was all about the location and the pace of the pass.

During our training sessions with PSV, we did more passing drills than I'd ever done with a professional team before. They were simple passing drills, but if you messed up and didn't send a firm pass or somehow missed your target, the whistle went and the practice halted. I felt pressure from the coaching staff right away. The coaches would be right on you. The demand was clear: an accurate, hard pass every time. No exceptions. Everything was crisp.

Those training sessions were more intense than anything I'd experienced before. If I made a pass that didn't have enough weight on it or was slightly off target, the whistle blew and everything stopped. I'd never experienced a more intimidating training environment. Everyone on the team bought into the same system. It didn't matter who you were: if you didn't execute properly, we stopped as a group until we got it right. The expectation was perfection.

Everybody pushed each other. It was always a battle. That's where I really felt the pressure to do better. Every player around me was so technically advanced. There were some very big names on the club: veterans like Dutch defensive midfielders Orlando Engelaar, Ibrahim Afellay, and defender Wilfred Bouma. We also had dazzling offensive talent in guys like Balázs Dzsudzsák, Jeremain Lens, and Ola Toivonen. Just being on the pitch with those guys set a higher bar. I had to be fit and ready for it.

It took me some time to get comfortable in a system like that. I'd never been challenged on the precise accuracy of my passes during training before. I needed to be better with my passing, to have the right touch. And the way that I'd approach the ball to take a touch—it was all new to me. There were technical approaches that I hadn't been taught when I was young. I was learning different parts to the game.

The expectation was that players showed up ready to treat every play like it mattered as much as it would in the final minutes of a tied championship match. In my experience training with Canadian clubs and with the national team, that certainly hadn't been the case, especially in practice. Even in Sweden and Denmark, that degree of precision was never enforced. With PSV, not only did I need to think quicker, I had to execute perfectly.

As nerve-wracking as that was through my first couple of months with PSV, I appreciated the high standard. It challenged me to be completely focused on what I was doing. My first touch had to be right. The weight of my pass mattered. My dribbling had to be swift and tight. There was no room for lost balls caused by careless mistakes. You had to be ready for it.

As a kid growing up in Brampton, I played for hours each day on a field with friends behind my house. My father coached all of the competitive teams I played for. He made me a midfielder.

I joined the Canadian senior national team for the first time in 2003. At the time I had no idea I'd represent my country for two decades. (Photo Credit: Canada Soccer / Munoz)

In the semifinal of the 2007 Gold Cup against the United States, my game-tying goal in the final minutes was called offside when it was clearly wasn't. It was one of many frustrations to come for the Canadian men's team. (Photo Credit: Canada Soccer / Mexsport)

After several years of trying to land a professional contract overseas, I finally got my shot with Östers in Sweden. I was just a kid, living on my own for the first time, clinging to my dream. (© Andreas Hillergren / Bildbyrån Photo Agency)

I met Sarah in Copenhagen. She changed my world. A couple years after we met, I signed with PSV Eindhoven and we started our life together in Holland.

At Copenhagen FC my career started to take off. I'll never forget the thrill of scoring my first ever Champions League goal, against Celtic. (© Bill Murray - SNS Group / Contributor via Getty)

I was a homebody until I met Sarah. We travelled around the world together.

I grew up in a very close family. Today, my own family is the most important part of my life.

When I first signed with Beşiktaş, I thought I might stay for a couple seasons. But Istanbul quickly stole my heart and became my family's home. (© Beşiktaş)

Ten years and three championships later, Beşiktaş became the club where I finally ended my career. I will be a Black Eagle for life. (© Beşiktaş)

As a father, it meant everything to share my third Süper Lig championship, after Beşiktaş's unexpected run in 2020–2021, with my three sons.

After years of frustration and disappointment, I thought my days with the Canadian national team and my dream of playing in the World Cup were over until John Herdman convinced me to return for one last run. (Photo Credit: Canada Soccer / Beau Chevalier)

Our run to qualify for the 2022 World Cup was one of the most thrilling experiences of my career. For the first time, our home games were packed with wild Canadian fans. I scored my final goal for Canada away against El Salvador. (Photo Credit: Canada Soccer / Martin Bazyl)

This group proved to the world that Canada belongs on the world stage. We celebrated after our 2–0 win in El Salvador during the World Cup qualifier. The future of football in Canada is in good hands. (Photo Credit: Canada Soccer / Martin Bazyl)

Two decades after I first joined the senior national team, we made it to the World Cup in Qatar. Though we didn't get the results we hoped for, I fulfilled my dream of representing Canada on the world's biggest stage. (© Photo by OZAN KOSE/AFP via Getty Images)

My boys Noah, Nava, and Ayo watching me play at the World Cup.

Without my family, I would never have had the chance to realize my dream, and it meant everything to me that they were able to be there at the World Cup.

Our daughter Lily-Rose was born in July 2023, a month after I officially retired. Even though my time as a player is done, there is so much to be excited about.

These kids keep me busier than my football career ever did. But I love everything about being a dad.

All four of our children were born in Turkey—Noah, Nava, Ayo, and Lily-Rose. Istanbul has remained our home since my retirement. It will always be a central place in our lives.

For club . . . (© Beşiktaş)

. . . for country . . . (Photo Credit: Canada Soccer / Martin Bazyl)

. . . for the generations to come. (Photo Credit: Canada Soccer / Martin Bazyl)

Those lessons helped my development so much. In the Eredivisie, the game was played at a much quicker pace than I was used to in Denmark. Though I'd developed into a quicker thinking, more intelligent player, I still wasn't as technically precise as I needed to be.

The Dutch style was more set on where players were to move at any given time. It was less free-flowing than I was used to in Denmark, under Solbakken. There was still a lot of movement with PSV, but it was more tactical than I'd experienced in Copenhagen. In Eindhoven, there was much more movement off the ball. There was always somewhere to be. How you received the ball mattered, as did how you moved it. Your first touch, your second touch—everything was to be considered and exact.

This excited me because I'd always been a player who didn't like to lose the ball. I loved to maintain possession. Now losing possession was akin to giving up a goal. But maintaining possession didn't mean holding onto the ball.

As a player in Canada, I'd developed while holding onto the ball as much as possible. I took time to get myself set and then make the right pass. I'd had to unlearn that instinct in Copenhagen, and in Holland it was another level entirely. Everything was a quick one-two touch. They didn't want us hanging onto the ball. If I had the ball, I moved it immediately. I had to know what I was doing next before the ball even came to me.

Under Rutten, we always worked in little triangles. So if my teammate had the ball, he needed to have two options to move it to. If he passed it to another player, I needed to be thinking about where to be to best receive the next pass from that player—in other words, making myself the third in that tight triangle. At the same time, I needed to think about where I'd move the ball next if it came to me.

We learned to think three or four passes ahead. I had to learn to read where the ball was going and make my movements according to that. The system forces you to become a smarter player; you are expected to see not only where your teammates and opponents are but where they will be.

In other words, in Copenhagen, I was playing checkers. PSV forced me to play chess.

◆

As I adapted at midfield under Rutten's system, I found my confidence on the pitch within the Eredivisie. I became less tentative and adjusted to the quicker pace of play—with a new degree of precision and care in the way I handled and moved the ball. Through that season, Rutten used me at right back as well as midfield, which wasn't my preferred position. But I viewed the new role as another adjustment that could only benefit my game. I learned to take better care of the ball and increased my pass completion rate tremendously.

We finished third in the Eredivisie that year and fell to Benfica in the Europa League quarterfinals. It was a disappointing outcome for a team that carried the same championship expectations I'd experienced with Copenhagen. Pass by perfect pass, it was a winning culture.

By the end of my first season in Holland, I knew that I was a better player than when I'd arrived. I was still moving in the direction I hoped to go, learning every day along the way.

In the years to come, the precision I learned with PSV would become apparent. In Champions League play, I would become one of the top twenty players in passing accuracy in the tournament's history with a 94.5 percent accuracy rate. I would have never been able to reach that level without the lessons I learned in Holland.

◆

Pressure can make you stronger. The pressure of being measured against talented and hard-working teammates, the pressure of demanding coaches and fans, and especially the pressure you put on yourself. That is what pressure is *for*.

Healthy pressure brings you closer to your team and your goals. But not all pressure is healthy. Pressure can also eat at you. As a professional athlete, there is nothing more unsettling than when your body begins to betray you. It's an inevitable reality—at some point, you will no longer be able to do what you were once capable of. You do your best to prepare. To train responsibly, with a focus on performance and longevity. To take care of your diet and prioritize sleep. The body is a machine that needs to be monitored and maintained. You can't replace it.

Through the early years of my professional career, I was fortunate to avoid serious injury. I was lean and light, which helped. And I was very focused on training effectively. There were oddball elements to my discipline as well. Each year, as a point of principle, I would commit to giving up one of my unhealthy vices for twelve months. One year, it was candy. Another, it was alcohol. There was nothing prescriptive about this approach. It was just something that I felt was a helpful way to focus on my health.

In my early and mid-twenties, I was reliably one of the fastest players on the pitch at any given time. That speed helped me establish myself as a versatile player who excelled in a box-to-box system. My speed made up for many of the elements of the game that I was still working hard to refine as I reached higher levels.

But in Holland, for the first time in my career, everything I'd relied on was in jeopardy.

The issue began in the summer of 2009, when I'd tweaked my left knee during training at the Gold Cup with the Canadian national team. We finished at the top of our group but lost 1–0 to Honduras in another frustrating finish at the Concacaf tournament. On top of that dis-appointment, I returned to Denmark for my final season with Copenhagen with a nagging pain in my left knee. I knew something was off, but I played through it. I didn't want to lose any time on the pitch, knowing that I was looking to impress a new club. But my knee continued to nag me throughout the season. I did an MRI while at the Gold Gup and learned that it was a torn meniscus. But it didn't seem too severe—my knee didn't lock up, which is usually when you have no choice but to operate. I'd have sharp pains here and there, but I was determined to stay on the pitch. There was too much at stake, as I prepared to move to a new team, to cast any doubt on my health.

After I'd agreed to join PSV and while I was playing out the final games of my contract in Copenhagen, I decided it was time to finally deal with it. We'd secured the Superliga championship with two games remaining in the season, so I underwent surgery right away and sat out the final two games so that I'd have the most time possible to recover before my first season in the Eredivisie. It wasn't consid-ered a serious injury, and it was a routine procedure. PSV agreed that it was best for me to get it taken care of. I had the surgery in Denmark. During the procedure, the surgeon found that there was more damage to my meniscus than we initially thought. There were three tears, instead of one. We decided against repairing the newfound tears, to avoid prolonging my recovery and because of my age. Instead, we removed the torn ligaments rather than stitching them up.

I missed the first two weeks of preseason with PSV, which made me feel anxious. I wanted to join my new team. There were all kinds of questions lingering about when I'd be ready to play. It's a terrible feeling when you're starting with a new club. I didn't want to miss much of the preseason with PSV because I was eager to play with my new club. Instead of taking the time I needed to recover, I rushed myself to be ready. I didn't complete the necessary rehab. When I got back on the pitch, issues persisted throughout that season, and the pain returned in fits and starts. I didn't feel one hundred percent comfortable, and I was often playing through agony.

Because of that self-imposed pressure, I hadn't taken enough time to properly heal and build up strength around my knee before I returned. Even through the pain, though, I played well. I continued to work in practice to bring myself up to the standard that I expected of myself and that the team demanded of me. Rutten started me off in the right back position, which was a new experience for me, but it wasn't an overly difficult adjustment. My ability to adapt and adjust remained a big strength in my game. By the midpoint of the season, Rutten moved me back up to midfield. I tried to minimize the pain that I was in and managed to limit the effect it had on my play.

After we finished third in the Eredivisie—not good enough to satisfy the high standards of the fanbase, but not drastic enough to be labelled a disaster—it was time to turn my attention back to Canada.

That February, in 2011, I'd joined the national team in Larissa for a friendly match against Greece. I received the captain's armband for the first time with the senior national group. It was an important moment in my career. I was deeply honoured. Despite a 1–0 loss in front of a boisterous Greek crowd, we held our own against the 2004 European champions, by far one of the strongest sides we'd faced. We rebounded with a 1–0 victory in a friendly against Belarus in Antalya, Turkey, that March. We were a well-balanced team guided by Stephen Hart. I was optimistic about where the national team program was heading, with an eye towards the 2014 World Cup in Brazil.

In June 2011, we gathered to take another run at the Gold Cup. We met the United States in our first match in Detroit; we were met by a surprising number of Canadian fans who made the trip across the border for a chance to cheer for us (or maybe against the Americans). It was another strong U.S. squad, led by Jozy Altidore and Clint Dempsey.

Despite the surprisingly loud Canadian cheers from the stands, we fell behind 2–0 in the first half and were unable to beat American keeper Tim Howard, despite several quality chances.

A 1–0 win over Guadeloupe in our second match set up a must-win meeting with Panama to round out the group stage. Anything less than our victory would put Panama through in our group's second spot behind the United States. In that decisive match, we carried a 1–0 lead through the second half off a penalty kick from De Rosario. But Panama wouldn't let up. They attacked relentlessly until finding the equalizer a minute into injury time. The 1–1 draw eliminated us from the Gold Cup. It was another disappointing result to add to an increasingly long list.

For me, it was even worse. I'd once again tweaked my left knee during the tournament, and the pain was too much to push through. After consulting with PSV, we decided on a second surgery to repair my damaged meniscus.

The surgery meant that I would miss the start of the Eredivisie season, which began that August. I didn't want to miss any time, but I couldn't continue to play without going under the knife again. I worried that I might be causing longer-term issues, making it worse by pushing through without surgery. But I also couldn't stand to watch the team play without me. Once again, I rushed through rehab to get back on the pitch as quickly as possible. After missing two games, I made it back as a second-half substitute in our third match of the season. But my knee still didn't feel right. I couldn't get comfortable on the pitch. I couldn't play the game at my usual speed. I couldn't twist or turn without feeling pain. My agility was the best part of my game. I wasn't myself.

Despite the lingering issues, though, I flew to Toronto to play in a World Cup qualifying game against Saint Lucia during the international window in early September. My commitment to the Canadian team was still frequently questioned by my European teammates and coaches, who couldn't understand why it mattered so much to me to take those long flights and play for my country when I could be using the break to rest. But I wasn't going to miss it. At twenty-eight, I was old enough to see the horizon of my career in the distance. There was still time for me, but it was slipping away quickly. The 2014 World Cup was two years away and I intended to be in Rio.

At BMO Field in Toronto, we played in front of another lacklustre crowd, easily defeating a scrappy Saint Lucia team 4–1. During the match, I felt another sharp pain in my knee. We flew to Puerto Rico a few days later for our next qualifying round match. The pain persisted. I spoke with the national team medical staff, and we agreed it was best for me to sit this one out. After a scoreless draw, I returned to Eindhoven to speak with PSV's experts. After more tests, the team's surgeon recommended that I have a third operation followed by a demanding rehabilitation program that would take me away from the team for a significant time.

I was devastated and anxious. I was beginning to see that I'd been my own worst enemy, pushing myself too far, thinking that I could push through the pain. I hadn't listened to what my body was telling me. My obligations to PSV and Canada were too important. My own competitiveness and refusal to slow down—what had once seemed strengths—had literally made me weaker.

Two surgeries had failed to fix the problem, and now they wanted to try again? I was running out of strikes. But there were no other options. That reality sent me into a spiral. Doubt set in.

"Will I ever be able to play without pain again?" I wondered.

I honestly didn't know. It felt like my entire career was on the line. How was PSV going to view me if I couldn't return as the player they'd signed? And would any club be interested in me in the future if they knew that I had knee issues? I probably wouldn't be able to pass a medical.

"I'm afraid we'll lose him for a while," Rutten told *Sky Sports*, when news broke that I was injured again.

A few days later, I missed the opening leg of our Europa League group play as I underwent knee surgery for the third time in eighteen months.

◆

This time, I had to get away. I couldn't be around the team anymore; there were always lingering questions about when I'd return, which added pressure to come back before I was ready. I'd done that twice— and this was where it had led. I needed to take more care this time.

I was told about an excellent physical rehab facility in Antwerp, which was only about a forty-five-minute drive from Eindhoven. A lot of the Belgian national team players went there when they needed to recover from injuries. PSV supported my decision to take some time away and heal properly.

Sarah and I rented a small apartment in Antwerp for a little more than a month, and I trained at the facility two times a day—doing rehab and strength training to build up the muscles around my knee and get it right again. It was the most demanding rehab regime I'd ever experienced. Each session lasted four to five hours, with challenging leg and knee exercises and mat work. Every day I went through the most gruelling training sessions of my life.

It was hard, frustrating work. There were dark days when I questioned if I would ever feel right again. There were good days, when I was certain the rehab was working. But with every good day came another bad one.

"I'll find a way," I kept telling myself. "It will get better at some point." I didn't always find myself very convincing.

That fall, I watched as PSV climbed to second place in the Eredivisie and secured the top of our group in Europa League play. The Canadian national team secured a spot in the third round of the World Cup qualifiers without me. The next round of games would start the following summer. For the first time, I doubted that I'd be there to help Canada earn its first World Cup berth in nearly three decades.

Sarah and I drove back and forth to Eindhoven as much as we could to see teammates and friends at the house and take our mind off the rehab. The rehabilitation pushed through autumn into winter. December came, Christmas passed, and 2012 arrived. I didn't return to PSV until that February, shortly after I turned twenty-nine.

When I was finally cleared to play, it felt like I'd been released from a mental prison. The anxiety of not being able to play—all the accompanying worry and doubt—had taken a significant toll. But I'd forced myself to take the time I needed. If I hadn't learned that hard lesson, my career would very likely have wobbled on its last legs.

In Holland, the Eredivisie season wound to its end. Once again, we finished third on the table, behind Feyenoord and our rival Ajax. I had played in only twenty-one matches all year, which was concerning as I headed into the third and final year of my contract with PSV.

In March 2012, I joined the national team for the first time since I'd been injured in September. I played the full ninety in a friendly against Armenia. The match was prep for the third round of World Cup qualifying, coming up in June. A young goalie named Milan Borjan split duties in goal with veteran Kenny Stamatopoulos, as Stephen Hart tried to decide who would join our team in the next round. Borjan hadn't been part of the four matches in the previous round, but the keeper carried a unique energy—exactly the kind of confidence and swagger we needed.

My return wasn't memorable. I was tentative and slow. I missed several passes. With PSV, I could have been benched. We lost 4–0—a brutal defeat. But I'd managed to play the full ninety relatively pain free.

After three surgeries and nearly six months of rehabilitation, I was back. I'd learned one of the most important lessons about what it takes to persevere through the grueling physical and mental challenges an athlete endures when an injury takes them out of the game. In life, there are often bumps and detours on the way to where we strive to be. Being able to push through those moments of doubt and frustration is what makes a professional a professional.

21

Family Secrets

Two months after our first date, Sarah and I had moved in together. She'd yet to meet all of my family and I'd not yet met hers. My friends were still strangers to her, as was I to hers. But none of that mattered. We knew right away—it was as though we'd known each other for years. This was it. We'd spend the rest of our lives together.

Even though we connected so well, we came from completely different worlds, and it wasn't certain how those worlds would connect. Sarah had never been to Canada. I'd never been to Iran, where her parents were raised. My family had raised us in a region that was quickly becoming the most multicultural place in the world, with our closest friends coming from a wide range of backgrounds. Since Sarah was a little girl, it was expected that she would marry a Persian man.

Sarah admired her father, Sifollah, for his intelligence and work ethic. He'd built a highly successful rug company in Denmark, selling to clients like the Danish royal family and LEGO. He'd left Iran to study in Germany when he was young, and then he started the rug company in Herning, a small town in central Denmark. He was a dedicated man. Sarah remembers him starting his workday before dawn and working through to midnight many days.

When the kids were little, the family moved to Los Angeles for several years. Then they moved back to Iran, where the children studied at an international school there. When her parents' marriage fell apart, Sarah and her brother moved back to Denmark with their father. He raised them. Sarah's mother, Fariba Valizadeh, was very young when she had her children and had left to find her own way after the divorce. She wasn't in Sarah's life at all when we met.

After high school, Sarah moved to Copenhagen to study—it was the only reason her father let her go. He was very strict. Growing up, she thought he was way too strict, but as an adult, she'd grown to understand that it came from a place of genuine love and concern. When Sarah and I met, she and father were very close. He lived in Aarhus, the second largest city in Denmark, about two hundred kilometres northwest of Copenhagen, but they spoke all the time. He'd become more like a best friend to her. To his daughter, he was a man of immense wisdom. Everything he said seemed to turn out to be right, whether he agreed to it or not.

When Sarah and I met, she didn't tell her father about me. She didn't know how. Her entire life, it was expected that she would marry a Persian man. So, dating someone who wasn't Persian wasn't an option. Sarah was scared that her father might cut her out of his life. Her father wasn't religious, but he was very strict about the family's culture. He would not accept his daughter marrying a foreigner. Nobody had ever done that in her family. It would have been against everything her father knew. Sarah was worried about hurting him. She loved him deeply and didn't want to upset him. I understood how much he meant to her.

♦

Just as Sarah and I were getting settled together, I'd committed to move to an entirely new country. Sarah had just returned to school, after several years working as an office manager for a law office in Copenhagen. She studied business management at Copenhagen Business School. But she also wanted to join me in Holland. After six months of long distance Sarah joined me in Eindhoven. She transferred from CBS to Fontys University of Applied Sciences, where she continued to study business management. Sarah's father wasn't happy that she was leaving Denmark, but she lied and told him that Fontys was where she really wanted to finish her degree, which helped soften his disappointment. He had no idea it was because of me.

I had a difficult time understanding Sarah's reluctance to tell her father about our relationship. Other people in her family knew. She was very close with her brother, so he was one of the first family members I met. Siavash and I connected right away and we became very close friends. Sarah was also close with her aunts who lived in Columbia. They'd also found out about us by the time Sarah moved to Holland with me, and they were very supportive. But no one told her father.

Sarah was still estranged from her mother when we met. She was living in Dubai at the time. It was hard for me to understand how Sarah and her mother could be estranged for so long.

My family was always so important to me. We'd remained incredibly close, even though I was only able to travel home to visit twice a year. We spoke all the time.

My sister Toyaa came to visit me for a month in Copenhagen early on after I'd met Sarah, and the two of them hit it off right away. My parents first met Sarah over the phone. It took a while longer for my parents to get to meet her in person, but that was only because of the distance between us. About a year and a half after we got together, they visited us in Holland. They immediately adored her, but it was hard for them to understand why I was such a secret to her family. It wasn't really something I could explain.

Sarah's estrangement from her mother weighed on me. I didn't want her to lose out on what could possibly have been a meaningful relationship, but I also knew that I was on the outside of an issue that I'd never fully comprehend. One night, when we were living in Holland, I had a nightmare that her mother had died, and Sarah would never see her again. I told Sarah about the dream and encouraged her to try to build a relationship with her mother. Sarah agreed that it was time. I bought her a ticket to Dubai. She got on the plane and went to meet her mother for the first time in at least fifteen years.

A short time later, Sarah's mom visited us in Holland. She was lovely and vibrant—just like her daughter. She seemed more like an older sister to Sarah than a mother. She was only eighteen when Sarah was born. Sarah was happy to have her mother back in her life; it had been difficult to live without her for so long. Her mother visited us often, staying with us for several months at a time. It was so nice to see them together. And it was a bonus for me, because Sarah's mother was excited about our relationship—and quickly became an ally for me in any disputes we had. She was also an incredible cook and made my favourites all the time—breakfast, lunch, and dinner. I was a lucky man. Her mother has been an important part of our family (and has remained my ally) ever since.

As time passed, Sarah believed that her father knew that she was living with a football player in Holland. Most of her other family members knew. When she visited him, she knew that there were people around her father who knew as well.

He didn't care about sports in the least, so it wouldn't have impressed him that I was a pro football player. But it also didn't really matter who I was or what I did for a living. Because I wasn't Persian, our relationship didn't exist to him. When Sarah would go to visit, or when they'd speak on the phone, neither of them ever mentioned a single thing about it. She loved her father deeply and didn't want to hurt him. He was a good man, and he'd been an excellent dad. But he was very traditional. It was easier to never discuss our reality than to grapple with the divide between his love for his daughter and his beliefs.

I wouldn't meet Sarah's father for another decade.

♦

During my first season in PSV, Sarah came to live with me in my small condo in downtown Eindhoven. It was a beautiful city to live in. Everything was walkable. The streets were a gorgeous mix of old and new—a tech hub that still boasted architectural remnants from its rich industrial past. There were old brick buildings with charming gables and ornate details beside stunning contemporary architecture. It was known as the City of Light because it was where Philips first produced light bulbs in the late nineteenth century. Eindhoven maintained a deep connection to its proud past, while advancing as a hub for innovation in Holland.

Sarah made friends at school and with the wives and girlfriends of my teammates. They went to lunches and dinners and explored the city. None of them had kids yet, so every day they were free to do what they wanted. Sarah and I would host them for drinks and dinner in the evenings. We played cards for hours.

But as much as we loved living downtown, there just wasn't enough space in the condo for both of us and her two dogs. After my first season at PSV, Sarah and I looked to rent a place with more space for us and her two dogs. (Peanut, the bichon, had since forgiven me for losing him on my first date with Sarah.)

Our real estate agent showed us several places that were still too small in the city, before mentioning that the house she and her ex-husband had lived in was now empty and that they were looking to rent it. The house itself was way too large for two people, even with two dogs. But we loved it. There was a beautiful French garden out front, and it was across the street from a forest. In the back, there was a large heated pool, a sauna, and a massive deck with an insane barbecue. The place was unreal. And the realtor offered it to us for an incredibly reasonable price—way less than we expected. We couldn't turn it down.

It was an incredible time in our lives. I was in the middle of the biggest contract of my career, we were living in a mansion (at a discount), and we didn't have kids or any dependents, aside from the pups. Sarah left for class every morning, while I went to the team facility to train, if we weren't away on a road trip. Sarah loved to study at Fontys. She met great friends there, whom she keeps in touch with today. We also became close friends with several of my teammates and their wives, so we played host often. There were always people over for dinner or drinks or to play cards. We were all from different places in the world, which made for such fascinating late-night conversations. Every day of my life off the pitch was an education too.

I became very close with guys like Ola Toivonen, a Swedish teammate, and Stanislav Manolev, from Bulgaria. We also often hung out with guys like Orlando Engelaar and Jagoš Vuković. These days of our lives in our late twenties would seem foreign to us in just a few years.

♦

Sarah loved to travel around the world. She possessed an inherent wanderlust. In Denmark, it's part of the culture. While in school, students travel to countries like Germany, Belgium, and Italy. They have so much access to the beauty and history of other countries. Sarah had also travelled so much with her father throughout her life. He'd recently bought a place in Cannes, France, and she was able to visit him often—always without me, of course.

I was still a homebody when we met. I flew back to Toronto to visit my family every chance I had. Maybe some part of me never really got over the homesickness. I spent so much time away from my family and my friends at home that I was eager to get back to them whenever I could.

But in our new life together, we decided to do both. There were two long breaks in play each year, so we agreed that during one we'd return to Canada and during the other we'd set off to explore the world. Early on in our relationship, we visited places like Thailand, the Maldives, and Mexico. We added more and more stamps to our passports. Travelling with Sarah brought me so much joy. She was excited to experience new cultures—the food, the customs, the languages, the history. There was always someplace else that Sarah couldn't wait to go. As I saw the world through her eyes, I gained the same gift of wonder.

I've since come to realize that she's always been the reason it was so special. The world was a brighter, more wondrous place with her beside me. Today I look back at all these postcards in my mind, memories of the faraway places we've explored together, and I know that none of them would be as magical without Sarah in the frame.

Of all the exotic places we went, the trip that I hold closest to my heart was the first summer that I brought Sarah home to Brampton. At the end of my second season with PSV, we decided to fly home so Sarah could finally meet my friends and the rest of my family. Though she'd spent several years living in Los Angeles as a child, she'd never been to Canada before.

In Brampton, I took Sarah to Morris Kerbel Park, one of the fields I played on when I was young, just a few minutes from my parents' house. We sat in the bleachers and watched my brother Haldon, cousin Kevin, and Alex play in a men's league game. The guys had their own cheering section with their girlfriends, family, and friends watching. The match was as serious and hard-fought as any of the summer pickup games, Brampton rep matches, or money tournaments we'd played together through the years. There was never a moment on a soccer pitch that these guys didn't take seriously.

Sitting next to Sarah watching the guys play brought back so many memories. It was as full circle as a moment can get. This was exactly where my beautiful dream began—alongside these guys, playing the sport we loved. Now I was playing for PSV, with a contract that set me up to be comfortable financially for years to come. I sat next to the woman that I wanted to start a family with. And I saw my own friends making their own dreams come true, building their lives, with successful careers and soon-to-start families of their own.

We'd all grown up from boys into men, now with busy lives filled with stress and pressure and all the adult things you never have to consider when you're young. But somehow, through it all, we'd remained the same. Sarah and I sat on those creaky bleachers, clapping and cheering as the old boys chased a ball across a patchy field, just like we did when we were young.

22

A Nightmare
in Honduras

Whenever we travelled with the national team for Concacaf matches—whether it was an Olympic qualifier, World Cup qualifier, the Gold Cup, or even a friendly—it was clear how much soccer meant to fans in the other Concacaf countries. These weren't just football matches, as they were in Canada. These were full-on national events. And instead of only playing the other roster, it felt as if we were taking on the entire country.

At home, in 2012, it still often felt as though our opponents' fans outnumbered our fans in the stands. Many of those fans were Canadian, of course, but they supported the country they or their parents came from. And many fans did travel alongside their team. Canadians tend to be polite to newcomers, so it was never uncomfortable for fans from countries like Panama, Honduras, or Mexico to fill the seats at BMO Field, BC Place, Saputo Stadium, Commonwealth Stadium, or anywhere else on Canadian soil. Our matches were usually scheduled during comfortable seasons; our opponents wouldn't have to adjust to the bitter cold that most of our team had grown up playing in through the winter months in our backyards or on frozen fields, when we refused to consider soccer a seasonal game. There was never a thought of gaining some kind of competitive advantage based on hosting privileges.

That was not the case elsewhere.

We played in stadiums where the home fans did everything they could to make sure we were intimidated. When I was coming up through the national program, you'd hear stories from players who had played in those places before, but when it actually happens to you, you're shocked.

In El Salvador during an Olympic qualifier, fans chucked bags of what seemed to be urine at us as we walked out onto the pitch.

"This is not real," I remember thinking the first time I saw one of those bags explode. I witnessed it first-hand—though I'd thankfully avoided the pee bomb splash. This was actually something fans would do. It was wild.

But there were other less aggressive realities to contend with.

Whenever we stepped on foreign soil as the Canadian national team, we were careful about what we ate or drank. It was common for players to come down with some sort of stomach bug if they weren't cautious. I remember during one match a player who will remain nameless had to come off the pitch because his stomach was running like crazy. He tried to make it back to the toilets in our locker room but couldn't get there in time. Desperate and out of time, he darted down some stairs and found a space where no one was and let loose there. After that, he came back onto the pitch. It was an absolutely heroic effort.

◆

Everywhere we went in Central America, we had a police escort, which was pretty standard for any national team visiting. In places with high crime rates like El Salvador and Honduras, we'd have to hire extra security who travelled with us from Canada, on top of the police presence. It was always a bit unsettling to require those kinds of measures.

It was also eye-opening to realize how fortunate we were to live in a country like Canada. As our bus moved through the streets, you'd see the contrast from the standard of living we were all used to. It was really tough to see. Those trips gave me a better window onto the world and helped me appreciate what I had.

But when I travelled for these matches, it was a quick visit. You drop in and get out—trying your best to focus on what you're there to do. Those trips always brought our team closer together. We wouldn't be able to go out very much for our own security. So we spent a lot of time in hotel rooms hanging out. The Canada Soccer Association couldn't afford to put us in our own rooms, so we always ended up sharing. As annoying as it was to not have our own space, it was also a bit of a blessing. The guys would pile into each other's rooms to joke around, chat, play cards—getting to know each other off the pitch.

Those were times where we could really bond. Iain Hume and I had been roommates since we started in the national program, back in our late teens. I got to know him better than any teammate I'd ever played with.

And then when we left the hotel to head to a match, people lined the streets to jeer at us, hurling all kinds of objects and insults, and they stayed on us all game as we tried to pull out a win. Those experiences made us come together as a group. It's our team against everybody else.

Those moments will always stick with me. It didn't matter if it was a win or a loss, a good experience or a terrible one. In the end, it was about the time that we spent there with our teammates, the places we saw, the intense experiences—the bond we formed. It's something I will never forget. All the travelling with the national team over the years created a lot of memories.

◆

In the summer of 2012, I began the final season of my three-year contract with PSV. After three surgeries, my left knee finally felt sturdy enough to play on—though I'd be lying if I said it was one hundred percent. Still, I was glad to be back on the pitch in Eindhoven. I was twenty-nine years old, unsure of where I'd be playing in a year's time. As with every contract year, it was an exciting but unsettling time. Our team had finished third in the Eredivisie for the second straight year, but we did manage to win the KNVB Cup, the Dutch knockout tournament, similar to England's FA Cup. Still, there was disappointment among our fanbase. On the pitch, we knew that we could play better. Fred Rutten was replaced partway through the season by Phillip Cocu. To start the fresh campaign that summer, the team hired Dick Advocaat—a veteran Dutch manager—as our new coach.

The year also brought a new challenge in the form of a Dutch legend. Mark van Bommel was an iconic midfielder with the national team who'd played six seasons with PSV, winning four Eredivisie championships. After playing with Bayern Munich, AC Milan, and Barcelona van Bommel returned to PSV for the 2012–13 season. His homecoming meant that I'd be pushed out of the centre midfield position to right back. I was able to make the move because I'd worked so hard on being adaptable—knowing how to adjust, making sure my skills were transferable, and being willing to accept my new role. Although I wanted to play centre mid, I accepted the responsibility that I had to my team and was determined to be as effective in my new role as possible. I was confident in my ability to play any area of the pitch. These were lessons that I'd first learned as a kid, playing under the guidance of my father. In sports, but also in life, I've come to realize that adaptability is one of the most valuable traits you can learn.

A month into the PSV season, I flew back to Toronto during an international window to join the national team on our quest to earn a spot at the Rio World Cup. Once again, I'd adapt—taking my place in the middle alongside my friends De Rosario and de Guzman.

There was a level of talent on our Canadian roster that we hadn't had before. And it felt like the best chance we had at a World Cup qualifier since I'd joined the national program. But we didn't have much depth. Our national program had produced world-class talent but not enough that we could go without certain people. If one or two players went out, we didn't really have anybody to replace those players. I'd learned so much from de Guzman and De Rosario throughout my career. We could also clash at times, as most competitive friends do. Once Dwayne and I nearly got into a fight during practice when he felt I was holding on to the ball too much. He kicked me and said I wasn't as good as I thought I was. I called him old and said he was done. The grudge boiled over until the next day, when we were already cracking jokes with each other again. Dwayne and Jules both brought so much to the team. Their experience and their technical and tactical abilities elevated our game. Maybe at times we could have been better at figuring out ways to get the team more involved. But it was a process. They were invaluable.

We had a group of players on that iteration of the national team who were all in similar positions. Kevin McKenna, our thirty-three-year-old centre back and captain, was in what would be his final year of international competition. De Rosario, our all-time leading scorer, was thirty-four and facing his last real chance to reach the World Cup; de Guzman was thirty-one and likely in the same position. He'd eventually surpass Paul Stalteri as the most capped player in men's team history. Iain Hume was on the brink of a new decade, like me.

I felt a sense of urgency during this round of the Concacaf qualifiers that I hadn't experienced before. In the past, I could see the urgency on the faces of our veterans and the disappointment that followed our elimination and the realization that Canada would miss another

World Cup. Now I was almost thirty years old with three knee surgeries behind me. I understood what it meant to worry about the
future. I knew that anxiety of wondering whether you'd be able to
continue to play or if you'd ever be the same player again. In 2014,
I would be thirty-one—on the older side of any World Cup roster, if
we made it. By 2018, I'd be thirty-five—reaching old-man territory in
the world of football. There was no guarantee that I'd make it that far.
In the past, I had seen other players realize that their last chance at the
World Cup had slipped away and I'd think, "That could be me one
day." Now that day felt far too close.

I carried that urgency into the third round of the Concacaf World
Cup qualifiers. We were in a group with Cuba, Honduras, and
Panama—from which the top two teams would advance to the Hex,
the final round of qualifying. A Canadian team hadn't made it that far
since 1998.

Earlier that summer, we'd opened the third round with a win over
Cuba away and tied Honduras at BMO Field. Back in Toronto on
September 7, we played Panama in front of 17,586 fans at BMO Field,
who cheered loudly and gave us tons of support. It felt like something
was changing in the way fans viewed soccer in Canada. We weren't
quite where other nations were, but then again it seemed very unlikely
that bags of urine would ever be hurled at BMO. The support was a
flash of the kind of passion I knew existed for soccer in Canada.

In the seventy-seventh minute, I lined up a quick free kick on the
right side close to the byline, which caught Panama sleeping. De
Rosario swooped in and fired his twentieth goal for Canada, a record.
We won the match 1–0. It was a relief after a series of lacklustre results
at home. (During the last World Cup qualifier in 2008, we'd managed
just two draws and a loss at home in our failed effort to advance.)

The win over Panama kept our hopes to advance alive, but we
faced a tough rematch in Panama City a few days later. They sat in

second place and needed a win as much as we did to advance, so there was a lot riding on this game.

When we arrived, they gave us the kind of welcome we'd come to expect. Our hotel was on a busy street in downtown Panama City with all of our rooms facing the street. We were told that the hotel couldn't switch our rooms.

At around two a.m., the onslaught began. Hundreds of people gathered on the street below. Cars and motorcycles lined up, honking horns and revving engines. They blared music through loudspeakers. An ambulance siren went off. Then they set off fireworks. They were doing everything you could imagine.

I lay in bed with my eyes wide open, unable to sleep, wondering how the police were allowing this. The noise carried on until sunrise at six a.m. We learned later that the street party was endorsed by the Panamanian Football Federation.

At match time, the fans at Estadio Rommel Fernández were on us right away. We buzzed through the first few minutes of the match, creating chances. The momentum was on our side right away. But early on, De Rosario went down grabbing his knee after what looked like an innocuous tackle. Then just after six minutes in, the lights went out. The entire north end of the stadium went dark. We were convinced they were cut on purpose.

Play stopped for nearly fifteen minutes. In the dark, our trainers confirmed that De Rosario had injured his knee. He'd be gone for the rest of the match at least. Our best striker was on the sidelines.

The lights turned back on, and we just weren't the same.

After play resumed, Marcel de Jong nearly managed a goal for us. But we couldn't generate anything beyond that. Panama outplayed us in every area of the pitch. They beat us to every ball. We didn't defend well. They out-passed us, out-chanced us. They simply wanted the win much more than we did. There was no excuse—hotel antics and light tricks aside—Panama showed up and we didn't. They scored in the twenty-third minute. In the second half, they added another to take a 2–0 and never let up.

The result meant that Panama held the top spot in our group. Despite the loss, we were still in contention, with the second spot belonging to either Honduras or us. A draw or win against them in our next match would secure our place in the Hex. The Hondurans needed to win outright to advance.

A month later, we flew to Honduras.

It looked bad for us from the start. First, our chartered plane had mechanical issues, which delayed our arrival and meant we got to our hotel much later than we'd hoped. The next morning, several of our players were suffering from food poisoning, including Kevin McKenna, who would take his position at centre back despite it. Ante Jazić, our left back, was so sick he couldn't play at all.

On the way to the Estadio Olímpico Metropolitano, our bus was held up by brutal traffic. The government had announced an extended national holiday, and fans had filled the streets waving white and blue flags. When we finally arrived at the stadium, we were met by soldiers as fans jeered at us.

Inside our crowded dressing room before the game, we heard rumours that players on the other team had been promised land or homes by their soccer federation if they managed to pull off the victory and advance to the Hex. Meanwhile, an executive from the Canadian Soccer Association entered and told us that we'd each receive an iPad or an iPod if we won.

The contrast was almost comical, highlighting the enormous disconnect between what the game meant for both teams. The promise fell flat. It was as if the CSA thought we were a bunch of teenage amateurs, not professional players who'd flown from top-tier clubs around the world to represent our country. It was a discouraging reminder of the lack of a world-class professional mindset within our federation.

As we walked out to the pitch before the match, it was clear how much this match meant to the Honduran fans. Along with Mexico and El Salvador, Honduras was one of the most aggressive places to play when it came to the vitriol in the stands. The Estadio Olímpico Metropolitano seats 38,000 people, but it is one of the most raucous, intimidating stadiums I've ever played in. And this was another level entirely. It felt like everybody in Honduras showed up for the game. It was so loud in that stadium that it was difficult to think. It was also sweltering hot. The match was scheduled at the hottest time of the day.

But once again, though, we answered the challenge early. Amid the fans' roar, we managed to get the Hondurans on their heels from the kickoff. Tosaint Ricketts nearly scored on an excellent chance that was turned aside by the Honduran keeper, Donis Escobar.

After that, everything fell apart. Honduras scored seven minutes into the match. The stadium shook. We nearly tied it a few minutes later, when Simeon Jackson hit the post and Tosaint Ricketts's shot on the rebound was stopped again by Escobar. Honduras added another on an easy tap-in off a rebound, making it 2–0 in the sixteenth minute.

At that point, we still had hope—but it was fading fast.

Honduras took it away in the twenty-eighth minute when Carlo Costly scored on a diving header to make it 3–0. Our World Cup ambitions were unravelling. A few minutes later, Honduras added a fourth goal. It was a complete nightmare. We went into the locker room trailing 4–0.

The room was silent.

What was there to say? I'm sure that our coach, Stephen Hart, said something, but I don't know if any player in that room would recall it. We were completely demoralized. We'd come here with our World

Cup hopes on the line, and we'd shit the bed. There was no way around it. It would take a miracle to get back in that match, and at that moment, none of us could find the faith.

The humiliation continued in the second half. Honduras scored two more goals by the fifty-sixth minute to make it 6–0. It was now an American football game. Every time Honduras scored, it felt like another kick to the stomach. They completely took the life out of us.

Iain Hume, who'd always been a source of never-die energy, managed to get us on the board, scoring in a free kick, after he was subbed in. But even the energy Iain brought couldn't save us. As the final minutes ticked away, Honduras added two more goals.

I'm still searching for a way to describe what I felt.

The final whistle was a small mercy—at least the onslaught was over. But there was no escaping the humiliation and anger that remained. It was the second worst defeat in the Canadian men's national team history, after an 8–0 loss to Mexico two decades earlier.

The Honduran fans celebrated as though they'd conquered some kind of giant. But we were far from giants. We were just another Canadian team that had failed to reach the World Cup.

8–1.

As I walked off the pitch, I pulled up my jersey and wiped my face in a mix of frustration, shock, and anger. Around me, my teammates hung their heads, feeling the same.

♦

In time, I would come to learn the value in those kinds of disappointments. I'd learn how pivotal they can be. I'd carry that loss for the rest of my career. The score still haunts me. But it became an emotional driver for me. All of those negative feelings turned into fuel for my desire to see Canada reach a World Cup. That's the thing about failure if you're willing to learn from it: it becomes a catalyst for success.

But on that day, in that moment—wiping away the sweat and tears from my face with the Canadian logo, while the Honduran fans celebrated—I felt nothing but dejection and humiliation. I'd never felt anything close to it on a soccer pitch before. It was the lowest point of my career. It hurt even more when we returned to Canada and realized that no one else in the country seemed to care about our humiliation. Our country was indifferent to our failure.

23

Istanbul

In the summer of 2013, Sarah and I took a trip to Istanbul, a city neither of us had been to before. Sarah planned the trip, as she usually does. She was usually great at it. But this time she must have received some bad advice or been feeling overly thrifty, because she booked one of the worst hotels either of us had ever stayed in. It was the kind of place that you'd be willing to check out when you're a student travelling with friends, trying to save as much cash as possible. It was in an overly touristy part of town with little charm. There were bugs in our room.

It wasn't the best introduction. After our first night in Istanbul, I would never have imagined that the city would become a place that I couldn't imagine leaving.

We fell in love with Istanbul right away.

Friends had told us to visit Turkey for years, but we'd never had the opportunity. I'd been told so many wonderful things about playing in Turkey by teammates who'd played in the country's famous Süper Lig. A couple of my teammates with PSV had played in the Turkish Süper Lig and they raved about it. They would talk about Turkey as if it was heaven.

"If you ever have a chance to go to Istanbul, don't think twice," one of them said. "It's a beautiful city. It's modern. A lot of people don't really know that it's like that."

I didn't know much about the city, other than that it was ancient and had a rich history. When I was with Copenhagen, we'd played a match against a team in one of the smaller cities in Turkey for a Euro League match. So, I had a sense of what it was like to play in Turkey. But that was the only reference point I had. I'd visited for a couple of trials with Russian teams several years earlier but had never travelled around or visited the country as a tourist.

Having heard such incredible reviews from my teammates about playing in Turkey, Sarah and I agreed that it was worth considering for our future. That's when we booked the trip to Istanbul, hoping to get a sense of the city. During that first visit, no one knew that I was a football player. We roamed the bustling streets of the old city, exploring the Grand Bazaar, marvelling at the Blue Mosque, and finding incredible food to eat. It captured our imaginations. It was a city full of life and energy. There was so much to discover. Sarah and I finished our trip to Turkey with a visit to Fethiye, a small coastal town—a vacation spot with stunning crystal-clear water. It was one of the most beautiful places we'd visited. The people we met there were so warm and kind, going out of their way to make us feel welcome.

♦

I was thirty years old and had just completed the final season of my contract with PSV. We'd finished second in the Eredivisie, after battling for the top spot all season. I'd played right back for most of the season, but I still managed to score two goals. After three knee surgeries in eighteen months, I finally felt like myself again on the pitch.

In December 2012, I was named the Canadian male soccer player of the year for the second time. I was very grateful to receive the honour, but it was a small consolation in light of the embarrassment I still felt over the loss to Honduras. I'd played sixty-two games for Canada in my career and was beginning to seriously doubt whether all of the transatlantic flights and days spent training and playing for Canada, when I could have been resting, were worth it.

I wanted it all to be worth it, but it felt like a fool's pursuit. In my decade with the national team, we'd yet to accomplish anything significant. It was just disappointment after disappointment. It also put me at risk for injury—and I couldn't afford to miss out on club contracts because of an injury sustained while playing for a national team that many of my pro teammates mocked me for caring about.

Despite the doubt, my heart was still with the national team. I knew that we were better than the world believed. One day, I hoped, we would shock them all. And not by losing 8–1 to Honduras. One day.

The player of the year award was particularly important to me because of everything I'd had to overcome with my knee injury over the past year and a half. It was validation that all of the work I'd put in had paid off.

"To come back from that and have a good year of playing football at a high level and feeling very comfortable and playing without pain, that was the most important thing to me," I told the Canadian Press after accepting the 2012 player of the year award. "I wanted to enjoy football and be pain-free, and it's just getting better and better."

In my early thirties, I needed to be careful and strategic about where that adventure took place. When you hit that milestone age as an athlete, you think about the end of your career much more than before. Especially after going through my knee issues, I had a new appreciation for how fleeting and vulnerable my career was. For the first time, I had to consider that the next contract I signed could very well be my last.

Questions naturally arose about my uncertain future. My contract with PSV was set to expire that June. I already knew that I was leaving Eindhoven. I was ready. PSV offered me a contract to stay for another three years, but there were no guarantees that I'd play my position. Over three years with PSV, I spent half as a midfielder, and the rest of the time as a right back. As much as I had learned from adapting my game, I wanted to return to centre midfield.

It was nothing against the organization. PSV treated their players well, and they were always good to me. I loved my teammates. We'd even been reunited with Zanka, who'd joined PSV from FCK in 2012. I appreciated the offer PSV put on the table, but it was time to move on. I told PSV that my mind was set on leaving.

Sarah and I loved our time in Holland, but we were ready for the next adventure. We'd certainly miss the Netherlands though. The people in Eindhoven were wonderful. They were very polite. They kept to themselves and didn't really bother players in public. People knew who we were around town, and they were always very kind. The PSV fans showed me a great deal of respect. I wasn't a star player there, but they supported me. They respected the work that I put into battling on the pitch—my defensive efforts and the hunger that I had to win.

Of all the places that I'd played, PSV had the most impact on turning me into a player who was confident that I could play at any level in the world. Those three years were massive for my career. I felt ready to dominate games.

I'd planned to play at least another two seasons in Europe, preferably in England, and to then possibly end my career in Major League Soccer with one of the Canadian teams. But even if I was offered a designated player contract, which would pay more than the MLS maximum salary, I wasn't ready to return home yet.

"I'd still like to see if I can go to a higher league here in Europe," I told the Canadian Press.

♦

I went into the summer of 2013 unsure of where I was heading next. My agent at the time was Niclas Jensen, one of my former teammates from Copenhagen. We spoke about several possibilities for where I might land. My focus was on moving to the Premier League in England, or perhaps playing in Spain or Germany. Wherever I ended up, I wanted to play my position at centre midfield. That was very important to me. As the weeks passed, there were rumours of interest from teams like Stoke City and Fulham, but nothing concrete. Then Jensen called one day and told me he'd received interest from a club in Turkey called Beşiktaş.

The team was named for the region of Istanbul it played in, in the heart of Istanbul on the Bosporus Strait, which splits the city between the European and Asian sides. Beşiktaş is on the bustling European shore. Istanbul is famous for being the meeting point of the two continents.

The Beşiktaş region of the city is home to about 175,000 people, which is relatively small in a city of sixteen million. But it has huge significance in the region as a centre of business, education, and historical sites, as well as for its location along the Bosporus. The region is close to Taksim Square—a hub of nightlife, dining, and shopping—which most tourists would recognize.

The club had just completed its final season at the historic İnönü Stadium, which had opened in the late 1940s. Vodafone Arena, a brand-new world-class stadium that would seat 42,500 people, was under construction. At that time, Beşiktaş was probably the third biggest team in Istanbul—though it's since become bigger. The other two big teams in the area, Galatasaray and Fenerbahçe, shared a massive rivalry with Beşiktaş.

Slaven Bilić was hired as Beşiktaş's new coach that June and had been part of the team's conversations with me throughout our negotiations. He was an experienced coach who'd previously served at the helm of the Croatian national team. I was excited about the potential of playing for him. Bilić told me that he viewed me as an important piece in the middle for his club. Once again it was important for me to know that a coach viewed me as important to his plans, while playing my natural position, and it helped seal my belief that Beşiktaş was the right club for me. After our visit, Sarah and I knew that Istanbul was a city we could see our lives unfolding in. If Beşiktaş was really interested, I was ready to take that step.

But that July, as the PSV preseason began, I still wasn't certain of where I would end up. Negotiations with the club broke down several times. Bilić kept reviving them. He was pushing for me. I stayed in Holland, working with a trainer on my own while talks went on with Beşiktaş. It was a weird time; I was uncertain where I would play next. It wasn't clear if the offer from PSV was still on the table, so I was in limbo trying to carve out the best deal possible. We went back and forth with the club for five or six weeks before landing on a deal that worked for both sides.

I finally signed with Beşiktaş just a week before the Turkish Süper Lig season began. The deal was for a couple of years, and in truth I initially only envisioned staying that long. I had no idea whether there would be more soccer in my future beyond this contract. Everything beyond thirty is an unknown. Whatever the outcome, this was a huge step in my career—the beginning of the inevitable end.

I joined Beşiktaş in Austria where the team was playing one last friendly before the season. I ran through a couple of training sessions before my first match. Our opponents had travelled there on a bus from Albania and were exhausted, but we still struggled against them. We were down by one at the half, and Bilić blasted us during the break. It ended up being a memorable start though. I entered the match as a substitute in the second half and managed to score my first goal in a Beşiktaş uniform. It was a header off a corner kick, which tied the match at two goals each. We held on for the draw and returned to Istanbul feeling lukewarm about the result, though I was satisfied to have made an impact so early. It eased some of the pressure of joining a new club.

♦

When we arrived in Turkey in August 2013, we had no idea how pivotal the decision to move there would be. I didn't know what it meant to join a club like Beşiktaş or the impact it would have on the rest of my life. I didn't know that being a Black Eagle was something so unique and special. Sarah and I were happy about living in one of the world's most interesting cities. But in the beginning, it was just the start of a new adventure.

The very first person we met in this new chapter would become one of the most important people in our lives. Ali was waiting for us at the airport. He was a driver the club asked to help us get settled in Istanbul. He kindly obliged.

As we left Atatürk Airport into chaotic traffic, which we'd come to know well, Ali immediately made us feel at ease. He wanted to make sure that we knew how to navigate the quirks and avoid the traps of Istanbul.

From the moment we met, we knew that he was someone we could trust. In his mid-fifties, Ali carried a presence that was genuine and warm, like a loving, protective father. He spoke perfect English, which was very helpful because neither Sarah nor I knew a word of Turkish. As Ali welcomed us to Turkey, we had a sense that we'd both known this man for decades. He made us feel at ease. Ali treated us as though we were members of his own family. He was so protective of us. He'd put his own life on hold to make sure that we were comfortable.

Over the first few days, Ali—of course—took care of everything we needed to do to set up our lives. He helped us find our house. He helped us buy a car. He took us looking for furniture and other things we needed to start fresh in a new place. Ali negotiated every deal for us. He made sure we got the fair, local price for everything we bought—rather than the inflated price that foreigners were often charged. Without Ali, we would have been lost.

In those early days in Istanbul, we were strangers in a new place. When I signed with Beşiktaş, the fanbase knew very little about me. I was an under-the-radar signing in the Turkish Süper Lig. We'd walk through the busy streets of Istanbul's many vibrant neighbourhoods, and hardly anyone would notice us at all. Before I became known as a player for Beşiktaş, everyone we met in Turkey was kind to us. We felt welcome right away. The people were so genuine. They would do everything for us, making us feel like we were part of their community. It was such a warm experience.

We settled in a suburban neighbourhood called Acarkent, on the Asian side of Istanbul, about fifteen minutes from the Beşiktaş training grounds. Several of the Black Eagles players lived nearby, which helped us feel like we had a community around us. As in Eindhoven, we would end up hosting dinners and drinks with my teammates and their families often, which helped build a bond among us. It was a well-off neighbourhood with very large houses. We rented a five-storey home with an elevator in it. It had a heated pool too. It was everything we could possibly need. And it was *way* too big for us. It was just Sarah, me, and the two dogs. It was so big that we'd bicker over who would have to go upstairs to get the phone charger if one of us forgot it. It was *way too much* house for us.

On the pitch, I quickly learned that I'd stepped into something special.

Imagine this: you're standing in the stadium surrounded by fifty thousand people, and as soon as the game starts, they all start whistling. Every time your team touches the ball, the whistling gets louder. It's piercing. It's all you can hear, even as your teammates are yelling for the ball. The referee's whistle is completely useless. You try to play through it, but the frequency is overwhelming. Soon it's all that you can think about. A constant barrage on your eardrums.

The first time I stood on the pitch as a Black Kartal, which means Eagle, it caught me completely off guard. We played Trabzonspor, one of our biggest rivals, in the first game of the season. They are one of the four biggest teams in Turkey, along with us, Galatasaray, and Fenerbahçe. Any match between these clubs is treated like a derby. Those games in Istanbul are on another level. It's almost like the classic Celtic versus Rangers matches in Scotland. It feels like there is much more than a soccer match on the line. Coverage of the upcoming game is all over the television and in the press for a week before the match kicks off. There would be a buzz around the city. There is a lot of history behind these rivalries, which are regarded as among the most intense in the world.

Galatasaray and Fenerbahçe are famous for their Intercontinental Derby, a fierce showdown that has carried over from its origins in the divide between the social classes of the two fanbases. Galatasaray is based on the European side of Istanbul. The team has roots in an elite boys school and tended to be supported by wealthier fans. Fenerbahçe is on the Asian side of Istanbul and has been viewed as the club of the middle class. It is proudly associated with a thriving Anatolia, rising after the fall of the Ottoman Empire under the leadership of Mustafa Kemal Atatürk, who is celebrated as the founder of modern Turkey. Both teams dominated Turkish football through the 1920s and 1930s, which fuelled the rivalry between the two. Beşiktaş's rivalry with Galatasaray and

Fenerbahçe grew over time. The club was founded in 1903, but it was less dominant than its crosstown counterparts until the late 1930s and early 1940s, when it won five straight Istanbul League championships.

♦

During my first season in 2013, Beşiktaş played out of Atatürk Olympic Stadium, while Vodafone Arena was being completed. The Olympic stadium seats seventy thousand people, the second-largest-capacity stadium in the country. In the western part of the suburban district of Başakşehir, it was about a forty-five-minute drive from Beşiktaş, the area in central Istanbul where we were based. For our games, our team bus carried us from the Beşiktaş training grounds to the Olympic stadium. Cars would honk and fans would wave Beşiktaş flags out their windows and sunroofs.

The stadium was always packed for a Beşiktaş game—even if it was the Olympic stadium that seats seventy thousand people. There were so many fans. From the moment we got on the bus, arrived at the stadium, and ran out to the pitch for warmups, the atmosphere was incredible. The stadium was full long before kickoff. I wasn't used to that. In other places in Europe, fans slowly come in during warmup, filling in right before the game starts. In Istanbul, it was packed. You feel the energy in the atmosphere. It was unbelievable. Beşiktaş fans were once deemed the loudest fans in the world, when the stadium was measured at 132 decibels.

That first game was electric. When we scored our first goal, the stadium erupted. It was unbelievable. I'd witnessed glimpses of that kind of energy playing in Central American countries like Honduras and El Salvador. Those were wild places to be a visiting team. But this was next level. I'd never seen the kind of intimidating organized chaos of a soccer match in Istanbul. Luckily it was our home fans, so the whistles weren't directed at us.

The whistling is a tradition for every fanbase in the Turkish Süper Lig. In all the stadiums I've played in around the world, there really is nothing like the Turkish whistle. When that piercing noise is directed at you, it's a completely different level of distraction and intimidation. Nothing can compare to it. *Nothing.*

◆

A few matches after my first game, we faced Galatasaray, arguably our biggest cross-town rivals, and the whistling reached another level—powered by decades of animosity that I was only beginning to understand. It was as though our fans were trying to drive Galatasaray to forfeit the match because the agony of playing against us at home was too much for them to handle. Some visiting players can't take the relentless onslaught of the high-pitched symphony.

During a Champions League match, a player on RB Leipzig, a German club, had to come out at half; he told his coach that he couldn't handle the noise. It was driving him crazy, and he couldn't do it anymore. His ears were ringing so badly that he couldn't play the final forty-five minutes. The story came out in the press later, which only encouraged our fans to do it even more.

I quickly learned that Turkish fans are some of the most passionate, animated, and dedicated fans in the world. They are right up there with the fans you can find in South American countries, like Argentina. In the Eredivisie, it sometimes felt like fans were watching the news rather than a football match. It was so proper and sophisticated. But at a game in Turkey, the energy is contagious. It overtakes you. Sarah, who was never a football fan, found herself standing in the crowd for Beşiktaş games screaming like a hooligan.

Thankfully the matches were much more civil than they had been before I came. In the past, it was really bad. During my first season with Beşiktaş, visiting fans weren't allowed in the home team's stadium. It used to be common for fights to break out in the stands or in front of the stadium before a derby match between rivals. The Çarşi ultras, a Beşiktaş fan group, has been part of social resistance movements since it was founded in the 1980s. They have demonstrated against tyranny and war and mobilized support for humanitarian aid. Minorities like the Kurds and Alevis are known to strongly identify with the club as well.

In recent years, the league started doing a better job of keeping the fans separate, so the two sides don't meet each other before the games unless they've deliberately planned something. When they are allowed to attend a match, away supporters have to get there hours before the home fans start coming in. They get escorted to their section with police all around, they're blocked off, they can't move. Maybe three, four hours before the game, and it's the same after the game. The fans have to wait for the opposing fans to clear out before they can leave. Because otherwise it would be a problem. But they'll be on the streets individually. Some of them go to the same schools. They live in the same city. And everything is fine. It's only when the groups come together that it gets dangerous.

◆

We were a decent team that year, but no one expected us to win a championship. We were led by a couple big time players like Hugo Almeida and Manuel Fernandes, both members of the Portuguese national team. Fernandes was one of the most talented players I'd ever play beside in the middle. Strong and unshakable on the ball, he was a central midfielder as well. Opponents couldn't take the ball off the guy. He was very gifted and played with a lot of quality. Tomáš Sivok was another excellent player for us at centre back. He was the captain of the Czech national team for a few years and had been a big player with Beşiktaş for five or six years before I got there. Julien Escudé was a veteran centre back who had played with Sevilla and Ajax before joining Beşiktaş the season before I arrived. He brought experience to our back line. Tolga Zengin, our keeper, signed the same season with me after a decade with Trabzonspor. He was a beloved Süper Lig veteran, who would become our captain the following year. We also had several talented young Turkish players like Olcay Şahan, Oğuzhan Özyakup, and Gökhan Töre.

I don't think that fans knew what to expect of me when I arrived, but they quickly came to appreciate what I brought to the club. I was viewed as a utility player who could play different roles, like right back or defensive midfielder. Through that first year, I played more right back than I'd anticipated when I signed, mainly because of injuries. That was where my team needed me most. I understood that we were building something, and it would take time. I believed in the vision Bilić had for our club and trusted in the vision he had for my role.

The year was a bit of a rebuild for the organization, with a lot of new faces under a new coach. Bilić really had an impact on the way the team played. He wanted us to play a tight possession-focused game, with lots of flair. He spoke English and provided a lot of detailed feedback. He was a real players coach. I enjoyed his coaching style. But this wasn't a championship team. Not quite yet. We didn't have enough quality and experience to win a title. That was one thing I'd learned from my time with Copenhagen. Young talent usually isn't enough alone, and quality builds with time. As the season went on, we started clicking and showed our potential.

We finished third in the league, which was a decent result for the team we had. There was lots of promise for what lay ahead. But I don't think even the most ardent Beşiktaş supporters could have predicted how quickly we'd get there.

24

Black Eagles

It seems like everyone you meet in Istanbul has a football team that they support. It's often the team of their grandparents, their parents—a tradition passed down to them. You're born into it. I can't tell you the number of times I was told someone's family history as football fans. The moment they recognize you as a football player, they stop you on the street and tell you all about it. Not just that they love your team, but *why* they love your team—what it means to them.

So what does it mean to be a Black Eagle? I don't think that I fully understood that until my second season with Beşiktaş, when I found myself standing in another one of the world's most famous stadiums playing in the Europa League and hearing our fans' cheers take on the home crowd.

Vodafone Arena was still under construction during my second year in Istanbul, the 2014–15 season. Rather than play all our home matches out of the Olympic stadium, we played part of our schedule there and the rest in half a dozen stadiums around Istanbul and across Turkey. Some of our home games were more than an hour-long flight away. We'd get there, and the stadium would be packed with our fans.

I mean, completely full of Black Eagles supporters. I couldn't believe it. It's not something that I'd experienced when I played in Holland, Denmark, or Sweden where most of your fans are in the city you represent. There might be some fans dedicated enough to travel, but if we had maybe one thousand fans at an away game with any of those clubs, it was considered a very good turnout.

But Beşiktaş had fans all over Turkey.

Every single time we arrived at an airport, the fans were there waiting for us, waving, lighting flares, and singing songs. I don't mean a small group of diehards; there was always a massive, loud crowd of people. It was almost like we'd won the championship—just by arriving. I'd never seen or heard anything like it before. The first couple times I experienced it, I didn't believe that it would happen again. But everywhere we went, the fans showed up and supported us. I used to take videos of the scene because it was so surreal.

That year, we added several players who'd become key pieces for us. Hugo Almeida and Manuel Fernandes left in the off-season, but the team moved quickly to fill the gap in talent they left behind. The biggest move was signing Demba Ba—a French striker who'd come to fame playing in the Premier League with West Ham, Newcastle, and Chelsea. When someone like Demba, who has had a successful career in the Premier League, signs with your team, the football world notices. All of our fans were ecstatic when the signing was announced.

Demba was one of the best strikers I'd ever played with. The way that he could score goals, finishing in different ways inside and outside the box was remarkable. The stuff I watched him do in training was jaw-dropping. He could create something out of nothing, in a way that reminded me of Thierry Henry. Demba could take on anyone one-on-one. He was very strong, so he could play with his back towards goal and then turn to create a chance for himself and finish. In the open field, you could give him the ball anywhere on the pitch, and he was comfortable receiving it. You don't see many strikers like that. He could get past one or two players, make a pass, and continue to go forward. Anytime I had the ball, I knew that I could connect with him. If I was in tight space, he was always there to help, providing an option. If I could give one piece of advice to young footballers, I'd say watch video of Demba Ba. Watch how he moves without the ball and puts himself in position to score. He's one of the best I've seen.

But even more than Demba's incredible football ability, I was impressed that he was a down-to-earth humble guy, despite his star power. Some top players are unapproachable, but Demba was never like that. He was easy to talk to and very smart. He was also very funny. Demba always had a story to tell—and it always ended with everyone around him cracking up. He was a guy that everyone wanted to be around. He's one of the teammates that I became very close with, and our families remain tight to this day.

In August 2014, we met Arsenal in the qualifying round for the Champions League. I was injured for the first leg of our home-and-away playoff against the Premier League giants. At home, the fans showed up ready to take on the world. Whenever Beşiktaş plays against one of the larger European clubs, our fans want to show that they are the bigger and better fans. At the Atatürk Olympic Stadium, seventy thousand fans let Arsenal know exactly how they felt. The match ended in a scoreless draw. We travelled to London the following week for the second leg of our meeting with Arsenal, at Emirates Stadium. Our fans travelled too. They filled the away section and large parts of the iconic venue, making sure that every Arsenal fan knew they were in danger of being drowned out at home.

We played very well, earning a chance to go in front early on, but we couldn't take advantage. We were right in the game though. I'd returned from my injury in time to rejoin the team. Bilić was still using me in a utility, moving me from left back or right back to midfield depending on our team's needs against our opponent. I understood that I had to accept that role for the team.

But at Emirates, I played in the midfield. It was one of my best matches in a Beşiktaş uniform. I won balls, broke up the Arsenal attack, kept us in possession, and helped advance us into good positions all match. We had several chances but fell 1–0.

After the match, legendary Arsenal coach Arsène Wenger noted my play. "The best player on Beşiktaş," he said, "I was impressed by Hutchinson."

I'd be lying to you if I said that I wasn't star-struck when Wenger said that. The man is a soccer icon. I often wonder why he said that. I remember playing a very simple game that match. I moved the ball well. I controlled the pace of play. But I didn't score a goal or even have any chances. Hearing those words from Wenger underscored what I had learned from my father as a boy: that football was about getting the details right and learning to see the future—knowing where the ball is going or needs to go before it gets there. Being aware of your strengths and perfecting them can help you go a long way.

"The best is still to come," I remember telling myself, after learning what Wenger had said.

That fall, Beşiktaş was all about putting ourselves on the map in Europe.

We entered the UEFA Europa League group stage in September, in a pool alongside Tottenham Hotspur, Asteras Tripoli, and Partizan. Everything clicked for us that fall. We improved drastically with the addition of José Sosa, who came from Atletico Madrid at the end of August. Sosa was a big addition, replacing what we had lost in Manuel Fernandes. He brought a lot of experience to our midfield; he had played for clubs like Bayern Munich and Napoli and was a member of Argentina's national team. He was a very intelligent player, hardworking, and unafraid to do the work both ways. A lot of players in his position only want to attack, but Sosa did everything. When the team was defending he always came back into position and helped the team recover the ball. His addition that January helped us find our rhythm and playing style. He was very influential in the way we played.

In early October, we drew Hotspur at ones, again shocking the London crowd with our Turkish turnout. By the time we faced Tottenham again that December, we were undefeated with three draws and two wins in our pool. Once again, the Black Eagles fans brought out their best performance against a big Premier League team. We edged them out 1–0, securing top spot in the group.

The win set us up to meet Liverpool in the round of thirty-two.

As the new year turned, Istanbul buzzed in anticipation of our meeting with the storied franchise. I was as excited and nervous as I'd ever been. I knew that 2015 would be the biggest year of my life. But it had little to do with football.

I was about to become a father. Sarah was pregnant with our first child, who was due in April. Before starting our family together, Sarah and I agreed that we needed to make our relationship official. I'd planned the proposal for months. I had a ring made in Holland, which was delivered to me in Turkey. It was an engagement band, because I knew she'd want to pick out her own wedding ring with a diamond. I wasn't about to mess that up.

It was a miracle that Sarah didn't learn about the ring.

Whenever we travelled, she'd always pack all our bags. But she didn't have a clue that I was planning to propose when we flew to the Maldives that January during the league's winter break. To her, it was the annual trip that we always went on. All of her friends knew what was up, but none of them gave it away.

The day I planned to propose in the Maldives, I kept bugging Sarah to get a manicure. She kept looking at me as if I was crazy, but I insisted that she needed to do something nice for herself. I told her that we were going to get dressed up and go for a nice dinner that evening. I'm not sure how she didn't figure something was up right then, but thankfully my insistence didn't ruin the surprise.

That evening, we took a boat from the resort our island was on to a private island, where we were met by a chef and a waiter. There was a table set up for us on the beach, with flowers on it. As we sat down, Sarah still didn't have a clue. It wasn't something that we'd ever really discussed, even though getting married—making this life together official in some way—was important to both of us.

Sarah was completely surprised when I proposed. It was a perfect moment, in the sand next to the ocean, just the two of us. Even the photographer I'd hired to be on the island somehow missed the moment. I don't know where he was, but he showed up after the proposal, so we had to pretend to do it over again, so we had the pictures to show everyone.

◆

We returned to Istanbul with the home-and-away series with Liverpool on the horizon. Of all the big European clubs that we could have matched up against, Beşiktaş fans relished a battle with Liverpool the most. In 2007, the club had been embarrassed 8–0 by Liverpool in the Champions League, and Beşiktaş fans have long memories. That loss was talked about a lot. Our fans wanted revenge.

We travelled to Anfield for our first match in the series, another surreal visit to one of the game's most storied venues. Once again, our fans showed up, making sure Liverpool fans knew that they were no match for the siyah beyaz, or "black and whites" as the team is often called. But we were outmatched on the pitch, maintaining only 36 percent possession and earning a single shot—a clean break by Demba Ba that was turned aside by Simon Mignolet. Still, we held on, keeping the match scoreless until Mario Balotelli scored on a penalty in the eighty-fifth minute. The 1–0 loss sent us back to Istanbul needing a win to survive.

A week later, the Atatürk Olympic Stadium was louder than I'd ever heard it. There were more than 63,000 fans in the building.

We played well, holding a scoreless draw. As the game ticked on, I wasn't sure if we had it in us to score a goal. Liverpool could settle for the tie and advance. But in the seventy-second minute, Tolgay Arslan—a German midfielder who'd signed with us a few weeks earlier—became an instant Beşiktaş hero when he took a pass from Ba at the top of the box and scored an unbelievable banger with his left foot, which curled beyond Mignolet's diving reach.

The stadium went wild. It was the most exciting goal I'd ever experienced. It was everything—the game, the play, the fans. It was one of those moments that I knew I'd always be able to feel. Our bench rushed the pitch. The fans leaped up and down in unison. It sounded like thunder.

We led 1–0 at the end of regulation, which meant we were tied on aggregate. Extra time solved nothing, so the series would be decided by penalties. I was set to kick fourth.

I was nervous. I watched everyone take their penalties, paying attention to what the keeper was doing. I had to decide which side I would go to. Should I go to my right? Should I go to my left? Each team scored on the first three shots. Then it was my turn. I walked from half up the ball, trying to stay cool. But I was a mess. Of course I was. We were playing against Liverpool in a Europa game, and the hope of an entire stadium rested on my shoulders. I tried to stay calm, but it was no use. I made up my mind. I lined up and felt the stadium go quiet. There was probably still a lot of noise, but I couldn't hear a thing. All I could sense was the pounding panic of my heart. I lined up the ball, took a breath, and moved to shoot. The ball went high and to the right above the keeper's reach. I felt a rush of adrenaline and relief. My mind turned the volume back on, and I heard the crowd's long, booming thunder. I had scored the biggest goal of my life. I'd never felt more relieved.

As my father always told me, when you pick your spot, never second-guess it. Just shoot your shot.

A few moments later, I was back at half watching Arslan score our fifth goal, after Liverpool had answered mine. The match came down to one more chance for Liverpool—and one chance for our keeper Cenk Gönen to secure one the biggest wins in Beşiktaş history. We put our hands on each other's shoulders and leaned forward, watching Dejan Lovren's shot sail over the top bar.

We sprinted forward towards Gönen. I swung my arms in circles as I sprinted. It was like we were little kids again. We'd just beat Liverpool. It was unbelievable. The magnitude felt incomprehensible—knowing not only what that moment meant to me but to every fan making that building shake. It was pure joy. I looked around at the fans, the coaching staff, the trainers—everyone—watching that joy explode. I'd never experienced anything like it before.

♦

That was when I first understood what it meant to be a Black Eagle. This was more than a win over a big club. This was about generations— about grandfathers, fathers, and sons—about a passion and belief that is passed on. It was about family. It felt like the kind of moment I'd been chasing my entire career. It was a feeling that is very difficult to describe, but you know it as soon as it arrives, and it becomes part of who you are. In that moment, you become part of something bigger.

A few weeks later, Sarah and I went to the Municipal Council of Istanbul—which is like a city hall—to get married. Mr. Ali, as we called him, came with us to be our witness. Fans noticed that we were there and started taking pictures of us. Sarah was sitting down at the time. She was seven months pregnant, but nobody knew, which was uncomfortable because Turkey is a majority Muslim country and people are very conservative. People usually get married before they get pregnant, not after. But there were at least a dozen people sitting in front of us, so we didn't really have anywhere else to go.

◆

Life had changed considerably since we'd first arrived in the city. After a season with Beşiktaş, it was difficult to go out in Istanbul without being noticed. Sarah was uncomfortable with the cameras that followed us. She is not interested in being famous. She'd much rather remain anonymous, so she was never into the attention we'd get in public—although she knew that with the fans, it came from a genuine place. When we were at a friend's house in Germany, a few people recognized us as we arrived. A few minutes later, a large group of kids were knocking on the door, asking for an autograph. We'd be walking down the street in places like Paris and Amsterdam and be stopped by Turkish football fans.

"How do they even recognize you here?" Sarah said.

It was very strange for me too.

Before playing with Beşiktaş, it was very rare to be recognized by fans for Copenhagen or PSV when we weren't in Denmark or Holland. But Beşiktaş fans—and even fans of the Süper Lig, regardless of the team they supported—could identify a player anywhere. That's how much the game meant to them.

As we waited at the Municipal Council that day, word spread through the building that we were there, and more people came to take photos and videos. Sarah politely asked them to stop, knowing that people would be shocked when they saw that she was pregnant. When it was our turn to see the official, she stood up with her round belly. She was embarrassed, but it wasn't as big of a deal as we'd worried about. Everyone was so gracious to us.

Sarah and I said our vows before the judge. Mr. Ali's phone rang as he signed to be our witness, and he fumbled to turn it off quickly. We all laughed. We were happy to be married—to have that officially done. But it didn't feel entirely complete for either of us. My parents, sister, brother, and friends were back home in Canada. Sarah's brother wasn't able to be with us, even though he was very close to both of us. She wished that her father could be, too, but he was still a long way from accepting our relationship. Sarah's father Sifollah knew that she was pregnant, but they didn't speak about who the father was. They didn't talk about it all. He didn't want to have that conversation.

We planned on having a proper wedding one day, but life got busy—and filled with kids—so it never happened. And neither of us needed a big party anyway. Aside from the absence of our loved ones, everything was perfect exactly as it was. That day in Istanbul, surrounded by Black Eagles fans taking photos and Mr. Ali by our side, under Turkish law, Sarah and I made our family official.

Our son Noah was born that April. When Sarah went into labour, Ali stayed at the hospital with us. He was there from eight in the morning to eleven in the evening, when he went back to the house to help fix up the nursery. Noah arrived in the middle of the night. I looked into his tiny eyes and teared up. It was the most magical moment of my life. When I walked out of the hospital room, Ali was there to greet me. He'd become like family to us. He was the only family with us at the time. Through the years to come, Sarah would often refer to Ali as her guardian angel. She had never met anyone like him before. At times, he would become like a grandfather to her. At other times, he was her therapist. Ali was one of Sarah's closest friends. It was supposed to be a one-day arrangement, just to help get us settled when we first arrived in a new country, but Ali still hasn't gotten rid of us. He became family for life.

The wonderful thing about families is that they grow with you— and often in unexpected ways. When Sarah and I arrived in Istanbul, we didn't know that the city would become as much of a home to us as Brampton or Copenhagen. We didn't know the people we'd meet in this new place would hold a precious place in our lives. It was supposed to be another stop in this beautiful dream. But standing there, holding baby Noah, surrounded by love, we knew this was the place where our greatest dreams would unfold.

25

A New Era

Vodafone Arena sat on the edge of the Bosporus Strait, just beyond the Dolmabahçe Palace, the ornate baroque and rococo revival master-piece where the sultans of the Ottoman Empire lived from the mid-nineteenth century to the abolishment of the caliphate in 1924. Beşiktaş's new home was a modern jewel in a bustling commercial district in the heart of Istanbul. The new stadium stood on the site of Beşiktaş's former home, İnönü Stadium, which had been built on the old palace's stable grounds in the 1940s. For seven decades, İnönü Stadium cradled the passion of Beşiktaş fans, who passed the fervour through generations. The old stadium's stone walls and pillars were incorporated into the new structure, paying tribute to the team's past.

For almost the entirety of my first three seasons in Turkey, Beşiktaş didn't have a proper home. We were a travelling team, finding our fans wherever we went. They'd filled the Atatürk Olympic Stadium and venues across Turkey. They'd flooded Anfield, Emirates, and White Hart Lane. Their tireless passion provided a sense of pride for our club—but until the spring of 2016, we had no consistent place to hold it. After all that invading, it was time for a home to defend. When it was finally time to open the new stadium, our team was ready to give Beşiktaş fans a new chapter in its long history.

The 2015–16 season brought a lot of necessary change to the club, which had improved drastically since I'd first arrived. Our coach Slaven Bilić left at the end of the 2015 season to become manager of West Ham United, his former club. He was replaced by Şenol Güneş, a beloved Turkish coach who had guided the country's national team to a third-place finish at the 2002 World Cup. Güneş had been a goal-keeper for Trabzonspor and later became the club's manager. The team would later dedicate its stadium to Güneş.

I was familiar with Güneş because he'd asked me to join Trabzonspor when I was still with Copenhagen. He was an intelligent coach who wanted his team to play an up-tempo game, which I liked.

That season, my good friend Demba Ba departed for a stint in China. His absence threatened to make us much weaker on the attack, but the team filled the void by bringing in veteran striker Mario Gómez, on a loan from Fiorentina. Gómez picked up right where Ba left off.

Ricardo Quaresma, a Portuguese international who'd played two seasons with Beşiktaş previously, returned after a season with Porto. He was playing at the top of his game at the time. We also added centre back Rhodolfo, another Brazilian.

At midfield I paired with Oğuzhan Özyakup, who was an intelli-gent, creative playmaker who was very comfortable in position, and could make a killer pass. We worked well together, putting up very good passing accuracy numbers and dictating the tempo of the game all season. We had a lot of fun playing together that year.

◆

Things clicked for us early on. We dominated games in the pre-season, in ways that we hadn't in the past. That gave us confidence, and we continued to build. Once the season started, we picked up a couple big wins in our first few games, playing really good football. We were flying.

Under Güneş, we played a quick, flowing brand of football. We always worked on that in our training sessions—building from the back, playing the ball quickly when there was pressure on us. We played stringent defence, but we also had a strong attack. With Gómez up front, we had a striker who could finish with world-class quality. He was the definition of clinical. He scored some wonderful goals that season, leading the entire league with twenty-eight. There was only one or two touches before we moved the ball. We didn't want to dwell on it and allow our opponents to close in, so the ball was always zipping around. After bringing in the right players for two years, we had the personnel to play that style. It was a very attractive brand of football—fun to watch and fun to play. You could almost liken it to tiki-taka football that Barcelona played, because there was a lot of short combination football, with lots of triangles and tons of movement.

The fans loved to watch us play. The Turkish game is fast-paced. It's very much up and down. In my first couple seasons, it took some time to adjust because the game never really slows down. It was rare to just possess the ball, knocking it around. The fans want to see goals. Often if you slow the tempo of the game down, by making a back pass or playing it back to the keeper, they'd be on us, because they wanted us to push forward. They want you to score a goal. Often when a game is scoreless for 10–15 min you would hear the fans scream Kartal! Goal! Goal! Goal!

In other countries, like Spain or Holland, fans appreciated that by playing it back, you get out of pressure. Imagine you're in one part of the pitch and there's a lot of pressure on you. To get out of that, you have to go back to the keeper, so you can go around the other way and outmanoeuvre the defence. In Turkey, you'd almost hear the crowd moaning, "Why isn't he going forward?" To return to the checkers and chess analogy, under Güneş we played speed chess—a fast-paced but cerebral style. And Beşiktaş fans loved it, because we moved the ball constantly and it led to a lot of chances.

◆

By the winter break, we sat atop the table and were well on our way to claiming the first league championship for Beşiktaş since the 2008–09 season. We carried a confidence that comes with knowing that you are the better team on the pitch. I never doubted that. We had the quality and connection that it takes to win a championship.

It was a fun time in my career. We had great fans. We were winning. And I was playing the best football of my life. I was sharp. I felt like I could control the game a lot more than I could before. I'd reached a perfect moment in my career: I had the experience to stay calm and execute, and I still had the speed and athleticism to stay a step ahead. I'd reached a peak—but I didn't know how long it would last before I descended to the far side of my career.

Beşiktaş fans were good to me. Turkish fans, like most fans, gravitate more towards the flashier players. But through my first few seasons with the club, they came to appreciate the way I played the game. They called me Octopus, which is probably one of the stranger nicknames out there. I'm not sure exactly how it started, but it had to do with my long legs and the way I seemed to be everywhere, by breaking up the opponents' attack and by sticking my foot in to win balls. Essentially, I everywhere with my body—playing as though I had eight legs, instead of two. The fans had started to view me as one of their own, rather than a player who was passing through, which happened often.

I still had another year on my contract and I was very happy. My wife loved every moment of it as well. We'd started our family in Istanbul. Noah was still an infant, and our second child was due in August 2016. We'd become very comfortable in Istanbul and had no intentions of leaving.

When we had first arrived in Turkey, Sarah and I took language classes to learn as much Turkish as we could. The language was much easier for Sarah than for me. She already spoke several languages, and there are some similarities between Farsi and Turkish, which helped her. I was hopeless. I had never been very good with new languages, and Turkish wasn't something you could easily pick up without the foundation of speaking multiple languages. It was kind of a doomed endeavour for me from the start.

With football being such an international sport, you're almost always on a team with someone who doesn't speak the same language as you. But that never matters on the pitch. Everyone speaks the same language in the run of play. It's universal.

Off the pitch, it isn't quite as easy. Many of my teammates with Beşiktaş didn't speak English at all. Under league rules, we were allowed six non-Turkish players on the roster. And all the foreign players, more or less, spoke English. There were several Spanish and Latino players on the team in my first few years there. There were also a few French guys. Our locker room was like a United Nations meeting. Several Turkish players couldn't speak English at all, so there was no way for me to communicate with them effectively. A fair amount of people working for the team spoke English, but a lot of them didn't. The team's chefs or massage therapist, positions like that, didn't speak English. But the team had translators who helped a lot. Bilić was fluent in English. But Güneş didn't speak a word of it. So everything was done through translators.

Beşiktaş had two translators. One worked in French and Spanish, and one worked in English. During a session, we'd be hearing voices all over the place. In Turkey, the translator is there all the time. During a game, anywhere the coach goes on the side of the pitch, a translator is nearby. He calls over a player; the translator is running to stand next to them to get the message to the player. But sometimes the messages don't come across as intended, or a player doesn't get what they need out of a conversation. Some of it gets lost in translation; the messages aren't delivered as powerfully as the coach intended. There were a lot of times when I would miss what the coach was trying to make me understand. I can't imagine how hard it would be to coach in a place like that: you're trying to get your message across while other voices are constantly echoing every word you say in what would sound like gibberish to your ear. But that's the only option on a team with that many players from all over.

Under Güneş, most of our tactical instruction was done on the pitch. The coach would physically show us where we needed to be, the runs we needed to make, and how the team needed to move as a whole. We were able to catch on by watching where everyone else was moving on the pitch. Then hopefully a few players could also help walk us through what we hadn't picked up on. The trick was to decipher what we could and then to not be afraid to ask for more detail through the translators about what we didn't understand.

◆

In February 2016, in the final stretch of the season, our team became even stronger when we signed Marcelo, my old teammate from PSV, on a loan from Hannover 96. We'd spent three years playing together and becoming good friends. Marcelo spent two and a half seasons in the Bundesliga when I moved to Turkey, before joining us with Beşiktaş. I spoke with him before he signed, but I don't think I played much of a role in recruiting him. Marcelo had already made up his mind about joining us in Istanbul.

In the second half of the season, we learned that Vodafone Stadium would be ready for the final few games. If we could hold on, there was a good chance we'd open the new facility while putting the final touches on the championship.

When we met Bursaspor for the inaugural match at Vodafone, on April 9, we were well enough ahead in the standings to be confident in our chances to win it all. The team was playing unbelievable football. We were playing for a championship. Everything came together at exactly the right time.

I remember walking into the stadium and feeling excited for what lay ahead. It was the best feeling. We'd been waiting for that stadium for so long. Everything was top-notch. The location was breathtaking, with a view out over the Bosporus. There were 42,000 white and black seats, creating a pattern across the sidelines that spelled out the team's name. The pitch was immaculate. And we'd be surrounded by our fans in our new home. Seven decades of history were in those seats—generations of family history being carried to start something new.

The game was sold out, and thousands of fans gathered outside the arena to be near the opening match. They were as loud as always, but their cheers and whistles seemed to carry a new weight. This was their home—their place to defend.

Gómez scored two goals, and Alexis—our Spanish defender—scored another as we held on for a 3–2 win over Bursaspor. When the final whistle blew, we rushed the pitch as though we'd won the championship. With this win, the title was pretty much secure. The grand opening of the new stadium created the perfect opportunity to celebrate. Our fans jumped and cheered and wept in the stands. We knew the title was ours. The thousands of fans outside turned the chaos into a party. Fans partied around Vodafone Arena. Some fans climbed lampposts and hydro poles, waving Beşiktaş flags.

The scene outside continued to grow, and groups of people were hit with tear gas and water cannons by the police to disperse the crowd. The overreaction was probably the result of the heightened security anxiety that gripped the country at the time. A series of recent terrorist attacks had rocked the country. In July 2015, at least thirty people were killed and nearly one hundred were wounded after an explosion in Suruç, on Turkey's southeastern border with Syria. The next month, a bomb attack on a police station in Istanbul injured five police officers and a civilian. In October, a suicide bomber attacked a peace rally in Ankara, the Turkish capital, killing one hundred people. Another suicide bomber blew himself up near the Blue Mosque in January 2016, killing ten tourists. In February, a blast in Ankara hit a convoy of buses filled with soldiers as it sat at a traffic light. Twenty-eight people were killed and more than sixty were wounded. In March, a car packed with explosives blew up in a public square in Ankara, killing thirty-seven people; a Kurdish military group known as the Kurdistan Freedom Hawks claimed responsibility for that attack. That month, a suicide bomber killed five people on İstiklal Avenue, a famous shopping district near Taksim Square. Several of the attacks were claimed by or said to be committed by the Islamic State of Iraq and Syria—better known as ISIS—which had been terrorizing the region for several years.

The celebrations that continued throughout the season's remaining games stood in defiance of that violence and turmoil. Football provided an escape and a common ground, as it does for so many fans around the world.

The matches were a formality and an excuse to gather and celebrate with our fans. It was incredible. I'll never forget it. I'd never been part of something approaching that kind of sustained joy. We officially secured the championship on May 15, 2016, with a 3–1 win over Osmanlıspor at Vodafone Arena. We'd finished with seventy-nine points, five points ahead of Fenerbahçe, to secure the top spot. Another wild crowd celebrated inside and outside the stadium.

After each championship, there is a parade, as with sports in North America. But Turkey takes it to another level. For our official celebration as a team, we rode a massive yacht down the Bosporus. We were followed by hundreds of smaller yachts packed with fans, who partied alongside of us. It usually took about fifteen minutes from where our boat docked to reach the stadium, but the streets were so packed that it took nearly half an hour. I'd never seen anything like it before. When we arrived at Vodafone, the stadium was full. We carried the trophy onto the pitch and hoisted it for our fans. The new building thundered and rocked. We were stood on top of the Turkish Süper Lig, the wildest and most passionate league in the world.

26

Martyrs' Hill

It had been a demoralizing few years for the Canada national team, since our embarrassing loss to Honduras during the World Cup qualifiers in 2012. Our coach, Stephen Hart, was let go shortly after that defeat. We had a series of interim coaches as the federation scrambled to find a new vision for our national team. Dwayne De Rosario, our all-time leading scorer, played his final game with the national program in January 2015. Julian de Guzman had recently become the most capped player in the team's history, surpassing Paul Stalteri who'd retired in 2013. But de Guzman was also on his way out. We had promising young talent in players like Junior Hoilett, Doneil Henry, and Cyle Larin—all Brampton boys. But we still didn't have the depth we needed to be a real threat at the international level, let alone to reach the final stages of Concacaf to qualify for the World Cup.

At the time, I wasn't sure how many years I had left with the national team. It was a period of transition and uncertainty. At thirty-three years old, I believed I only had one World Cup cycle left in me. I intended to be there through the 2018 World Cup qualifiers, which would continue that September. The outcome would dictate my future.

Shortly after the Beşiktaş championship season ended, Sarah, Noah, and I travelled to Bahamas for a vacation and then to Canada to visit with my family.

It was nice to be home again—especially with Noah. By now, most of my lifelong friends had also started families of their own. Being away for so long meant that I wasn't able to be around for some of the biggest moments in their lives, though we'd done very well to stay close despite the distance between us. It was great to see Haldon and Toyaa too. I felt fortunate to have siblings that I was so close with, and who cheered for and supported me more than anyone. And now that I was a father, I was able to appreciate what my own parents had given me in my life. Being home with them, seeing their joy as grandparents to our little boy meant the world to me.

As it always does, the end of our visit came too soon. I had to return to Istanbul for training camp and Sarah was due with our second child in August. We said our goodbyes once more. But when we checked in at Pearson International Airport, we were told that the doctor's clearance we'd received in Istanbul for Sarah to fly in her third trimester wasn't valid in Canada. We weren't allowed to fly without approval from a Canadian doctor. We couldn't believe it. Our flight to Istanbul took off without us, while we rushed back to Brampton to find a doctor to let us leave the country. We went to the hospital near my parents' home, but we were told they couldn't help us. We visited a walk-in clinic where we were again denied. It looked as though we were stuck. As we continued to search for a doctor to give us approval, we started making plans for Sarah and Noah to remain in Canada until the baby was born. I'd have to return for training camp and the start of the season. I always missed home, but I knew I had to leave. It was a nightmare until we finally found a doctor at a walk-in clinic who confirmed that it was safe for Sarah to fly.

We booked the first possible flight out of Toronto heading to Istanbul the next day—June 28, 2016. We landed at Atatürk Airport around four p.m., disembarked at the international terminal, collected our luggage, and met our driver. A few hours later, a friend texted me, concerned that we were still at the airport. Two gunmen armed with automatic weapons and explosive belts had approached the security checkpoint at terminal two, the international wing, and opened fire. As police returned fire, both attackers detonated the bombs strapped around their waists. A third attacker set off an explosion in the parking lot across the street from the terminal. At the end of the horror, forty-five innocent people were killed in the attack. Another 230 people were injured. It was the sixth attack in Turkey since October. In early June, a car bomb had destroyed a police vehicle as it idled near a tourist district in Istanbul, killing eleven people and wounding dozens more, adding to the devasting tally.

It was a frightening time—scary for anyone living in Turkey and heartbreaking for anyone who loved the country and its people. After three years with Beşiktaş, we'd come to know and love this place as much as we loved Canada or Denmark. We felt fortunate to have missed the violence at Atatürk Airport; it was close enough to feel its chilling reality.

Life carried on in Istanbul, as it does in a city that large and important. The spirit of the Turkish people couldn't be diminished by violence, even if it created a heightened concern. Everything calmed down after a few days. We were assured that there was little risk of anything else happening. But the violence shook Istanbul. It was impossible not to feel uneasy.

Training camp opened in July, as our team prepared to defend our championship in the shadow of the ongoing tension across Turkey.

I'd stayed late after training to get some extra work in on July 15, when I received another worrying text from a friend.

"Something is going on with the military," he wrote. "You should get home right away."

I rushed to my car without any further information. I drove across the Bosphorus Bridge, heading home as quickly as possible in the dense Istanbul traffic. A couple hours later, everything started going off. There were helicopters and fighter jets in the sky and tanks in the streets. There were shootings and bombings across the country.

It wasn't immediately clear what was happening. But a faction within the Turkish army—organized as the Peace at Home Council— was attempting a coup d'état against the government. The armed rebellion attempted to take control of key locations across Istanbul, Ankara, Marmaris, and other cities across the country. The group attempted to take over the Bosphorus Bridge. The Turkish parliament and the presidential palace were both bombed.

That night, we lay in bed listening to fighter jets roaring and helicopters hovering above us. It sounded like there were gunshots in the streets. We didn't sleep at all.

During the coup attempt, more than three hundred people were killed and more than two thousand were injured. The next day, there was uncertainty over what had occurred. It was a scary time. We had a scheduled training session the next morning, but I wasn't leaving our house or my family until I knew for sure that everything was safe. We stayed inside all day. The team tried to assure all the players that everything was okay and that we'd be taken care of. But I didn't leave the house until the next day, when it seemed like calm had been restored. In the aftermath, more than forty thousand people were detained, and the underlying tensions and ramifications of the coup attempt persist to this day.

◆

Turkey was in turmoil after years of being viewed internationally as a country of stability and prosperity, leading the Middle East during a time of turbulence. Over the past four years, increasing violence and political problems within its borders had left the country on edge. Tourism had collapsed. The city centre lost businesses. Some trendy shops and restaurants shut down. It was a hard time for a place that we had come to love.

We thought about leaving Turkey. Or to get out of the country while there was so much violence and uncertainty. But everything was shut down. There was nowhere for us to go. The airports were closed. There were no flights in or out. I'd never experienced anything like it before. We didn't know how long it would last or when we'd be able to leave. We were also a month away from the arrival of our second child.

Amid the violence, several of our international players decided to leave Beşiktaş. Mario Gómez, who'd joined us on loan, didn't return. José Sosa also left the club to join AC Milan. But we remained a quality team despite the players we'd lost. Talisca, a Brazilian midfielder, joined us on loan from Benfica. He could score goals from anywhere. In games where not much was happening, he could pop up and score a goal. Adriano, a smart, quality Brazilian defender, came over from Barcelona. He was a very good player for us—he was usable in so many positions. And Vincent Aboubakar, a Cameroonian striker who would become a Beşiktaş legend, joined us from Porto. He was our main offensive threat. Cenk Tosun, a Turkish striker, was also an important attacker on our team.

Despite our concerns, Sarah and I decided to remain in Istanbul. Fans returned to the stadium for the start of the 2016 season that August, carrying forward the same excitement from the previous spring. Despite the tensions across the country, soccer provided a sense of escape and passion.

Nava, our second son, was born later that month. Even within the turmoil, Istanbul was beginning to feel like home. It was where our family had started and where we saw our future, which made the violence and uncertainty even more difficult to grapple with.

◆

In September 2016, I left Sarah and the kids in Istanbul to join the Canadian national team for the fourth round of the 2018 World Cup qualifiers. It was a tense time to leave, and it was difficult to not worry about my family as I once again tried to realize my dream of helping Canada reach the World Cup.

We had only two games left to determine whether we'd advance to the Hex, or whether we'd be denied another chance to qualify for the World Cup. Mexico had dominated our pool and held the top spot.

We were tied with Honduras for the second spot, with two matches left in group play. Our next match was in San Pedro Sula, a place that still haunted me. More than forty thousand fans showed up for the game, once again doing everything possible to get in our heads.

We needed a result, but we messed things up again. The Hondurans beat us 2–1. It wasn't a replay of the 2012 disaster, but it put us in a tough position to advance. Once again, we left Central America disappointed. Due to the goal differential, we'd have to win our final match against El Salvador by five goals to advance—and that could only happen if Honduras lost to Mexico in their final game.

We still had hope. In football, you always hang on to that, and you hope things go your way with the other result. But hope and confidence are not the same thing. After several difficult years, we'd slipped to a dreadful 122nd in world rankings. Benito Floro had taken over as our head coach. He was a veteran Spanish manager, who'd spent his career coaching club teams in Europe. Julian de Guzman had taken over from Kevin McKenna as captain, as he played out the final days of his national team tenure.

We'd hit a patch where we didn't have chemistry. We didn't have that rhythm. We couldn't put a string of games together. There wasn't any confidence that this team was good enough to qualify for the next round, let alone the World Cup.

It was a rebuilding phase for our program. We were trying to find the right team, going through several coaches in a short period of time. Federations need that kind of a rebuild sometimes. The turnover is important. But everything felt stagnant. It was extremely frustrating. I was one of the more experienced players on the team, and I was hoping—wishing—that this could be my time to help the team go forward and qualify for the World Cup, but we weren't good enough.

What was missing?

We were slowly starting to get more talent over the years but still not enough. It was an issue of depth. An issue of opportunities for our talent to play top-quality soccer and grow. There were fewer players on the 2016 squad who played top-quality soccer in Europe or in MLS than we'd had with the team that had been blown out by Honduras in 2012. If a player wasn't able to join a camp because of commitments to his club team or due to an injury, we didn't have the players to replace him.

We faced a nearly impossible situation at BC Place a few days later, on September 6. El Salvador was a weak team, but the goal differential was insurmountable. We scored three goals and gave up one—the 3–1 victory sealing our defeat.

As the final whistle blew on our chance to reach the 2018 World Cup, I felt all the hope I'd been carrying fall away. I was completely dejected. I still believed in what Canada was capable of in football.

I would never stop believing in that. But I was getting older, and leaving Turkey to fly across the ocean was taxing on my body. It was much easier for a European player to take a short trip to represent their country in international competition, but the travel for anyone heading to North America was brutal. And it meant time away from my family, which was a factor I'd never had to consider before. As a father, every day away from my children felt like an eternity. Every time I left Turkey to play for Canada, I was putting a strain on my club career and missing days with my family that I'd never get back. After another loss to Honduras and then failing to beat El Salvador by enough goals to qualify, in my head I was done.

In the locker room at BC Place, I walked around the room saying goodbye to everyone with tears in my eyes. I signed shirts for some of the younger players and took photos. It was a proper farewell. In the frustration of that moment, as I said goodbye to my teammates, I believed that was it.

◆

Back in Istanbul, Beşiktaş continued to play well under Güneş's leadership. Though we weren't as dominant as in the previous season, we remained a strong contender for a repeat championship. We had a good start in the Champions League group stage, playing against Napoli, Benfica, and Dynamo Kyiv. We made it through our first five matches with four draws and one win, which came over Napoli.

We faced Dynamo Kyiv in the last match of our group stage in December 2016. A draw would have been enough to put us through to the second round for the first time in the club's history in the Champions League. But we were undone by horrible refereeing. Early in the game, one of their wingers and Andreas Beck, our fullback, chased a 50-50 ball. As Beck gained a little edge, he was nudged from behind. As Beck fell, he accidentally clipped their player with his foot. It was clearly not intentional—he was falling and had no control. But the referee called a foul on Beck. There was no VAR replay at the time, which surely would have overturned the crucial mistake. It was reminiscent of the false offside that cost Canada a chance at the Gold Cup against the United States back in 2007. The match snowballed from there. Kyiv scored three goals in the first half. Aboubakar was given a red card early in the second half, for picking up a second yellow card violation. Kyiv added three more goals in the second half. The 6–0 defeat eliminated us from the Champions League, putting us in the Europa League instead.

Four days later, we were back in Istanbul, playing Bursaspor at Vodafone Arena in front of 43,000 fans. It was a hard-fought match, which we scraped out 2–1. The victory made us joint leaders atop the table with our local rivals Başakşehir.

Our fans flooded into the streets after the match, celebrating the win—and the possibility of a second straight championship on the horizon. Police monitored the revellers, making sure that the scene didn't get out of hand.

I stayed at Vodafone Arena late after the game. Sarah was at the game with the boys, and we always spent time together at the stadium, eating dinner, messing around, having fun. A lot of the guys go home right away, but I stayed around a bit longer that day. We were the last family to leave the stadium. We drove out of the private underground parking lot about an hour and fifteen minutes after the match had ended. We drove through another vibrant Saturday night in Istanbul, alive in the way that a megacity of thirteen million people always seems to be. The streets, bars, and restaurants were packed. A few minutes after we arrived home, my phone rang.

"Where are you guys?" my friend asked. He sounded panicked. "They just bombed the stadium."

On the road next to Vodafone Arena that we'd passed only min-utes earlier, a car bomb packed with about eight hundred pounds of explosives and iron pellets had exploded. The attack targeted a bus full of police officers as it pulled away from the stadium. Less than a minute after the first explosion, another bomb went off in nearby Maçka Park. A person wearing a coat and carrying a backpack had been ordered to stop by police officers. The bomb detonated and killed four officers and a civilian.

The echo of the explosions could be heard across Istanbul. Sirens blared through the night, as ambulances rushed to the stadium. Helicopters hovered overhead. A large cloud of smoke rose over the city. The scenes were reminiscent of the coup attempt and airport attack that summer.

Thirty-nine police officers were killed in the attacks. Vefa Karakurdu, Beşiktaş head of security, and Tunç Uncu, a member of the club's congress, were killed in the blast at Vodafone Arena. They were among the seven civilians who died. The Kurdistan Freedom Hawks claimed responsibility for the attack.

Seeing such horrible things happening to the people around me was hard to deal with. It was so close to home. It's difficult to see how it hurts people. A player in the league had lost his father in the Ankara car bombing in March 2016, shortly after he watched his son play for Galatasaray. It was horrible. It was felt around the whole league.

We had a lot of anxiety after that. Sarah didn't want to go anywhere—and she didn't want the kids to go anywhere either. We avoided going to malls or anywhere crowded and public. More attacks happened in Belgium and France, and for a while, it felt like we weren't safe anywhere. It was always in the back our minds.

The tragedy hung over Beşiktaş through the rest of the season. We played with heavy hearts, knowing even our best efforts couldn't shake the pain and fear that our teammates and our fans carried. The location of the bombing was known as Free Hill, a section on the northwest edge that had an open view of the old İnönü Stadium where spectators had been able to watch football matches for free. After the December 10 bombing, the section around the stadium was officially renamed Martyrs' Hill—Şehitler Tepesi—in memory of the victims who died there.

On the pitch, we did the only thing we could do—as small as it seemed in the shadow of Martyrs' Hill.

We received a big boost in the second half of the season, when Demba Ba returned on loan from the Shanghai Shenhua. In the Europa League, we eliminated an Israeli team, Be'er Sheva, and then we defeated Olympiacos to move on to the quarterfinals—which matched the club record. We still had a good team.

We were in a good position all season, but the standings became tighter as the games wound down. In early April, we played away at Trabzonspor—at Şenol Güneş Stadium, named in honour of our coach—sitting atop the league table by a narrow margin over Istanbul Başakşehir. Trabzonspor was eager to play spoiler in our quest for a back-to-back championship. It was a wild back-and-forth match.

We were tied 3–3 at the end of ninety minutes. We pressed during the first minute of injury time, going for the win. As the ball was played out wide, I ran into the box and cut towards the first post, anticipating a cross. I read it correctly: the ball sailed towards the goal. The Trabzonspor defender didn't see me coming. He jumped for the ball, thinking he could head it safely away—but I leaped in front of him and managed to get my head on it first. The ball looped just over the keeper. I couldn't even see the ball cross the line as I fell. I looked over and saw it sitting in the back of the net.

We shocked the stadium. The Trabzonspor fans were silent as we celebrated like crazy. We held on to win 4–3, putting us in a good position and feeling confident about claiming the title.

The championship went down to the second last match day. We were away at Gaziantepspor, a city in south-central Turkey close to the Syrian border. When we walked into that stadium, it was full of Beşiktaş fans. It was only our fans. I still don't know how that stuff happened. Imagine being the team playing us, hoping to stop us from winning a championship—and they look around their own stadium and see nothing but our black-and-white jerseys and hear nothing but the piercing barrage of whistles directed at them.

Once again, the Black Eagles came and conquered. We won the match 4–0, securing our second straight league championship. We finished with twenty-three wins and seventy-three points, four ahead of Başakşehir. Beşiktaş flags waved throughout the stadium. Fans rushed the pitch as we celebrated, taking selfies with us in our championship jerseys. There was so much joy in that place. It felt wonderful to find it again.

Part V

27

New Canada

After Julian de Guzman retired in 2017, I was named captain of the national team. I still hadn't changed my mind about my future with the national program, however. My passion for the national team was difficult to quit. I was committed to helping out where possible, transitioning the club to a new era of players. But as far as I was concerned, I was only able to take part when it made sense for me.

I skipped the 2017 Gold Cup that summer, opting to rest and spend time with my family. It was the first time I'd missed the tournament while healthy. In September 2017, the national program asked me to take part in another training camp. I agreed, but in the back of my mind I'd decided this was the last camp I would go to. It was a short trip with a match in Toronto and training sessions in Nottawasaga. I considered it a one-off. I didn't see myself as part of the 2022 World Cup qualifying cycle. I was more focused on finishing off my career in Turkey. The national team had become a wait-and-see endeavour for me.

After that trip to Toronto, I wouldn't play another game for Canada for more than a year.

It was never an easy decision to make though. Canada was always in the back of my mind, even as I focused on continuing our success with Beşiktaş after back-to-back championships. At my age, I had to do everything I could to prolong my career so that I could provide as much as possible for my family. The window on my life as pro athlete was closing.

A new generation of talent was emerging in Canada at the time. For years, new talent cropped up sporadically, but now talent was rising all over the place. The MLS had helped a lot, with three teams in Canada. Younger players had more chances to play. The teams were looking at more Canadian players than ever before and developing them in their local programs. Private soccer academies also played a big part. A few of them developed some of our best talent; Sigma FC, a Mississauga-based academy, for example, helped develop national team players like Cyle Larin, Richie Laryea, and Tajon Buchanan, a rising star who made his first appearance with the national team in 2021.

Back in the fall of 2017, I could see that there was so much potential on the horizon for Canada. I first heard of Alphonso Davies and Jonathan David through Paul Stalteri, our old captain, who started coaching the men's national youth program when he retired in 2013. But I didn't know much about either of them when they arrived at the national team training camp and I had the opportunity to see them play first-hand. Davies was only about sixteen years old when he made his way to the Vancouver Whitecaps, which is when everyone started to take notice. But before that, I didn't know anything about him at all. Both players were about to have a major impact on how Canadian men's soccer was perceived within our borders and beyond.

The next generation was emerging, and maybe it was time for me to step aside.

◆

Back with Beşiktaş that fall, our team looked good enough to win a third straight Süper Lig championship. We had lost a few key players, including defender Rhodolfo, Marcelo, and Andreas Beck. But once again, we brought in talent. This time, we added Pepe, an outstanding defender who had won three La Liga championships with Real Madrid and Euro 2016 with the Portuguese national team.

We made another memorable run in the Champions League, finishing atop a group that included Porto, RB Leipzig, and Monaco. Cenk Tosun, one of our main strikers after Gómez and Ba left, scored four goals in our six matches. We won each of our away games in our opponents' stadiums, again showing the world how well Black Eagles travel. It was the first time a Turkish team had ever gone undefeated in the group stage in the Champions League. Usually finishing first in our pool was good news, but we drew Bayern Munich in the round of sixteen.

Before we met the Bundesliga powerhouse in February 2018, Tosun joined Everton in the Premier League, for a reported 27-million-pound transfer fee. We added forward Vágner Love from Alanyaspor and my fellow Canadian Cyle Larin, who joined us from Orlando City in MLS. I'd known Cyle well for several years, since he'd been a young talent rising in our national team program. He had also grown up in Brampton, one of several who continued to build the city's reputation as a soccer hub.

I was playing some of the best soccer of my career at thirty-four years old, but even as a veteran player, I made costly mistakes at times. As with pretty much everything in life, missteps are part of the game. As an athlete, you have to learn to move past costly errors, making sure you don't allow them to become an even bigger problem—stripping you of your confidence and taking away your focus.

Early in our first match against Bayern Munich—away at Allianz Arena in front of seventy thousand people—I played a risky pass back to Domagoj Vida, who was put in a tough position as Robert Lewandowski pressed. Lewandowski stole the ball, and Vida tried to win it back but was given a red card for a hard tackle. I felt terrible that my misplay had led to a play that put us down a man so early in the match. But there was no time to dwell on mistakes. We played well despite the disadvantage, holding off Bayern through most of the first half, but we conceded a goal in the forty-third minute.

The floodgates opened in the second half. We completely lost control of the match, and Bayern scored four times, including two goals from Lewandowski. The five-nil loss put us in an almost impossible position during our second leg a few weeks later at Vodafone Park. We lost the second match 3–1.

Our Champions League run became the primary focus for our team through the first half of the season; our softened focus on league play caused us to slip in the standings. We had only thirty points through our first seventeen games. But we fought hard to make up for it in the final stretch of the Süper Lig season that spring, knowing that we were talented enough to still make a run of the championship. Talisca, in particular, had a monster second half for us. We pulled ourselves back into contention in a tight race, trying to reach our rivals Galatasaray who held the top spot. In the end, we finished in fourth place with seventy-one points—four shy of the champions, Galatasaray.

Despite our strong showing in the Champions League, it was a disappointing finish for our team and our fans. Beşiktaş had last won three championships in a row in the early 1990s, and we had had a chance to match that. We were by far the most talented team in the league. In my career with Beşiktaş, we wouldn't have another roster with the kind of talent we'd showcased over those previous three years.

When the season finished, Sarah and I took the kids on a trip to Thailand. There was a lot on my mind that trip. I'd just had surgery to repair an ankle injury that had plagued me that year. I wasn't sure whether the injury would become a recurring problem. I was in the middle of a contract negotiation to return to Beşiktaş. Everything about my future was up in the air. Our family had also gotten bigger. Ayo, our third son, was born in December 2017. Sarah and I were now outnumbered by three kids under three years old.

At the time, Canada wasn't really on my mind. I was focused on figuring out the next year of my career—maybe two years, if I was lucky. I was focused on my family and on the future. I sat on the beach in Thailand, resting my throbbing ankle after struggling to walk through the sand, when my phone rang.

It was John Herdman.

He'd been hired as Canada's new head coach in January 2018, replacing Octavio Zambrano. John moved over to the men's team from the Canadian women's national team, where he'd had remarkable success and coached one of the greatest women's soccer players of all time in Christine Sinclair.

John told me that he hoped I'd return to the national team. Having worked with Christine Sinclair on the women's national team, he believed it was important to have a strong leader on and off the pitch to provide experience and guidance for a core of young players. John knew that he had talent in players like Alphonso Davies, Jonathan David, and several other rising stars, but he hoped my experience playing in championships and in the Champions League would have a powerful influence on them. John told me he believed I had more to give on and off the pitch.

"You haven't reached your full potential yet," he told me. "And you can do it in a red shirt."

It was a very real, emotional conversation. I shared my frustrations with the program and the federation, the years I'd spent playing for Canada feeling like there was no one behind us. Of being mocked by European teammates for caring about my national team at all. Of losing to countries that should have no business beating us. I told John about my concerns about coming back to play for Canada—the reality of my shifting priorities and responsibilities that come with age and family. And of playing through the fleeting years of a career, at thirty-five, not knowing how much more my body would give before the ability I'd worked my entire life for was gone.

It was a conversation that I needed to have.

It wasn't only a sales pitch for Canada. John asked if I'd join the team in St. Kitts for the Concacaf Nations League qualifiers that fall. That was all—no commitment beyond that was necessary.

I was conflicted. I told John that I needed some time to think it over and discuss it with my wife. But I really appreciated that he'd taken the time to call me. I was impressed by John's vision and energy for the team. It was enough to convince me to return for one more camp, if only to see what his energy was all about.

That October, I joined the team in Toronto for a Nations League qualifier against Dominica, which we won 5–0. A month later, I joined the team again for our camp in St. Kitts.

I was immediately impressed by the way John communicated with his players. He respected our input—in fact, he sought it out. And he was so confident about what we could achieve. He gave his players leadership roles, leaning on our experience and insights on and off the pitch. John looked to veteran players like me, Scott Arfield, and Milan Borjan, who had seen a lot in our careers. He also brought in some of the younger guys, like Sam Piette, as leaders on the team, connecting with a younger generation in our group. There was always a core group of guys, but John also changed the leadership group often, bringing in a younger player each cycle, so they had an opportunity to gain some experience in a leadership role.

During one meeting, John often asked us what we wanted to do for the country. We all decided that we wanted to leave the shirt in a better place than when we first put it on. We wanted to put Canada on the map. We came up with a saying that we used often, referring to this era as "New Canada."

John set goals for our team. He'd actually go to the drawing board and talk about exactly what we wanted to see with the team. We had missions right from the start—like how many goals we'd be happy with scoring against St. Kitts.

During our match against St. Kitts, I intercepted a pass and played the ball to Junior Hoilett, who dashed through several St. Kitts defenders and moved the ball to Russell Teibert. As he moved down the left side, I drove towards the goal, leaped in the air, and got my head on Teibert's perfect cross through the box. It was the only goal in our 1–0 win over St. Kitts.

It felt good to score for Canada again. More importantly, there was something about this cycle that I hadn't felt before. There was new energy. There was belief. The players were buying into John's approach. He told us that we would qualify for the 2022 World Cup. The players looked at each other, thinking this man was crazy—but also that maybe he was right.

"Okay," I thought, when I left the Caribbean, "I'll just take it one game at a time."

The energy kept building each time I returned. We were fighting for something together, pushing for a goal we'd yet to achieve. The way he brought everyone together was something I'd never seen before. I'd had coaches who looked to their older players, but the way John approached it was unique. He gave us a role where we collectively set expectations and high standards. John encouraged us to gather and speak to the team often on our own, so that we were setting a tone without him—something that belonged to the players. We started singing the national anthem proudly as a team after John came in. I hope that never changes.

As I watched the dynamic of our team evolve, I wasn't completely sold on my continued place within it. Every time we would finish a game or camp, John and I agreed to check in to discuss a little further and see where we were at. But we never looked too far out. We never discussed me participating in the World Cup. We played a few friendly games, and then John convinced me to come play in the Gold Cup. In my head, I was thinking, "Okay, maybe it's a chance to have a bit of success with the national team, maybe hoist a trophy." That came and went, and he'd hop on a call with me again. He kept talking to me about how I could still be involved with the team.

◆

I was ancient in the world of professional football. I was having issues with my body, battling injuries, getting old. It was frustrating, because all the things that I used to be able to get away with on the pitch, I just couldn't anymore. At times I used to feel like I could control the game. When I lost that, my mind filled with doubt. I started to wonder if I actually had anything to give to the team. Do they really need me? Or am I hanging around too long? Am I keeping younger players out of the squad who deserve the opportunity to take my place?

John seemed to understand those anxieties. He kept reiterating that I was important to the team. He'd show me stats to back that up. It wasn't only about my presence as a veteran; it was about what I offered on the pitch and the impact that I had. He used GPS data to analyze the distance I covered on the pitch and my effect on building up the attack, as well as my defensive efforts and the velocity of my runs. That confidence went a long way for an old guy.

I was learning to not quit on myself.

I missed a few games to take care of my health and make sure I was rested, but I didn't skip many. We kept going one step at a time—and we inched closer to qualifying for the World Cup. Every time John called, he asked how I was feeling—where my head was at, how my body felt. But he never put pressure on me to return. He supported me and told me that he wanted me involved if I could still do it. That trust and respect meant a lot to me.

John spoke often about leaving the program in a better place—a lasting legacy. That resonated. He'd send me messages trying to convince me to join the team for the 2022 World Cup qualifiers. In one message, he sent an image of what he envisioned to be our starting line-up against our first match that spring against Bermuda. He sent a picture of a pitch with each player's face in the spot he intended to play us, with mine right in the middle. In a text below the image, John wrote:

"It's a very exciting team to take on a tough Bermuda squad . . . It's one game for you, 4 days away from home/club—a massive game for the country and will set the tone for the journey (no pressure haha we lose we are out). Your presence with these men is undeniable and irreplaceable."

John was a hard man to say no to. And with the visual, it was that much harder to turn down.

In March 2021, I joined the national team in Orlando for the very first match of the qualifiers for the 2022 World Cup. It was the lowest bar we had to clear, playing Bermuda and the Cayman Islands. I only played in our first match, a 5–1 win over Bermuda. Being on the pitch, I marvelled at how good our younger players were. These were guys who hadn't been on my radar at all. They'd never been to camp before. It wasn't only Alphonso Davies and Jonathan David. There were players who added the kind of depth we'd always lacked. It was the first time I saw Richie Laryea play. I saw an even younger rising star in Jayden Nelson. The future looked bright. Bermuda wasn't a tough team, but the way we dominated that game felt new. We had complete control. Everything was in their half.

We really did seem like a new Canada.

"Maybe we're on to something here now," I thought. "I don't want to miss out on this."

28

Captain

I looked around a near-empty stadium in İzmir, as tense as I'd ever been on a pitch. We had no business being in a position to win the league championship—but somehow we'd fought our way there.

It was the final match day of the 2020–21 Turkish Süper Lig season.

The pandemic had shortened the previous season, and we were playing without fans in the stands. On paper, our team wasn't nearly as strong as it had been during the back-to-back championships a couple years earlier. I'd signed a one-year contract with Beşiktaş, playing out the final chapter of my career on a year-to-year basis. I was playing as well as ever, with a sudden spark of offence in my game. I'd scored four goals in 2018–19 and six during a pandemic-shortened season the following year. I hadn't put up those kinds of offensive numbers since my days with Copenhagen.

After battling through injuries, I felt as good as I could have hoped for. The limited travel had helped. I was also very conscious about my diet, avoiding gluten for a time, like tennis star Novak Djokovic. I'd been doing a lot of work with Pablo, a prehabilitation and athletic trainer who I'd worked with in the past and later hired privately. Pablo was influential in keeping me fit and saving my career a few times. He helped me stay on top of my fitness and reduce my risk of injury. It felt like everything was clicking at the right time, keeping my career alive at thirty-eight. I was blessed to have such longevity, but I'd also been meticulous about aging as well as possible and extending my career. For so long, I'd felt like I was improving every season, still fine tuning the rough talent I'd arrived in Europe with. I'd gotten better with age and experience. My friends back home in Brampton often joked that I was like Benjamin Button, aging backwards.

Before the 2020–21 season, I had been named Beşiktaş's captain. Wearing that arm band was one of the biggest honours of my career.

From the start, we weren't considered contenders to win the league, but a couple key additions helped give us a spark. Vincent Aboubakar transferred back to Beşiktaş from Porto in September 2020, along with Gökhan Töre who returned from Yeni Malatyaspor. After having a hard time and not finding his feet through his first couple seasons with Beşiktaş, Cyle Larin had a breakout year, scoring nineteen goals in league play. Cyle had taken a lot of heat from media and fans, so I was glad to see him finally show Beşiktaş fans what I'd always known he was capable of. We surprised everyone that year, including ourselves. Sergen Yalçın, a former star Beşiktaş player, had taken over as head coach, and we thrived under his system.

Through the first half of the season, we sat near the top of the standings. After the break, Cenk Tosun also returned on loan from Everton. Our momentum picked up in the second half, led by Larin. We held a large lead in the standings with about six games left in the season, but we dropped two key games against Galatasaray and Karagümrük.

By the final day, Galatasaray and Fenerbahçe had caught us. Each team played its last game at the exact same time, with the results set to decide who would celebrate as champions. We needed a tie or win to secure first. It was pressure I had never felt before, because we had had it in our hands and let it slip away.

We played Göztepe in İzmir on the Aegean coast—watching our phones and checking the stadium scoreboard for updates from Galatasaray and Fenerbahçe. It was odd to feel so much pressure amid relative silence. Although there wasn't supposed to be any fans, a small group found their way into the stadium, which gave the atmosphere a little life. But it was nothing compared to the chaotic noise of football matches in Turkey I'd become used to. The calm was eerie and almost added to the pressure. We were tied 1–1 at the half, anxiously awaiting updates on the pitch.

I got word from one of our teammates who was on the side warming up that Galatasary had scored and had a one-goal lead in the second half of its match.

"Oh shit," I thought. We were done if we didn't press for a goal. It was all or nothing now. We attacked Göztepe with everything we had.

In the sixty-ninth minute, Cyle Larin drew a penalty. I felt a rush of adrenaline and relief as Rachid Ghezzal, who took the penalty, fired his shot past the keeper into the net.

From the pitch, I kept glancing towards the bench, waiting to get reactions from the boys about the other games. With about five minutes to go, I saw that both matches were over. All we needed to do was hold onto our lead for a few more minutes, and we'd be champions. But if Göztepe scored one more goal, we'd be done.

A few minutes and an eternity later, the final whistle blew on injury time. I rushed my teammates, and we celebrated as wildly as we had after our back-to-back championships. We'd won it by a single goal. The tightest margin possible. I don't think I've ever seen anything like it.

It was one of my happiest moments on a football pitch. Maybe it was because we'd been counted out before the season started. Maybe it was because I was wearing the captain's band. Maybe it was because I knew our fans were out there, somewhere, celebrating like only Black Eagles fans do. I knew how much they deserved this.

I also knew that it was likely the last championship I'd win in my career. It was a reminder of how far I'd come, as I neared the end of this dream. I couldn't stop believing now.

◆

Four months later, I was home again for one last run.

That September, we entered the third round of the 2022 World Cup qualifiers in an expanded eight-team format of what had previously been called the Hex. After drawing with the United States and Honduras, we played El Salvador at BMO Field.

Something felt different this time. There were still flecks of blue in the crowd, but it was mostly red. The crowd was loud and excited. We fed off their energy right away. Six minutes into the game, I made a run from the top of the box towards the near post as Richie Laryea cut around an El Salvador defender. His pass found me in stride, and I tapped the ball between the keeper's legs into the goal. I turned and found a red sea rising. The stadium was as loud as I've ever heard it, finally in favour of us. Canadian fans roared as my teammates put on a display of what Canadian soccer was all about. Jonathan David scored a few minutes later, and Tajon Buchanan added a goal in the second half in our 3–0 win.

We had somehow captured the attention of the entire nation. The electric play of Alphonso Davies and Jonathan David captivated Canadian audiences. Stephen Eustáquio's quality in the midfield captured the attention of seasoned fans. Cyle Larin showed everyone why he was on his way to becoming Canada's all-time leading scorer. Alistair Johnston played with poise and confidence on defence, alongside Kamal Miller. Richie Laryea continued to dazzle opponents and fans alike. Milan Borjan fired up our team from the goal line and endeared himself to fans with his animated passion.

A few weeks after our win against El Salvador, on a cold November day in Edmonton, we sat near the top of the pool in the final round of World Cup qualifying—with Mexico in town. With a win, we'd go to the top of the table.

Normally we had a pregame meeting the day before a match. This time, John had us meet him in the lobby of our hotel. We followed him across a bridge into Rogers Place, where the Edmonton Oilers play. We walked down a large set of stairs into the lobby and then into the Oilers dressing room. John had called in some kind of favour. Inside, for each of us, there was an Edmonton jersey with our name on it hanging in the stalls. We sat in the Oilers locker room and held our team meeting there.

It was the kind of gesture that had never been made for the national team in the past. I could see how much it meant to the players. It was a small thing, really—but it took thought and effort. It took one of John's connections. It helped solidify what we had built as a team over the past few months.

This was a new Canada, for sure.

The buildup to that game was the most incredible thing I had witnessed in men's soccer in Canada. It seemed like the entire country was watching. The next morning, before we left the hotel for Commonwealth Stadium, we were shown a video of Wayne Gretzky wishing us well.

I walked out onto the pitch and couldn't believe what I was seeing. The entire freezing stadium was full of Canadian fans. More than 44,000 people had packed in to watch us play. It was a first for me against Mexico or any of the Central American countries. Throughout my entire career, whenever we played a home game, the stands were always predominantly filled by our opponent's fans. The moment we would come out onto the pitch, we deflated, playing at home and feeling as if we'd already lost. The majority of the people in the stadium would be cheering against us. But everything about this game was different.

It was a first for Mexico, too, used to the comfort of a home game on Canadian soil. The –9 degrees Celsius chill was the coldest temperature a Mexican team had ever played in. Commonwealth Stadium was nicknamed Iceteca—a pun on the enormous Estadio Azteca in Mexico City, which is notoriously tough to play in.

The way we approached the game, the way we played was an eye-opener for everyone. It made me extremely happy to see how far the country had come. We played with confidence and poise against a bewildered and freezing Mexican team. It was an exceptionally rough match. Our players came to the side of their teammate after every hard tackle or skirmish after a play. The game was scoreless until injury time in the first half, when Larin finished off a rebound off a shot from Johnston. The stadium erupted, sending snow falling from the rafters. I had a feeling all game that we were going to win. There was this weight off our shoulders, and it showed in the way we played. This was our time.

Early in the second half, Larin blew by the Mexican defenders to finish a perfect pass from Eustáquio off a free kick. Larin rushed towards a snowbank as we ran to mob him. Sam Adekugbe sprinted right past us and dove right into the snow. It was the first time in my career that I was teary-eyed in the middle of a match.

I could feel it. We were right there. This was what I'd been waiting for my entire career. It was the twenty years of disappointment. It was all the shit we went through. I'd tried this so many times, and we'd always fallen short. We never had the luck, or we just hadn't been good enough or had what it takes. I thought of all those memories and of all the players who stood and battled beside me, experiencing the same frustration, who weren't there to feel this now. To experience this looming victory for the team, for the country.

You could see it on the Mexicans' faces. They knew it too. We had them beat. Between the weather, the fans, and our play, they didn't know what had hit them. The tables had turned. We felt like we were the best team in Concacaf. We felt untouchable.

For the first time, we had the respect of the other countries. They didn't look at us like we were a guaranteed three points anymore. We knew that we had been viewed as an easy win by opponents like Mexico. Not anymore.

Mexico did manage to get one goal back though. They scored late, nearly bursting my emotional bubble. With almost no time left in the game, Milan made an unbelievable save on the goal line on what would have been the tying goal, to save our win. It was one of many world-class saves he made throughout the cycle.

I felt the sharp shout of doubt in the back of my mind. "Jesus! Not again!"

But we held on.

At that moment, in the freezing cold, I felt a rush of confidence. We were going to the World Cup. It was an overwhelming moment.

We weren't there yet though.

In early 2022, we continued our unbeaten run in the final qualifying round with a 2–0 win over Honduras in the Estadio Olímpico Metropolitano. A week later in El Salvador, I scored a goal that some have jokingly called a Canadian Heritage Moment. The match was scoreless twenty minutes into the second half when Cyle Larin won the ball from an El Salvador defender and cut towards the right side of the goal. As I crossed half, I saw Larin break free. I sprinted towards the goal. Larin crossed the ball from the right side as I cut towards the post. I threw myself forward towards the ball, trying to get my head on it. I made just enough contact to tip it towards the goal. As I fell forward on my side, the ball ricocheted off the post, facing away from the net. The ball hit the back of my right thigh and bounced off my back—and then somehow looped up and past the keeper into the goal.

I looked up as the ball fell over the keeper and bounced on the line. He dove backwards trying to swat it away, but it rolled into the net. It was the craziest goal I'd scored in my life.

I got up, arms stretched wide, and sprinted to my teammates. That 1–0 lead held until the final minute of injury time, when Jonathan David scored to secure the win. Afterwards, Herdman said that no one else would have made the run to score the backside goal that I had. I don't know about that. But I did come to see that goal as reflective of how I've played the game and pursued my goals. I ran as hard and as far as I could. When I got close, I threw myself at the opportunity, knowing I had to sacrifice to succeed. Then I got lucky as hell. That's just how life works. But I had to put myself in position for that luck to find me. If I hadn't taken that chance, if I hadn't thrown myself into the opportunity, I would never have had the chance to stumble one win closer to the World Cup.

We were one win away from clinching a spot at the World Cup. The Canadian Soccer Association flew us to our next match in Costa Rica in a private jet that was swankier than anything I'd ever seen the federation pay for. It was decked out with everything. When I walked on, I thought, "This is not for real." In the early days, we usually flew economy—which did a number on our bodies. More recently, it was common to fly charter if we were all together, but this private jet was a different level. It was John again, knowing the importance of making the players feel special and appreciated. It was the first time we felt that we were being looked at differently than in the past. The federation even got us our own private chef to make sure that we were eating properly, especially on the road when it was hard to trust the water and food we were given.

Despite the first-class treatment, we lost 1–0 in Costa Rica. It was a disappointing reminder that we couldn't take anything for granted. This wasn't done. We weren't there yet. We had to stay focused. These teams were too good, and the stakes were too high to lose sight of what we needed to do to get over the line.

A few days later, on March 27, 2022, we met Jamaica back at BMO Field in Toronto. It was another matchup that would have felt like an away game in the past, but this time the seats were filled with nearly thirty thousand fans cheering for us. The energy was unbelievable. It was just what I'd always hoped to see on Canadian soil. This time, there was no doubt.

We dominated the match, winning 4–0.

After the game, as we celebrated on the pitch, several of my old teammates joined me. Dwayne De Rosario, Julian de Guzman, Paul Stalteri, Craig Forrest—the legends of Canadian soccer. This was their victory as much as it was ours. Iain Hume didn't come down to the pitch, but I found him up in the stands. He was elated. We hugged. It was our dream finally realized: Canada was going to the World Cup. This wasn't just about the current roster. It was about all the blood, sweat, and tears that fell in the decades before so that this moment was possible. It belonged to them. It belonged to all of us.

29

On the Other Side

Once I became a father, I started to understand the sacrifices that I had to make to sustain my career. It required travelling all the time. I spent a lot of time being away from the people that I'm really close to. I missed my family.

Back home in Istanbul, Sarah and the boys woke up in the middle of the night to watch Canada qualify for the World Cup. My eldest son, Noah, always wanted to watch my games—regardless of where I was in the world at the time.

It was hard to be away from them. But at the same time, they were part of what drove me to fight to achieve my dreams to the very end. I played to make them proud—and to show them that they can achieve anything they set their minds to and work as hard as they can for.

But with the World Cup on the horizon, I also knew that it was time to let go.

All three of the kids were in school. Sarah was taking care of them while I was off living my dream. It wasn't easy for her, and she was the reason that I had been able to play so long. She knew what playing for the national team meant to me. She understood my dream of making it to the World Cup. Without her support, I would never have been able to play this long. When I was home, I was often on the road playing for Beşiktaş. Every time I joined the Canadian team, it meant more time away from my family and more time leaving her to care for our three kids. That was always in the back of my mind.

◆

I'd learned a lot about family over the past decade, as Sarah and I started our own. I learned that family isn't only the people who raised you or who you were raised beside. It's the people you grow up around and become part of your journey. It's the people you meet along the way. The unexpected strangers who stand beside you in new worlds.

Family can be complicated. Before I met him, Sarah's father came to Turkey twice—both times while I was away playing with the Canadian national team. The first time he came, Sarah took down all of our photos because she didn't want to make him feel uncomfortable. Our son Noah was there. Sifollah adored him. As Noah grew, they became very close. He was the best kind of grandfather a kid could have. But he still refused to acknowledge that I existed.

Sarah's aunt came to Istanbul to visit us, and we connected right away. Afterwards, she told Sarah's father that he needed to come and meet me. Sarah had spoken to her father several times about it. He'd met her children, and he was a wonderful, loving grandfather.

"It's time for you to meet the father of my children," she told him. But he resisted again and again.

Then one day, in 2019, he called Sarah. "I'm ready to meet your husband," he said. "I want to come now."

I was so nervous before he arrived. We'd spoken on the phone a couple times before his trip, which was nice but not the same as meeting someone in person. It was strange to finally meet a man who already knew all my children and whom my wife loved dearly. It was hard to know that he'd refused to acknowledge my existence all those years. But I wasn't angry. It hurt, but our cultures were so different. I knew that this was something that I couldn't understand. It was beyond my experience. Sifollah loved her very much, and he'd extended that genuine love to our children. I hoped that he'd come to love me too.

Our driver picked up Sarah's father at the airport. We waited anxiously at the house for him to arrive.

The moment we opened the door and he walked in, all of my nerves rushed away. It was as though we'd been friends for years. He was genuine. It didn't feel like there was anything fake or forced about him being there.

He stayed with us for several days, and he and I sat and spoke for hours. I asked him a lot of questions. Sifollah is an incredible story-teller. He's seen so much of the world and has had such unique experiences. He's the kind of guy who knows everything about everything. I could sit there and listen to him talk endlessly. Every story he told led to so many more questions. We didn't talk much about me and Sarah, but that was alright. There was plenty of time for us to get to know each other now. It was like he was an old friend.

It was an emotional time for Sarah, who'd been hoping and waiting for so long for us to meet. She knew that if her father could get past the cultural barriers, he and I would connect, just as I had with her brother Siavash, who was now one of my closest friends. Sarah called my parents to tell them that her father and I had finally met. They were so happy. It was hard for them to understand why he hadn't wanted to meet me for so long, and it was impossible to explain. It meant a lot to them to know that her father and I had hit it off so well.

It was emotional for me too. It was a huge weight off my chest. It felt like someone who had been missing from our life was finally here.

Sifollah wasn't a football fan at all. But in Turkey when he visited bazaars and shops and he saw a Beşiktaş sign, he'd tell the shopkeepers that I was his son-in-law. He was amazed by the way they reacted. He'd come home and tell Sarah, stunned that they knew who I was. It made him very proud—which made me very proud too. He was a bit too old to come to the stadium by the time we met, but he would watch my games with my sons on our television in the living room. Whenever the camera panned to me, he'd point and yell excitedly, "It's Tiba! It's Tiba!" Sifollah never really knew what was happening in the game, but he always made sure to point me out to my kids.

The boys call him Baba Joon. *Baba* is Persian and Turkish for *grandfather*. And *Joon* means *dear* in Persian. (The kids also call me Baba because it means *dad* as well.) He'd bring fruits and candies for the kids whenever he'd visit. And if any of them acted up and got in trouble, he was always on their side. He and Noah, in particular, had something special. Whenever Baba Joon came to visit us, he'd rush to give him a kiss on the cheek, which is something he never does for anyone else.

To this day, my father-in-law and I often go out in Istanbul, just the two of us, to grab a coffee and tell stories.

As I've gotten older, I've come to understand that, regardless of what I've achieved in my life, the people around me will always be the most important thing.

♦

In December 2022, I stood in a tunnel in Qatar on the edge of a life-long dream. Even in that moment, it seemed impossible.

We stepped onto a stage against Belgium, ranked number two in the world—with players like Kevin De Bruyne and Eden Hazard—and thoroughly outplayed them as people watched around the globe. We missed a penalty kick and had several chances to score. But we couldn't find the net. Belgium scored just before halftime and held on to win 1–0; even they knew they should have lost.

In our next game, we shocked the world again: Alfonso Davies scored a brilliant header off a gorgeous cross from Tajon Buchanan in the first moments of our match against Croatia. For the first twenty-five minutes, we put the former World Cup finalists on their heels. Then, led by Ballon d'Or winner Luka Modrić, the Croatians remembered who they were. We were undone by their poise, talent, and speed. Modrić was mesmerizing as he dismantled us. We lost 4–1. And just like that, any hope we had of advancing at the World Cup was erased.

It happens that quickly. You work your entire life to reach a pinnacle, and in a flash, it passes you by. And suddenly, you realize your legs are just that much slower than before, and the game is somehow so much faster. In that moment, you realize that your dream has come and gone. I could almost feel that dream receding into the past.

My time was almost up.

We faced Morocco in our final World Cup match—a team that was playing some of the tournament's most inspired football. At that point, all we hoped for was to return home with Canada's first win. Herdman brought me into the match at the sixtieth minute, as we trailed 2–1. With twenty minutes remaining, I leapt for a pass off a perfect corner kick from Junior Holiet that found me at the top of the goal area. I was bit late on my timing, but I managed to get to get my head on the ball. It ripped towards the goal, just beyond the reach of Morocco's keeper. The stands behind the goal were filled with roaring Canadian fans. It was scene taken directly from one of my boyhood dreams. The ball clipped the top post and ricocheted down. I didn't see it land. I thought it was in. Jonathan David put his arm up to celebrate. The fans jumped. The joy lasted a fraction of a second. The ball had fallen directly on the goal line. I put my hands on my head in disbelief, looked up and covered my eyes. At the end of this long journey, I was mere inches away from scoring Canada's biggest goal at the World Cup.

I'd left it on the line.

The final whistle blew. We lost our last World Cup match 2–1. Both Morocco and Croatia advanced to the semifinals.

It was a disappointing result, but I left Qatar feeling content. Several dozen family members and friends had made the trip to Qatar to be in the stands when Canada played. My sons witnessed their father play in a World Cup. I'd refused to quit, and I had found a way to finish my journey well.

There was nothing to be sad about. I found the most important thing in life years ago, on a neighbourhood field around the corner from my family's home. The magic of a dream is never about its ending.

◆

I returned to Istanbul after the World Cup to finish my final season with Beşiktaş. The team had extended my contract that year, mainly so I could stay fit and prepare for the World Cup. Beşiktaş fans took pride in my appearance at the Cup, especially because Turkey hadn't qualified. In the weeks leading up to Qatar, a billboard with my image on it was put up in the city.

As the season wound down, everyone knew my final game was coming.

In our second last game of the season, away at Kasımpaşa, I subbed in one last time as a Black Eagle. We were up 4–2 in injury time—the match was essentially over. But a penalty was called in the final seconds. I was on the sidelines, as I had been through most of that final stretch of the season as Şenol Güneş, who had returned as head coach that fall, focused on playing his younger players. As the Kasımpaşa fans realized a penalty shot would be awarded, they started to chant my name: "Ati-ba, Ati-ba." The chants grew louder and louder as Güneş sent me in. These were Kasımpaşa fans; visiting fans had been banned from stadiums that year. I was touched by the honour. I was also more nervous than I'd been in ages.

I was usually strong on penalty kicks, but I'd missed two earlier in the season.

"What if I miss now?" I wondered. The "Ati-ba, Ati-ba" chants continued as I stepped back from the ball. I usually stuck with my routine, deciding exactly where I would kick a penalty before a game to avoid winding myself if the moment came. I always kicked to the right side. Now I second-guessed it.

"Go straight down the middle," I thought.

I lined up. The crowd hushed. I took a deep breath—and then changed my mind midstride. It was as if my father was standing behind me, saying, "Just shoot your shot."

And I did.

The keeper dove to the left and the ball hit the back of the net, low on the right side.

It was my tenth season with the club—by far the longest tenure of an international player in the club's history. It was hard to put into words what that time meant to me. Three championships. Two appearances in the Champions League round of sixteen. Those would always be career highlights. But my connection to Beşiktaş was deeper than that. I didn't consider myself a foreigner anymore. My sons' entire lives existed within that wonderful city. The life Sarah and I had built together was there. Istanbul was home. I knew what it meant to be a Black Eagle. And I knew that I would be one for life.

30

Full Time

I was an old man ready to say goodbye to the game. I'd flown to Vegas knowing that this was the end. I was forty years old, long past the age when most players hang up their boots. I was lucky to have made it this far. But every dream, no matter how beautiful, comes to an end.

There was still one thing that I hadn't checked off my long list of goals. With Canada, I'd never raised a championship trophy. In fact, it'd been twenty-three years since we'd reached a final. The 2023 Concacaf Nations League finals were my first and last chance. We'd toppled Panama in the semifinals, setting up a chance to win gold over the United States in the final.

It was June 2023, two decades after my journey with the Canadian national team had begun. The 2–0 win over Panama was my 104th cap, more than any player for the men's national team. But this would be the last time I'd wear the Canadian jersey. That reality didn't set in until I did an interview with Canadian journalists in Vegas the day before the Nations League final. I'd let word slip that I planned to retire. There had been speculation that I might carry on for one last run at the Gold Cup. But I needed to put my family first. I had three young boys at home who'd spent so much time watching their father on a screen; I was done spending time away from them. And Sarah was pregnant with our fourth child. This trip across the Atlantic, while she stayed home with the boys, was asking more than I should have of her. But she was gracious, as always. She knew what this final run meant to me.

Our baby girl was due to arrive in July, and I'd be there to meet her in Istanbul.

After a long series of interviews, I went to my hotel room. That was when the reality started to sink in. This was the last time I would suit up for Canada. This was the last game of my career. The next morning, I tried to run through my normal routine, getting ready for the game, but I couldn't stop thinking that I was doing everything for the last time. The intensity grew as the game neared. I tried to focus but couldn't.

"This is my last walkthrough . . . This is my last team meal . . . This is my last stretch . . . This is my last run . . ."

Before the game, I spoke with John Herdman. It was something we always did to check in on how I was feeling. He often left it up to me to decide if I was ready to play. As long as I felt good, he wanted to get me in.

"This one is for you," he said. "But we're going for the result this time."

"Absolutely," I said. "Don't even think about me. We'll make it happen if it's the right time."

I would only play if he felt the team could use me. I had no intention of being a liability for our team, especially with a trophy on the line. It was all about the result. All I wanted was a win for Team Canada, regardless of my role in the victory. It was more important that we were holding that trophy at the end of the day.

John agreed. He knew even before coming into these games that I wasn't making the trip to get minutes. We were open about everything. That's what I loved about playing for John.

In the locker room before heading out for warmups, I stood up and addressed the team.

Several weeks earlier, I had done the same with my Beşiktaş family. At the last home game of the season, I arrived at the stadium to find players and staff wearing shirts that read "Thank you Atiba." For the game, the team wore special jerseys on which the numbers were made up of tiny photos of my face. Later, in the team facility, I addressed all of the players and staff who'd gathered, trying to put into words a feeling that I was still trying to process. I broke down in tears. It took me several tries to compose myself enough to say thank you to a club that was family to me.

In Vegas, the same emotions flooded back. I teared up right away. I couldn't speak at first. I hadn't had an opportunity to thank them for giving me the chance to play in a World Cup. It hit me all at once.

But when I was able to gather myself, I told my teammates how grateful I was for all of the time we'd shared, the friendships we'd forged, the brotherhood that we had. I looked around the room and saw players I had stood beside for years. I was so proud of how far we'd gone and what we'd become. I remembered all the years I'd put in playing alongside so many of those guys and the newer faces. I said a few words about some of the guys who'd been there the longest. Guys like Cyle Larin, our nation's leading scorer. And Milan Borjan, the heart and soul of our national team. I felt so fortunate to be among this group. To have played long enough to see what we could become. Ours was a story of ups and downs—many more downs than ups. We'd had good teams in the past, but we had never been strong enough to qualify for a World Cup. Even though the program and the federation had a long way to go, it was incredible to think about how far we had come.

This was a room full of champions. Players who'd won in some of the best leagues in the world. I looked at a room full of the kind of talent that Canada had never produced before: guys like Alphonso

Davies, Jonathan David, Ismaël Koné, Ali Johnston, Richie Laryea, Stephen Eustáquio, and Tajon Buchanan.

I told them that I knew Canada would play in many World Cups from here on out. That was a given. We had too much talent to be stopped. But this had been my last chance at it. And the run we had to get there had been the most unbelievable and fulfilling time in my career.

"Thank you," I said, wiping away another tear.

I loved these guys like brothers.

And now we had one last game to play.

"Let's focus on the game," I said, collecting myself. "Let's go out and get the win."

Canadian fans filled in a full corner inside Allegiant Stadium and were scattered among the Americans throughout. My family and several of my friends made the trip to Vegas from Brampton to be there for the end. I spotted them up above our bench during warmup. My mother and father watched quietly, nervously. Toyaa screamed the loudest. Haldon ripped into the American players as the game began. Alex sat beside them, challenging every terrible call made by the referee.

It was the same as always. Just right.

I stood beside my teammates as the national anthem played, knowing this would be the last time I felt the joy of singing the anthem alongside my brothers and country.

There are few perfect endings though.

The Americans played a strong, confident game—and we looked nervous and underprepared. In fact, we were. The U.S. had had a week-long training camp before the Nations League finals, and we'd only had four days to prepare for our two matches. We fell behind in the eleventh minute and never really found our footing. They added another in the thirty-fourth minute, and we felt our chance slipping away.

As the second half began, I started warming up in our corner to make sure I was prepared if the call came. I knew that John was in a tough spot. We were chasing a 2–0 deficit. We needed goals. Years before, my speed would have been an asset. But I didn't have that extra pep now. There were other players on our bench that Canada needed more.

As the clocked ticked towards ninety, I felt the hope of hoisting a trophy tick away. That's just the way it works out sometimes. Of course, it would have been nice if things had worked out the right way. I was sad we didn't get the result.

I watched from the sidelines as the final second ticked away.

As the Americans rushed onto the pitch, celebrating their championship, I embraced my brothers on the pitch. The boys were upset. A few hugged me, apologizing as if they'd let me down. They hadn't, but it meant a lot that they wanted that win for me. They wanted to give me that trophy.

"It's a game," I said. "Don't worry about it. We keep going from here."

It was a weird feeling. I was upset and happy at the same time. I felt a lump in the back of my throat, as I thought, "That's it? It's over now?"

For so long, I'd envisioned holding a trophy for Canada. That moment had run through my head so many times. But at the end of it all, I was also happy to be there, to live in that moment. To have had the career I had. And to still be playing for something on the very last day. That was special. It had been a great run. If this was the way it ended, so be it.

I'd played one last season in Istanbul and I'd played in a World Cup. That was all the fairy-tale ending I needed. I was finally satisfied.

I looked around the stadium as the American fans clapped for their team and streamed for the exits. The Canadian fans stayed. In the stands, Haldon and Alex were still complaining about the referees.

Toyaa and my father commiserated with the families of other players. My mother sat a row above them alone, quietly watching me on the field. A few people came over to speak to her, but she didn't take her eyes off me. She wouldn't leave until I did.

I heard the cheers coming from the corner, where all of the Voyageurs sat.

"Ati-ba! Ati-ba! Ati-ba!"

They were calling me over, but I wasn't sure what to do. We'd just lost, so I didn't want to celebrate while everyone was down. It was one of those moments where I really didn't know how to proceed.

But a couple of my teammates nudged me. "Go."

I walked over to the diehard fans, clapping my hands. They cheered louder and continued to chant. I waved and clapped for them—for these fans who had been with us when it seemed like no one else was. These were the supporters who'd cheered against visiting crowds that dwarfed them in our own buildings. And here they were, still. I was honoured. I tried to let them know how much it had all meant to me. I stayed as long as I could, until it was finally time to walk away.

I turned towards our tunnel. The Americans' celebration continued beside us. The chants of "Ati-ba! Ati-ba!" echoed behind me, growing fainter.

My family and friends were still in the stands. My mother still sat alone. Afterwards, as the stadium emptied out, the four of them—Mom, Dad, Haldon, and Toyaa—would pull each other tight in a family hug, holding onto the moment.

My name was a distant echo now. I reached the tunnel and took one last look around. I thought of a boy chasing a ball across a patchy field in Brampton. What a beautiful dream it had been. And the best part was that my end was only our beginning.

Epilogue

At the end of my journey, I found myself thinking about the start.

I can close my eyes and hear the joy of kids falling in love with a game. I recognize the laughter and intense chatter. The goal celebrations. The trash talk and arguments. The excited crescendo of a win, the silence of defeat. The sound of grass and frost crunching beneath our feet.

Those moments of my childhood are as vivid as any Champions League match, championship win, or World Cup appearance. They were the days that set the course for everything that followed. Without Arnott Charlton, there would be no Parken. No Eindhoven. No Black Eagles. Old Trafford wouldn't be in my story. Without the passion I found playing with my childhood friends, there would be no Qatar. No 104 caps for Canada.

The beginning was essential.

I see it now in my children. In my boys Noah, Nava, and Ayo—wild and full of wonder—teaching them the game, the way my father did for me. I see it in my baby girl, Lily-Rose, as she smiles and laughs and sees the wide world for the first time. There is so much ahead for each of them. I'm excited to see where their journeys take them. I know that wherever they find their unique passion, it will be guided by what they learn about themselves now.

I see myself in them and I'm excited by all the possibilities that lie ahead for them. Looking back at my own journey, I've thought about what I learned along the way—what lessons I can share with my own kids and with others who set out to achieve goals that seem so far away.

♦

The pitch before me was just as I'd imagined all these years. A group of kids chased a ball, their shoes crunching on the crisp, artificial turf—no form or strategy, just the carefree pursuit I recognized from when I first fell in love with the game.

I saw myself and my friends in the kids running across the green, shouting and laughing as they went, at the grand opening of the soccer courts that the City of Brampton unveiled after my retirement.

I'd approached the city council a couple years earlier with a vision to create boxed soccer courts for local youth to easily access to play drop-in pick-up games, like I used to on the patchy sandlot at Arnott Charlton near my childhood house. As I travelled around the world through my career, I often saw community soccer courts in cities where football was a part of everyday life for young people. They were safe places, where kids could come to play for hours, losing themselves as they developed skill and imagination in the beautiful game.

The hope was to create a similar space in Brampton and develop an after-school program for students with my foundation through which a passion for the sport could be fostered in future generations.

That passion was already rising. In the years since my youth, my hometown had become a soccer hub.

Soccer's popularity exploded with Brampton's population, which put pressure on the municipal government to improve old facilities and build new ones. Today, there are professional quality pitches around

Brampton, some which are bubbled in the winters to make sure players of all levels have access year round. New community centres are built with indoor soccer facilities and old hockey rinks have been repurposed for soccer. Brampton Soccer Club, which I played most of my youth soccer with, is still the largest league in the city. Several soccer academies and club teams have emerged to make the environment even more competitive. All of this has had a huge impact on the quality of soccer coming out of the area.

✦

In the 2021 Canada census, nearly 80 percent of the city's population identified as "nonwhite." That means there are many new families arriving from places in which soccer is likely one of the most popular sports, and parents pass that influence on to their kids. Both Iain and I benefited from the connection our family made with football elsewhere. It was an imported passion. It makes sense that as more people arrived in the city with those kinds of connections—and as the grassroots soccer programs in the city continued to improve and club teams became more competitive—we would see more talented players emerging.

Soon some of the nation's top talent would rise out of Brampton, with national team players like Junior Hoilett, Doniel Henry, Jonathan Osorio, Cyle Larin, and Tajon Buchanan all coming out of my hometown. Of the twenty-six players on the Canadian men's national team in 2022, seven were born or raised in Brampton. Younger players from the city like Jayden Nelson and Jahkeel Marshall-Rutty are just starting to make names for themselves.

Brampton's Kadeisha Buchanan won gold at the 2020 Olympics and represented Canada on the women's national team at the World Cup for the third time in 2023. Kadeisha, a three-time Canadian player of the year, also won five UEFA Women's Champions League titles with Lyon, before signing with Chelsea.

We can count on more and more talent rising out of Brampton soon. In the same 2021 census, there were 117,000 kids under fourteen years old living in Brampton, a massive fraction of the population.

Part of my hope was that these soccer courts would foster that rising talent. That some of the kids who step on the turf will become that pro player, on fields thousands of miles away—or wearing the Maple Leaf on their jersey as opposing fans jeer and spit at them—fighting to prove to the world what they will already know: that Canada is a soccer nation.

They will carry on what names like Forrest, De Vos, Stalteri, Hume, De Guzman, De Rosario, Sinclair, Huitema, Beckie, and so many others began decades before and carried through recent years.

But it was about much more than that.

Most of the young people who step on the new courts won't go on to become professional players or members of the national team. The best friends who grew up playing outside beside me on those long summer afternoons went on to achieve different dreams in their lives. They became a banker, a real estate agent, an optometrist, a businessman, and much more. They became parents. They became leaders in their communities. They remain the most competitive people I know, now chasing ball every weekend in the same men's league my father played in—way back when I believed he and his teammates were the greatest footballers on earth.

In the same way, most of the kids who play on these soccer courts will become something beyond the soccer dreams they might envision there. They'll become teachers, lawyers, doctors, contractors, police officers, bus drivers, social workers, and any other myriad of paths that life might take them.

They will become parents. They will be coaches. They will be leaders. They will be fans, cheering from the stands. Or at home, watching a faraway team on a weekend morning, next to their daughter or son.

They will become the fabric of that nation, with all its unique histories and cultures. And football will be a part of who they are—an aspect of the values they carry, the passion and pride they feel. And they will pass it forward, through the generations.

Football is life that way.

They will be what my father was for me. And what I hope to be for my own kids.

The lessons learned and passed will transcend the pitch, as they always have. The grand opening of the soccer pitches was celebrated by the first annual Atiba Hutchinson Invitational, which included a challenge for each player on the youth teams competing to complete a series of 13 assists—deeds of kindness, positivity, and responsibility—as part of the competition. The good deeds were a celebration of what football is really all about.

◆

In the end, it's not the success you find in the game that matters. The game is universal because it's about much more than a scoreboard or the trophies you hoist. It's what it teaches you about friendship and respect. It's what you learn about the value of dreams and the importance of hard work.

The game gives us passion. It gives us a sense of what magic is possible if we are relentless in our pursuits.

It shows you what you can achieve on your own, but also with a group. That you can play in the back, or the middle, or the attack—and that each role is an equally valuable part of the bigger picture. It doesn't matter if it's on a soccer pitch.

Whatever your gifts allow you, there is an important position to play in something bigger than yourself.

The soccer courts in my hometown will host endless World Cups, where all of these values are learned and shared every day.

That was the vision that brought me back to where it started, hoping to create a grander version of what me and my friends found as we carried our handmade goal to that dusty field, rolled out the bumps, and played to become champions in this world.

Acknowledgments

Atiba:

From the beginning, I've been fortunate to have been blessed by the people who surround me. This book is just a brief reflection of those who made my path possible. There is not enough space to properly express what you have meant to me, so please forgive my brevity.

To the friends who shared a love for the game with me at the very beginning in Brampton, and who still stand beside me—thank you. You are the heart of my story.

My endless gratitude to all the coaches and teammates who helped me find my way in this beautiful game. To all the mentors who showed me that my dreams were possible and provided guidance on how to get there. To those who inspired me, who believed in me—and especially those who helped me see that I still had more to give, long after I imagined I'd still be playing—thank you for keeping an old man going.

Thank you to the fans who have cheered for me throughout my career. To the Canadians who followed this sport with passion when it seemed as though no one else did. And thank you to the ones who've come to love this game and are excited for what this new generation will bring. And to the fans of each club I've played for, who always made me feel welcome and loved.

To Östers IF and Helsingborgs IF for giving me a chance to show that I belonged. To FC Copenhagen for giving me some of the most memorable years of my career. To PSV Eindhoven for giving me the chance to play for one of Europe's greatest clubs. And to Beşiktaş, for welcoming us into this massive family and making Turkey the place we call home. I hope this book has reflected what the privilege has meant to me.

Thank you to Alex Della Sciucca, one of my oldest friends, for always passing me the ball and finding ways to help me succeed. Thank you for convincing me to write this book and being a driving force behind getting it done.

Dan Robson, thank you for your help in bringing my story together in these pages. It was fun reflecting on my journey with you.

Rick Broadhead, thank you for your support as my literary agent. Thank you to everyone at Penguin Random House Canada for giving me the opportunity to share my story and for believing in its reach.

Most importantly, thank you to my family. To my father, for sharing this game with me. To my mother, for being my biggest champion. To my brother and sister, for being there with me every step of the way. And to Sarah, for allowing me to see the world in ways I never had before—and for being the best partner and the most incredible mother to our children.

And finally, to my children—Noah, Nava, Ayo, and Lily-Rose. Being your father is the most thrilling and rewarding privilege of my life. I can't wait to see you reach for your dreams, as you discover that with hard work and courage, nothing is impossible.

Dan:

Thank you to everyone at Penguin Random House Canada who had a hand in making this book possible, from editing to design and marketing. It's an honour to work with such a talented group.

Thank you to Alanna McMullen for guiding us throughout this process and helping bring shape to this book. And to Crissy Boylan for your help copy editing the manuscript.

Thank you to Nick Garrison and Nicole Winstanley for seeing the potential in Atiba's incredible story.

Rick Broadhead, thank you for championing this book and for your tireless effort as my literary agent.

Thank you to all of the journalists and commentators who have covered the Canadian national soccer team and Atiba's career, whose work was essential background in writing this book. In particular, thank you to Kaan Bayazit and Alexandre Gangué-Ruzic who shared their insights on Atiba's career and legacy with Beşiktaş and the Canadian men's national team. And to Joshua Kloke, my colleague at *The Athletic*, whose book *The Voyageurs* helped provide important context.

I'm indebted to all of the family members, friends, and teammates of Atiba who took the time to share stories about his life and career. Thank you to Alex Della Sciucca for being a driving force behind this book and for your endless passion to celebrate and share your friend's story with a wide audience.

Atiba, thank you for trusting me to help tell the story of your remarkable career and legacy. It has been a joy and a privilege to get to know you and to see the beautiful game through your eyes.